Essays in Understanding Latin America

Essays in Understanding Latin America

KALMAN H. SILVERT

With a Foreword by Joel M. Jutkowitz

A Publication of the
Institute for the Study of Human Issues
Philadelphia

Manufactured in the United States of America

For information, write: Director of Publications, ISHI,
3401 Science Center, Philadelphia, Pennsylvania 19104, U.S.A.

Library of Congress Cataloging in Publication Data:

Silvert, Kalman H.
    Essays in understanding Latin America.
    Includes index.
    1. Latin America—Politics and government—1948-   —Addresses, essays, lectures.
    2. United States—Relations (general) with Latin America—Addresses, essays, lectures.
    3. Latin America—Relations (general) with the United States—Addresses, essays, lectures.
    4. Latin America—Social conditions—1945-   —Addresses, essays, lectures.   I. Title.
    F1414.2.S52   301.5'92'098   77-2340
    ISBN 0-915980-02-9
    ISBN 0-915980-82-7 pbk.

A slightly different version of "Leadership Formation and Modernization in Latin America" was
published in the *Journal of International Affairs*, Vol. 20, No. 2 (1966), pp. 318-331. Copyright by
the Trustees of Columbia University in the City of New York. Permission to reprint, granted by
the Editors of the *Journal*, is gratefully acknowledged.
    "Fate, Chance, and Faith: Some Ideas Suggested by a Recent Trip to Cuba" first appeared as an
American Universities Field Staff Report, North America Series, Vol. 2, No. 2 (September 1974).
    "An Essay on Interdisciplinary and International Collaboration in Social Science Research in
Latin America" is reprinted, slightly modified, from *Latin America in Transition: Problems in Train-
ing and Research*, edited by Stanley R. Ross, by permission of the State University of New York
Press. © 1970 State University of New York.
    A different version of "The Relevance of Latin American Domestic Politics to North American
Foreign Policy" appeared in *The Americas in a Changing World: Including the Report of the Commission
on United States–Latin American Relations* (New York: Quadrangle, 1975). Copyright 1975 by the
Center for Inter-American Relations.
    A slightly different version of "Turning Ideals into Reality: Democracy in Latin America" was
published in *The New Republic,* March 22, 1975, pp. 19-21.
    "Frames for the Caribbean Experience" appeared in a different form in Tad Szulc, ed., *The
United States and the Caribbean* (New York: American Assembly, 1970).
    An adapted version of "Latin America in the World in the Year 2000" appeared under the title
"Latin America and Its Alternative Futures" in *International Journal* (Canadian Institute of International Affairs), Vol. 24, No. 3 (1969), pp. 403-425.

Contents

Foreword

JOEL M. JUTKOWITZ

KALMAN HIRSCH SILVERT'S intellectual activity focused on understanding the possibilities for democracy, while his research experience centered on Latin America. This book combines these two elements of his work. The insights he acquired through his research in Latin America were the basis for his "essays" at comprehending the crises in U.S.–Latin American relations, the crisis in his profession of social science, and above all the future of democracy in the United States as well as in Latin America.

The writings included in this volume were selected and arranged into sections by Silvert in the period just before his untimely death. Had he lived he would have added an introduction to the book, to discuss the significance of the selection of essays and their arrangement. It would be presumptuous to assume that task in his absence. However, to assist the reader, this Foreword will provide an examination of the principal themes treated in all of Silvert's work—themes that are reflected throughout this volume.

Before we enter into that discussion, one further note about the book's structure should be added. *Essays in Understanding Latin America* was intended to be an exemplification and a summation of Silvert's work over the past decade. Following his design, each essay bears (on its final page) the date when it was written. And none of the essays was altered by the author or the editors to achieve consistency after the fact. Thus, the consistency in the work is that given by the development of a man's thought through time. The basic

continuity of all his writing can be illustrated by the relationship
between the Prologue and the concluding section. The Prologue,
"Coming Home: The U.S. Through the Eyes of a Latin Americanist," was the last piece in the volume that the author produced,
while the concluding essay, "Latin America in the World in the Year
2000," was one of the earliest. However, it will be clear to every
reader that the two are linked not merely by their polar positions in
the text, but by common concerns.

These common concerns can be divided into four major themes
that appear throughout Silvert's work:

- A student of the development of the modern industrial state, he
  sought to understand the conflict that arose between the *nation* as
  an expression of the public interest and *class* order as an expression of private interests.

- Concerned about the possibilities of making rational and effective
  choices, he explored the basis for the establishment of public
  freedom and a democratic political order.

- Since he was concerned with the centrality of ideas in social and
  especially political behavior, he sought to understand the ways in
  which men, through their conceptualizations, have shaped their
  political options. Therefore, he pressed for the development of a
  social science that was both politically relevant and truly intellectual—oriented toward constant critique of the existing political
  order.

- He was concerned with the dependence of states upon each
  other. He studied the ways in which the formation of nations
  enhanced the possibility that each nation would be able to control
  its own destiny. He strove to understand how the creation of
  transnational power combinations limited the freedom of *all*
  states, not merely those usually considered "dependent."

Nation and Class.   For Silvert, the *nation* as a concept
defines the political community who may participate and how they
may participate. Such a definition is given form through the operation of the *state*. These two elements, nation and state, ideally reinforce each other. The conception held of the nation should infuse
the state with purpose. The state should provide the organizational
support for the maintenance of the social consequences of the pre-
vailing definition of the nation.

The extreme cases in contemporary Latin America, as Silvert
sees them, are Chile and Cuba. The latter, as he indicates in the

essay "Fate, Chance, and Faith: Some Ideas Suggested by a Recent Trip to Cuba," has reached the point of full nationhood. Class as a limiting factor has been overcome, and the nation includes virtually everyone. Chile, on the other hand, has become in recent years a "society organized to maintain hierarchy and existing privilege" (page 152). The Chilean junta has attempted to "break the Chilean nation," to turn the clock back to the eighteenth century and "repeal the French Revolution" (page 10). Class interests override and in effect are substituted for any notion of the public interest.

Choice and Freedom. The Chilean and Cuban cases, as well as the Argentine case alluded to in the Prologue, represent more than examples of the search for nationhood. They represent different modes of confronting the questions of political choice and political freedom, the foundation stones of a democratic order. Throughout Silvert's writings these components of the democratic order are continually examined. It is in this sense that Silvert "comes home," as he says in the Prologue, with insights into U.S. problems gained in his study of Latin America. As he contends, many in both Latin America and the United States share the same worry—the failure of governments to fulfil the democratic possibilities contained in the growth of the industrial order. The consequence of this failure is that in the United States and also in Argentina, Chile, and Cuba people are asked to choose between loyalty to the state and loyalty to the nation. The state in all of these cases has become rigid, unresponsive, and therefore increasingly irrational. The choice that arises, as Silvert puts it, is between being loyal to the concept of a fully participant nation based on an expanding ability to make rational decisions about public affairs (Silvert's definition of political freedom) and being loyal to a state that embodies just the opposite of this freedom.

The emphasis on choice arises from Silvert's rejection of deterministic views of history, a rejection based on his belief that central to all social processes are the values with which men shape their perceptions of social institutions. To focus on values is to focus on man as a generator of his own social circumstances. Man either controls through or is controlled by his ability as a shaper of symbols to obtain an understanding of his social situation. With this ability he may open up or close down his opportunities for choice among alternatives.

A Relevant but Independent Social Science. If values and understanding are the underpinnings of a free political order, then social science as the intellectual pursuit of social understanding is an integral part of that order. As Silvert sees it, the task of the social sciences is to overcome those theoretical constructions that hamper social understanding. To do this requires taking into consideration all of those phenomena that are the categories of social analysis—individual idiosyncrasy, institutions, social structure, and ethos—within a single intellectual frame.

To achieve that end, social scientists need to understand the limitations on their theoretical constructs. They have to probe, as Silvert does continually in these essays, into the philosophical bases of their approaches. They have to be political in the sense that they are conscious of their role as citizens as well as their role as "experts." They have therefore to be relevant in the sense that they must treat issues significant to society as well as those related to the expansion of their technical proficiency. On the other hand, they must not let their politics undermine their intellectual independence as scholars.

It is this constant concern that led Silvert to include in the section "Ways of Knowing" a number of the commentaries he had produced on the social sciences. "An Essay on Interdisciplinary and International Collaboration in Social Science Research in Latin America" argues the case for both professional competence and professional ethics on the part of his fellow social scientists. There he concludes that the future of interdisciplinary and international collaboration rests on "competence and the understanding that professional and social integrity are goals to be simultaneously pursued" (page 129). And the last essay in the section, using the example of the Camelot incident that troubled U.S.–Latin American scholarly relations in the late 1960s, reiterates the importance of professional competence by advocating the institutional separation of the academic task from policy making. That separation is necessary for the scholar to preserve his capacity to think critically about his society and to distinguish his role as citizen from his role as scholar. The argument here reinforces the point Silvert made on a number of other occasions: in a democratic society, whether a man be a scholar or a shoemaker, his prejudices are equal to anyone else's. No man's opinion is more equal than others in the making of public policy.

Dependence and Interdependence of Nations.   Finally, Silvert expresses in this volume his concern with the growing interdependence of nations. He does that, however, within an awareness of the historical evolution of the nation-state. He argues in the last essay that the difference between the best possible and worst possible situations in Latin America at the close of this century will rest on the strength of the nation-state. The answer to the dependence of Latin American states on foreign power centers lies in the expansion of the effective nation. As Silvert suggests, the limitation of direct foreign intervention is a consequence not only of major power decisions, but of the strength of Latin American public opposition to such intervention. (The clearest example of this was, of course, the repulse of the Bay of Pigs invasion.) The limit of indirect intervention also rests on the strength of the nation-state: the degree to which the nation expands to eliminate areas of privilege and the degree to which the state acts in the public interest rather than as an agent of domestic or foreign private interests. Thus, the road to independence is the realization of the process that concerned Silvert constantly throughout his research and writing—the building of a fully participant nation-state endowed with a populace capable of making rational and effective choices. He believed in this process not just as a means of raising the downtrodden, but as a way of establishing a more reasonable international order that would benefit the major nations as well as the developing ones.

To close this Foreword in an analytical vein would be to fail to do justice to Kalman Silvert the man. This book represents more than his academic understanding of Latin America; it represents Kal's commitment to the need for democracy both in Latin America and in his own country. It also represents Kal's faith in the ability of his fellow Americans, from whatever part of the hemisphere, to learn from their past, to be free from the dictates of fate or the "iron laws" of history.

Kal, I am certain, would have dedicated this book, as he did his others, to those he felt closest to him—his family, his intellectual "brothers." I will not presume to make that choice for him. Rather, I shall merely suggest that this book most properly should be dedicated to Kal himself, because of his faith in his fellow men and in their inherent good—the good that flowed from their ability to reason, if they so chose.

Prologue

This Prologue is adapted from the Charles W. Hackett Memorial Lecture given at the Institute of Latin American Studies, University of Texas at Austin, April 1976.

Coming Home:
The U.S. Through the Eyes
of a Latin Americanist

MUCH OF WHAT I have been worried about—and I suspect many in Latin America as well as in the United States share the same worry—is complex yet elemental to our times. One could use the shorthand word "democracy" to try to describe it, or one could use the grander word "freedom." One could use the very narrow concept "human rights," or the slightly larger one of "civil rights." But whatever may be its label, it is global. The issue turns on the relationship of man and woman to the state, and persons to themselves.

It is, of course, fortuitous that 1976 is a bicentennial year for us in the United States. Thus "coming home again" is a theme very much in keeping with the general tone of our celebrations. For me, "coming home" is not only to return in a geographical sense, it is more profoundly connected with coming home to my own youth. I have heard many of my colleagues talk about the difficulty of developing a coherence between what we think now and what we used to think as children. For me, what we thought then was in large measure what I was taught in civics classes. It is a cultural, political, and intellectual return that motivates me and, I think, others of my generation. It is a long and difficult journey. For years I used to think that it was somehow not proper to be patriotic because people with whom I was politically uncomfortable had wrested the flag from my hands and pasted it on their car windows. Then there were other people who had wrested the flag away and pasted it on the back of their pants. Yet, when I was a kid, it used to be great fun to attach a

3

little bouquet of flags to the emblem of the car radiator. That was a big thing to do on the Fourth of July. Several questions arise: Since when has love of country become shameful? In giving it up, what have we lost? Is the break of the mythology good or bad? What have we done to ourselves when the words "nation" and "nationalism" become pejorative, when it is *good* to be international, but *bad* to be national? What kind of peculiarity is it when we decry "isolationism" and the "new isolationists" while the loudest accusers are the very ones working overseas by themselves? To act unilaterally overseas is the essence of isolationism.

If one begins to reflect on the twisting of concepts, of ideas and of words—and the even more serious implications of the way of looking at things that dominates our social science teaching, our political discourse, and our construction of reality—then it is time to ask very basic questions about both the nature of one's own intellectuality and the nature of one's relationship to country. They are old questions—about civil society and state, about citizenship and participation, about loyalty and legitimacy and the roots of power. However, it is to them I must return in order to make sense of the experiences of Latin America and the United States. Both Americas are grappling with the same problems, but with very different sets of abilities and resources to solve them. In both I find an enormous vacuum of ideas about a relevant theory of democracy.

Recently, I have been chairing a seminar in New York, comprised of Latin Americans and North Americans, on the subject "Democracy, Authoritarianism, and Development in the Hemisphere." It is amazing how the group can talk endlessly about authoritarianism, endlessly about development, but cannot find five sentences to say about democracy. It is time, then, for a bit of self-examination, for asking ourselves: "What intellectual construction do we have left to us, which we commonly and ordinarily use, that makes the idea of publicly ordered freedom something more than sentimentality and the evocation of times past?"

It is my thesis that a reconstruction of what we mean by terms like dignity and freedom will serve us well in understanding why certain things have and have not happened in Latin America, and equally well in reassessing our own situation. This reconstruction, I suggest, will give us the basis upon which to decide whether our society is "sick," and, if we so decide, to determine what the nature of the sickness is. Prescribing the "brand of medicine" is not my business as a social scientist; that is a matter for the political process. But diagnosis is certainly the business of a social scientist as it is equally that of every other citizen.

In discussing either the United States or Latin America, I have been exposed to the usual common wisdoms. The first is an obvious one: You can know your country only if you leave it. It was invariably said to me on my returns home, "You must have a fresh view of the U.S. now that you have been away." Latin Americans, for their part, asked me, "Tell us about ourselves. You come from abroad, you can understand us better than we can understand ourselves." But then, as with all wisdoms, I was subject to the opposite: "As a foreigner you cannot understand us. You have not grown up in our culture, have not had the experience of kindergarten, of primary school, or of our family life. You have not experienced how we relate to others. Since you cannot know these things, you cannot really, truly experience us." Obviously there is truth and falsity on both sides of the common-wisdom coin. What I will attempt to do here is to use a particular framework to understand the different sets of empirical occurrences found in Latin America and the United States.

Let me confess immediately from whence I draw this framework—or, as I might better call it, this common wash of ideas. They start with Machiavelli and Locke, are heavily influenced by Rousseau, even more heavily by Kant, and, finally, are made current through the interpretations and insights of Max Weber and Ernst Cassirer. I mention these social philosophers because they are not normally the sources for the current construction of the world. In this country, understandings of how things happen stem from Utilitarianism—the view that we are moved by something "natural and equal for all," that each one of us operates merely according to a "pleasure/pain calculus," and that if we simply agglutinate all of this "instinctive" behavior we have a self-adjusting or homeostatic way of understanding societal change. The Utilitarian view puts reason in second place. It assumes that reality is "out there," that we somehow feel it and "learn" it by its impingement upon us. Our heads reason only to manage our intestines. The contemporary evocation is the idea that "good" politics simply uses reason in service of a self-sustaining, automatically working mechanism. Thus "good" politicians are "technicians," and because they have the "facts" they know much more than we mere citizens do. What they are, in effect, are managers. The point of the modern-day saints of Utilitarianism is that politics should be depoliticized.

The deterministic Marxism developed recently in the United States shares some of the Utilitarian logic. The automatic grinding of the dialectic sets up a scene in which, once again, reason has no comfortable place. Neither in standard Marxism nor in Utilitarian-

ism is there any theoretical room for the creative use of the mind—
thus there is no theoretical room for freedom. Freedom becomes
epiphenomenal—superstructural for Marxists, a matter of manage-
rial technicism for Utilitarians, restricted to "policy elites" for technocrats like Nathan Glazer, Daniel Moynihan, and Samuel Huntington.

There is, however, another kind of theory, deeply rooted in
Western tradition. It is the one from which I draw my "wash of
ideas," and the one that informed the writing of the American Constitution. The Constitution is based on a notion of ethicized institutions and on an idea of the primacy of reason in secular affairs. It is
designed to permit reason to operate *institutionally*; but it has been
interpreted by Utilitarians. We have a document that, in its fundamental conception of reality, indicates one direction, but an administrative structure that has attempted to use it in a different way.

North America and Latin America share the same fund of
philosophical precepts. Despite the different partisan and ideological
meaning of classical Liberalism in Latin America, it has exactly the
same *philosophical* meaning. Latin Americans knew long before John
Rawls wrote his book *A Theory of Justice* that Liberalism and Utilitarianism were philosophically extraordinarily different. They also
knew that Liberal parties had decayed into Utilitarian parties. It is
only recently that we in North America have become aware of the
epistemological as well as the partisan political differences involved.

It is also true that Marxism, as a general philosophy, has had
more fertile soil in Latin America than in the United States, at the
level not of partisanship but of culture. It is an idea more attuned to
the Latin American experience, or at least to certain groups in Latin
America, because it is grounded in history rather than in the individual. It is an idea about structures and relationships, and has in it the
notion of *fuerza mayor*, of blind forces at work. Latin American
culture, especially the Catholic ethos, leans more to the idea of
persons being caught *organically* in a totally evolving situation than
does the American liberal interpretation. Here in North America the
emphasis is on a *pluralistic* set of institutions pulled together by a
common ethic.

I have tried to explain my motivating values, perhaps too rapidly. But it is not *what* I am saying that matters so much as the *act* of
attempting to explain. The reason for this is simple: what distin-
guishes free politics from unfree politics is that, in a society where
people are free, the "doing of politics" is its own reward. It is an
expressive, not an instrumental, function. It is like making music. It
is platonic. The act of revealing my ideas to you is the making of
freedom. If I do not afford you the ability to defend yourself against

me, I destroy the interplay of reason. Thus I may not lie to you, because that will create differing realities, differing phenomena. Thus I may not corrupt this act by bringing in other interests that fit differing institutional spheres. Thus I may not pick and choose among my listeners by religion or color or age or sex, because that is an ascriptive exiling from community of the persons involved. And I may not be discourteous, because that destroys communication. In short, for reasons of epistemology, values, honesty, and courtesy, I may not interrupt the process; if I do, the act ceases to be expressive—it ceases to be a freeing act.

Enough, then, of describing my cargo. I have told you that I have come home. It is a very long way for me to go—to get all the way back to understanding my civics classes, my first- and second-grade teachers, the whys and wherefores concerning the nature, joys, and pains of political community. Without the Latin American experience, in truth, I do not think I could have come home.

But one more word is necessary about the "wash of ideas," because it will explain the method behind the following paragraphs. The thrust of Utilitarianism and of American social science has been to universalize, to talk about what is equal in all persons. The drive of the classical Liberal and Enlightenment thinkers, on the other hand, was to draw categories, either historical or conceptual. In effect, they drove their cases to the borders—the point being to form distinct and specific categories. This led to the Weberian idea of clusters of uniqueness, an idea I will draw upon here. For what Latin America can do for an understanding of freedom—and it is amazing in this—is to provide the world with a series of outer-limit cases.

Let me start to examine these cases, sentimentally at first, and later in a more rigorous fashion. During 1947–48 when I was studying the Chilean Development Corporation, I read in the *New York Times* that there had been a great snowfall in New York which paralyzed the city. I received a letter from a friend describing the great joy after that event. In snowbound New York persons felt drawn together; they talked, community developed, there was joy, people were cracking jokes and helping each other—a sense of euphoria had overtaken the metropolis. The letter from New York caught precisely the general social feeling that my wife and I had for almost the entire year we lived in Chile. It was the postwar period, the beginning of a developmental, industrial, urbane euphoria, a time when bright young people were emerging. They and the country had been bottled up in World War II politics. Suddenly the lid was off and the country flourished. The Chilean Development Corporation, which I was studying, was only one locus of this euphoria;

it showed in the government as a whole and in everyday life. Among persons in the professional groups and the upper middle classes there was simple social joy. They were caught up in a task larger than they; they were *forjando nación,* forging nation, and they loved it. I felt this again, for a short while, on another occasion in Guatemala. I felt it for a very long time among the middle-class groups in Argentina after the fall of Perón—simple, continued, day-to-day happiness. Imagine, when you have behind you twenty-five years of off-and-on dictatorship (from 1930 to 1955), and all of a sudden you are permitted to reopen your universities. For years you have been clogged and clotted, your best sociologist has been translating science fiction and publishing *Galaxia* (*Galaxy,* in Spanish) and writing in women's magazines. Your best publishers have been putting out trash. Now, all of a sudden, this talent can be put to work rebuilding the university, the communications industry, and the intellectual life of a country that has been living in sadness and despair. The joy is palpable. You feel it. It is nothing to stay up all night long and go right to work. You don't even miss the sleep much. That was standard in Chile, standard in Argentina. And, of course, it was this euphoria everybody commented upon in Cuba after the Revolution. You could feel the radiating joy in Cubans who were going to "make nation."

It is almost all gone, of course. And although this is a limiting case—a sentimental limiting case—it is worth thinking about. It is worth asking ourselves why, after the longest war in our nation's history ended in 1973, nobody said anything. Nobody celebrated or went to the streets. Can we remember 1945? Can we remember the tears upon the death of a President? I was in Africa at that time and marched in the military through streets lined with Arabs crying their hearts out. Has anyone cried for an American politician since Kennedy? For good or ill, what was the symbolism of social joy or tears, and what is it that was lost?

As euphoric openings are limiting cases, so are the despairing and apathetic closings of Latin American societies. Their transposition to the United States matters. There are many among us who have never felt social joy. I can only be very sad for them. It is the tastiest and headiest of all brews, though it is very dangerous. It is the poison used by demagogues, but also the joy that can be institutionalized and sustained in a society which, as Franklin Delano Roosevelt put it, "has decided that nobody should be left out."

We can talk as well in structural terms, which are more familiar than the vagueness of sentiment. Today the problem of great moment in the United States is how to reconcile equality before the laws with the fact that material and educational differences divide us. That is to say, there is a stress in the United States between nation—which covers all of us in our political beings—and race or class or special interest, which are anti-nation. We know, too, that those who say there is no democracy in America, because blacks, chicanos, Puerto Ricans, or members of some other group are shabbily treated, are not correct. We know that the fabric of liberty *is* divisible, despite the common aphorism that liberty is indivisible. The United States has managed to live half free, or more than half free, since its beginnings. That is the history of classical democracies, and Latin American countries are part of that history. It is not sufficient to say that Chile from the 1940s until the early 1960s was an undemocratic country because a large percentage of the population did not have enough to eat, was not doing well educationally, and was unable to move up the occupational ladder. That reveals nothing about the other half of the population, which was living in relative equality before the laws and had relatively free access to the institutions of the country. In short, significant numbers were living a relatively democratic life, while many others were not. Chile was a partial nation-state.

Partial nation-states, of which we are one, are very powerful instruments. Those of us who are legitimizers, who are "loyal," who give our government consent by anticipation, who do not need more than a letter to report for military service, who wait with baited breath at the beginning of each year to get our tax forms (which almost all of us fill out dishonestly because we pay more than we should)—we create power. However, those without that created power, and without access to it, can be held in a bondage that appears mysterious and difficult to shake off. Completing the democratic job, the job of national community building, is a difficult proposition. It has been accomplished by some countries—Sweden, Denmark, and Norway, for instance. It is not an impossible task, but neither is it an easy one. It is especially hard for a country as big as the United States, split by ethnicity, class, and race. And it is not simple for Latin American countries, where the past three or four hundred years of Western history have been collapsed into fifty-five or sixty years.

The limiting cases of nation-state building in Latin America are two: Chile and Cuba. For good or for ill, what the Allende administration set out to do in Chile was to maintain a democratic structure and at the same time change the marketplace economy. The goal was to involve *all* Chilean citizens in the production and consumption of goods and services while increasing the wealth of society as a whole. Hindsight affords us the luxury of cool reflection: there were mistakes made and there was disorganization. The point now is simply that the attempt failed. But, in that failing, what choice was being made? Allende attempted to complete the Chilean nation. The present Chilean government has made the opposite choice: to break the Chilean nation. With this choice comes the necessity to rid the country of the entire idea of citizenship. That, indeed, is what the Chilean junta has done. Citizenship in Chile matters not; nationality matters, but only because you have to have a passport. Today there is no such thing as a Chilean *citizen.* There is no voting, there is no body politic, there is no polity. The Chileans have managed to repeal the French Revolution. They have even reduced those ascriptive cushions that used to protect people in traditional Latin American society from the greater barbarities of the state. It matters not whether you are old or young, whether you are man or woman, whether you are Catholic or anti-Catholic. It matters not whether you wear clerical garb or a regular suit. If your politics are wrong, you are at the complete and absolute mercy of the state. Twelve-year-old children *have* been executed in Chile; women have been subjected to all kinds of indignities, including torture and death, as have men. Priests have been imprisoned and killed. The destruction of the nation carries with it the *necessary* destruction of citizenship; for citizenship is that role, that function, which permits us to say that no matter what divides us—accidents of individual experience, of birth, or of religious belief—for the purposes of our interaction as secular human beings in a transitory secular world, we are *fellow citizens.* That conception is totally absent in today's Chile.

Cuba went in the opposite direction. The point of the Cuban Revolution was to break class bounds and to create a nation-city-state—to turn everybody in Cuba into a citizen. That is the reason Cubans always talk about *participación, participación,* until it drives a visitor mad with desperation and finally with boredom. But theirs is a success, they have done it; and the result comes as no surprise to people who think about development not in Utilitarian but in classically Liberal, constitutionalist terms. John Kenneth Galbraith has asked us to remember Dresden, bombed to the ground in World War II and rebuilt in two years. The moral of the Dresden tale needs to be understood. All of those mechanical tasks of development that we think of as so difficult can in fact be done, and much more quickly than Utilitarians suppose. They have been accomplished in Cuba in no time—without those terrible twists of torture that the Chilean junta tells us are necessary for material development. It is easy enough to make a total population literate if you want to. One probably couldn't make any more Cubans literate. There is practically no educational pyramid in the primary schools: if you enter school, you go straight up. Now they are working hard to erase the secondary-school pyramid. In short, there is no problem in getting people into school and keeping them there if one decides to do so. There is also no problem in extending life expectancy. For Cuban men and women the average life expectancy is now longer than it is for North Americans, despite the fact that in 1962 there were only twelve professors in the School of Medicine of the University of Havana. In general, "development" *can* be achieved. If you want cows that will give a lot of milk, you experiment enough and you will get them. If you genuinely want to grow rice, you can—at least until the price of petroleum goes up and you are forced to solve another "problem" in order to get the necessary fertilizers.

These, however, are technical achievements. They do not give you freedom. Nation-building is a precondition for democracy, but not a sufficient condition. What we see in Cuba is a victory of nation over class, threatened by technocracy, by the children of the managers, by a Yugoslav-like new class beginning to emerge, and by a Soviet kind of managerialism. Cuba has a totalitarian *national* government with a highly participant *local* government, and is attempting to make the two meet. If the Cubans manage this, it will be quite a victory. Their success will take more than partisan politics, and more than simple ideological maundering. It will take hard, conceptual reasoning.

Two discussions I had in Cuba might help illustrate the harsh reality of this problem. The first came when I pointed out to some Cuban leaders that Nazis participated enormously, that perhaps "participation" is not a *good* in itself. To this they had no answer. On another occasion I was told that the liberal-bourgeois notion of human rights must cede to the new socialist version—food for everybody, *techo* (roof) for everybody, and so on. I suggested that perhaps those were not human rights, but feline rights, because my cat has all of them—milk, shelter, and the best training I could give. My cat is very good; it does what it is supposed to do, and it is secure. Why call these human rights? Human beings are not pets, they are significance-creating persons. The issue is how to develop an institutional structure that will permit persons to create and re-create that significance.

These Latin American limiting cases, both sentimental and structural, invite us to a rethinking of the North American situation. They clearly suggest faults, in the seismic sense, in the American political and social scene. For example, they lead to the diagnosis that governmental dishonesty is not a light matter and that corruption is not to be shrugged off as "natural." They suggest that the deterministic linealism so prevalent in the World Bank and in the work of the "population" experts—to mention only two groups among many—leads to a misdefinition of the problem. I return from Latin America with a surer knowledge that ecology is *not* a problem, pollution is *not* a problem, and population is *not* a problem, because problems have to do with relationships. The words in themselves do not contain relationships. Thus, is pollution our problem? Or is our problem unemployment? Maybe we need unemployment, as William Simon tells us, in order to contain inflation. The problem becomes one of inflation, not unemployment, by that logic. On the other hand, if the problem is poverty, as it was defined in President Johnson's Great Society programs, one has only to change the definition of the "poverty line," as the Nixon administration did.

I come home, not with some such "problem" encapsulated in a word, but with the diagnosis that the major American problem is the same as for all developed Latin American countries—how once again to start the process of the contained use of reason operating through accountable institutions. That is a functional definition of democracy. It is not a loose statement about freedom, or about accountability. It is a recognition that, at least in our lay lives, at least in our pursuits as secular citizens, the structured institutionalization of reason is something we have permitted to slip away from us. We are told, by some social scientists as well as officials, that we do not have the "facts," and that therefore we should be quiet. Nathan Glazer declares, for example, that we ought not to bother government because, if we push for reforms, "things" will happen that we will not like. We are asked to throw away the notion of self-correction, a suggestion I find simply incredible. I would agree with Al Smith, who said that "When Democracy is in trouble, what it needs is more Democracy." I do not see a solution in delivering ourselves to the hands of our so-called intellectual betters.

If I have learned anything from Latin America it is the following: that unreason is inefficacious; that, by and large, American behavioral social science is inefficacious; and that tyranny and dictatorship are inefficient and inefficacious. Tyrannical regimes last for a little while; they may or may not do something; they are enormously wasteful, irresponsible, and corrupt. And they end up blinding even the dictators to their own interests. I have as yet to see in Latin America any authoritarian government that pretended to change, to improvement, to progress, or to betterment, which could keep itself going for more than six or seven years. The Peruvian government has now bogged down. The Argentines managed for two or three years at a time; perhaps the present government will also manage for a few years. The Uruguayan government? It is reigning over a national disaster—poverty, increasing ignorance, brain drain. The Chilean government? Brutalizing, losing its best brains. Everything it gets in foreign aid it has lost in the educational value of the talent that has had to export itself or has been killed. Even on a simple bookkeeper's balance sheet, that is inefficacious, wasteful, and stupid.

But there is always the Mexican case. That becomes a much more difficult matter to deal with, because, in truth, Mexico is a single-party dictatorship that has lasted for more than a few years. It is extraordinarily developmental in certain ways, and not in other ways. The mixture yields an interesting statistic: there are more illiterates in Mexico today than there were Mexicans in 1940. There are strains in the Mexican system, cracks that appear to be widening as the obvious need for flexibility and institutionalized reason begins to emerge.

The country in Latin America that is by far the most developed, socially, economically, and otherwise, is of course Argentina. This is true by any standard measure—literacy, the length of time for which Argentines have been literate, the number of universities, the percentage of university graduates, the consumption of newsprint, aluminum, automobiles, and so on. Argentina has held the position of being the most developed for a long time. And if any country in Latin America indicates the need for a democratic solution, it is Argentina. It is a country whose population has learned to live without its state. Clearly Argentines live in a very democratic *nation,* with a very authoritarian *state.* Their informal political organization, complex and rich, has permitted them to survive their governments. The question we should ask of Argentina is not why the country is in such a mess, but how it managed to avoid disaster from 1930 to 1950. Why is Buenos Aires still a great and vibrant city? And why is Havana such a boring city—with the same number of literates, *más o menos,* in the population? These are perplexing questions worth the asking. A sentimental answer to them would be to recall walking down the beautiful streets of Buenos Aires, window shopping, talking, and later eating in a restaurant where a waiter comes up and interrupts you, saying that he doesn't like the way you're telling a joke and that he tells it better. (And he does tell it better, by far.) That was an experience I had recently with seven other persons. At 2:30 in the morning we looked around to discover that the great Cabaña restaurant had been closed for an hour and a half; not a one of us had known it because the waiter was too busy being a comedian while passing the desserts around, and the other waiters were too happy listening. There was a civility in this, an informal attachment, an expression of the way the nation as a political community had knit. But what is occurring in Argentina at the present moment is that to be loyal to the state is to be disloyal to the nation.

Much the same threatens to become the case in the United States. Have we not been told by our own governors that to disagree with them is to be disloyal? But disloyal to what? Disloyal to an unresponsive, rigid, and increasingly nonrational state, but perhaps loyal to ourselves as a democratic nation? The *Argentinization* of the United States is something that worries me severely. What we have, however, which the Argentines do not have in as full a measure, is the philosophical and epistemological tradition that forged the democratic ethos of my civics classes in grade school—a tradition I see being attacked and dismembered by technocratic elites nurtured by colleagues of mine who have become mere homeostatic systems analysts. My "coming home" is not made only of nostalgia; it involves as well the firm belief that we must reconstruct the democratic temper.

1976

I. Categories

Leadership Formation
and Modernization
in Latin America

EFFECTIVE LEADERSHIP cannot, by itself, ensure modernization. Indeed, no one causal agent—be it change in economic structure, in values, in formal political institutions, or in educational levels—is sufficient to transform traditional behavior patterns into their modern counterparts. The modern situation is a totality: the *presence* of one major element of modernity does not guarantee the automatic emergence of the others; the *absence* of one will provide difficulties for the development of other elements of the system.

But leadership is, nonetheless, a crucial variable for political development. Leadership groups influence to a considerable extent the direction in which their societies will evolve. It is easy enough to point out that leadership groups in developing lands must be analyzed within the frameworks of their societies. Providing such a framework is, however, a most difficult undertaking, involving an understanding of the level of technology, the social order, the existing ideological and value beliefs, interest groups, and political parties, and the situation in the international marketplace of ideas, power, and money. Any analysis of leadership must include these elements, because leaders cannot exist without followers and because their power is generated by consensus and legitimacy. The instruments of overt control are only the most obvious evidence of the leaders' power. This author has written elsewhere:

> The identification of elite groups, leaders and followers is in certain
> respects an even more treacherous task in underdeveloped than in

17

developed lands. By this time it is platitudinous—even though still valid—to state that underdevelopment is also asynchronous development. This statement means that we should expect to find within some "national" boundaries hunting and fishing cultures, stable village patterns, other groups moulded in feudal organization and attitudes, and sometimes even highly industrial urban complexes verging on the megalopolis. This array exists within contemporary Brazil, for example. Clearly there can be no single elite group, no single set of leaders or masses of potential followers within such complicated systems of only partially interacting coexistence.[1]

This essay is a study of the Latin American sociopolitical context, of the types of leadership which this context has produced, and of the values and ideological norms which have shaped the goals of these leadership groups.

STRUCTURAL CATEGORIES OF LATIN AMERICAN STATES

National averages are misleading in Latin America, especially for the larger and more complex countries. Crude as such figures are, they are nevertheless of some utility in permitting us to distinguish the most underdeveloped from the most developed of the Latin American states. Our purpose in this exercise is only inferential: to discuss the varying kinds of societies which offer potential for different types of leaders.

Of the many typologies of Latin American countries, perhaps the most sophisticated is the one created by Roger Vekemans and J. L. Segundo. They use six general categories (the economy, the social stratification system, cultural factors, the standard of living, ethnography, and political behavior), subdivided into such standard indicators as literacy, ratio of physicians to inhabitants, and voting characteristics, to suggest the classification shown on the following page, advancing from the least to the most developed.[2]

The spread of the real numbers involved will reveal the differences hidden by the simple distribution. To take extremes, Argentina has a per capita income of $460 per year, Haiti $64; the former has 128 physicians per 100,000 population, the latter 9; 74.6 Argentines per 100,000 are university students, only 9 Haitians per

[1]K. Silvert, "National Values, Development, and Leaders and Followers," *International Social Science Journal,* Volume XV, Number 4 (UNESCO, 1963), p. 560.

[2]"Essay of a Socio-Economic Typology of the Latin American Countries," in Egbert DeVries and José Medina Echavarría (eds.), *Social Aspects of Economic Development in Latin America* (Paris: UNESCO, 1963), pp. 88–91.

Group I	Group IV
Haiti	Brazil
Guatemala	Mexico
Honduras	
Dominican Republic	*Group V*
Nicaragua	Panama
El Salvador	Costa Rica
	Venezuela
Group II	Cuba
Paraguay	
Bolivia	*Group VI*
	Chile
Group III	Uruguay
Peru	Argentina
Ecuador	
Colombia	

100,000; 14 percent of the Argentine population is illiterate, while the figure for Haiti is 89 percent. For almost all such social characteristics, the distances are much wider between Argentina and Haiti than between Argentina and the United States.

Reasonable political inferences from this typology are not as evident as they may seem. Stability, for example, does not correlate with socioeconomic indicators. The susceptibility of leadership elements to political extremisms of left and right also seems to fall randomly. The most important correlation between this typology and contemporary political data is the relationship between political leadership and followership: *type of followership* may be inferred from these numbers, but *not type of available leadership*. In other words, leadership is more variable than followership.

The emergence of extreme modernizers as well as extreme traditionalists can occur in the socially less developed lands, but the effective public reactions cannot vary so widely. Marxist leadership in Bolivia, Guatemala, and possibly the Dominican Republic could not find the same degree of human availability for mass political mobilization as lay at hand in Cuba. The corporate organization attempted in Vargas' Brazil and Perón's Argentina was made possible by the existence of disorganized and unorganized blue-collar elements, especially those recently recruited from rural areas to the industrial city and still imbued with the traditionalist desire for personalistic leadership.

The typology is especially useful for countries at the extremes of the developmental spectrum. The most developed (Chile, Argentina,

Uruguay) are also the most homogeneous, and the least developed (Haiti, Guatemala, Honduras) have the smallest upper groups. Averages work best for the two extremes, in the former case because of the similarity of the units being averaged and in the latter because the very smallness of the elite groups permits them to be lost in the general averages with little numerical skewing of the means. The countries in the middle underscore the importance of going beyond the averages to the social structural distributions.

SOCIAL STRUCTURE, POWER, AND LEADERSHIP

Aside from the differences between Indians and *mestizos,* no social distinctions are more obvious in Latin America than those of class. With the possible exceptions of Uruguayans and Argentines, it is possible to determine the social origins of Latin Americans by their manner of speech. Latin American classes are also sharply differentiated from one another by dress, housing, customs, aspirations, schooling, and political participation. The structural rigidity related to these harsh distinctions is most important here because it produces vast differences of power and activism among the various classes.

The more developed Latin American countries seem to have complex and indeed almost "modern" social structures. The view that all Latin Americans are either rich or poor may be a justifiable stereotype if derived from Central America, but it has not been true of Mexico, Argentina, Uruguay, Chile, Venezuela, Cuba, and Brazil for the past twenty-five years. As early as 1950, according to a reliable estimate, the percentage of the population in middle and upper income and occupational categories was, for each of the more advanced countries: Argentina (36), Chile (22), Brazil (15), Cuba (22), Venezuela (18), and Colombia (22). The operation of Latin America's great cities, of course, requires a substantial number of persons in intermediate positions of training, income, and occupation. One-third of all Argentines live in Buenos Aires; half of all Uruguayans live in Montevideo; a fifth of all Chileans in Santiago. Rio de Janeiro and São Paulo together have a population of over ten million. Mexico City contains over five million.

"Middle-class politics" were visible in Latin America long before the massive industrial urbanization of the postwar generation. The emergence of the Radical parties in the southern cone countries (Argentina, Uruguay, Chile) occurred in the last century. Socialist parties have always drawn their leaders from middle and even upper elements, and increasingly their rank and file membership has come from the growing middle groups. The social origins of the leaders of the Mexican Revolution were almost invariably in favored social groups, and their populist politics led to the enlarging and empowering of middle groups.

Perhaps the mythology of the allegedly two-classed nature of Latin American society is a result of the romantic belief that stability and growth occur automatically with the presence of middle groups. If there is little stability and spasmodic growth, then it must follow that middle groups are absent or powerless. Such reasoning is untenable. As C. Wright Mills has put it,[3]

> To understand the occupation, class, and the status position of a set of people is not necessarily to know whether or not they (1) will become class-conscious, feeling that they belong together or that they can best realize their rational interests by combining; (2) will have "collective attitudes" of any sort, including those toward themselves, their common situation; (3) will organize themselves, or be open to organization by others into associations, movements or political parties; or (4) will become hostile toward other strata and struggle against them. These social, political, and psychological characteristics may or may not occur on the basis of similar objective situations.

If class position, then, tells us something immediate about potential power as actually distributed, it tells us nothing directly about how power is used, for what ends, through what means, and with what rationalizations. The concept of social class does indicate the loci of power and, of course, in general terms whether we are dealing with a more modern or less modern society *in a structural sense,* but not necessarily in a functional one.

Power may be defined for our present purposes as the ability of an individual or of a group to make others do what it wants them to do. Naturally, there are many subtleties surrounding this concept. For example, how does one estimate potential power? The consent of the governed is not merely empty phraseology; refusal to accede to the wishes of others even at the cost of death is, of course, to destroy the power of others over oneself.

Another facet of power analysis concerns the means of its application. It is a truism of politics that the greater is the reliance on overt sanction for the enforcement of law, the more brittle the political structure; the more institutional legitimacy is expressed in the acceptance of law as the temporarily absolute arbiter of social interaction, the greater the strength of the political community. As obvious as are

---

[3]I. L. Horowitz, ed., *Power, Politics, and People* (New York: Ballantine Books, 1964), p. 320.

these statements, they cannot be fully understood without reference to class and caste factors as these factors define the nature of community. If caste lines locate qualitatively different kinds of human beings within the same political boundaries, then by definition there does not exist a single uniform rule of law applicable to everyone. The same conclusion may be true of class differences. If the distance between class groups is extremely wide, then a sufficiently broad community of interests cannot be found for the purposes of the adjustment to change, law, and articulated interests demanded by the high degree of differentiation inherent in industrial society.

This brings us back to our original proposition: the nature of a given social structure sets the limits for possible power and leadership-followership relations, but the type and quality of those interactions depend on ideological and value factors, on how individuals within their social situations understand those situations. To think that class interest magically reveals itself to man is to fall into another of those fatalistic analyses which have so bedeviled our understanding of the social process. The Marxists, assuming a long-term correlation between "real" class interest and its ultimate recognition by the members of each class, are engaging in essentially this type of analysis. With these analyses, short- and middle-range phenomena are practically inexplicable. Why do Brazilian industrialists fight with Brazilian industrialists, Argentine generals with Argentine generals, Guatemalan aristocrats with Guatemalan aristocrats? If class interest will eventually override all other interests, why do the proletariat invariably prefer identification with their own bourgeoisie inside national boundaries to alliance with other proletariats across national frontiers?

These questions have been asked often enough, of course. They would appear to need constant restatement, however, to remind us that the "natural" is not so natural as many of us would like to think. Leaders both create and group power; they employ that power toward certain ends, inevitably affording differing benefits to the various groups and individuals in the society. We cannot fully understand the role of leadership in Latin American until we know for what ends power has been used. For this, we must consider the value orientations which influence leadership groups.

Values, the Uses of Power, and Leadership

In a social sense nothing merely existentially happens. The objective *social* happening is the melding of a positive occurrence with the social understanding of that event. How such happenings will be understood, how they will be imbued with significance, is a function of the value orientation of the persons concerned. And that value orientation is in itself a primary defining characteristic of cultures.

The common division of the world into traditionalists and modernists is a current manner of incorporating value elements into the analysis of development. These two categories are insufficient to cover all Latin American cultures from nomadic tribes to industrial urban persons. Merely for convenience, however, and because the immediately important political actors in Latin America are all within the greater Mediterranean cultural continuum, let us distinguish an Iberian kind of traditionalism from attitudes which, *grosso modo,* we may call "Western Modern."

It is fairly conventional to describe modern values as rationalist, relativist, and self-adjusting to change. To be a rationalist in public affairs involves pragmatism and experimentalism, a seeking for a relationship of means to ends that permits an enlargement of the area of rational choice in the future. Rationalism carries with it the necessary correlate of relativism. Pragmatism involves making choices in terms of the less bad against the bad, the better against the not so good—and not exclusive choices involving utopian statements of the best or the worst. The individual effect of rational relativism and its accent on process is to lead to a dynamic, to the ability of individuals and groups to adjust themselves easily to change after it occurs, and hopefully to anticipate changes and to adjust beforehand.

The Mediterranean traditionalist, and perhaps all nonmodern persons, holds values of ritualism, absolutism, and stasis. The traditionalist does not justify his actions by pragmatic reasoning, but rather in conformity with the dictates of custom and rite. He does not test his actions against their relative validity, but judges them according to absolute standards legitimized in beliefs concerning the supernatural. Change is abhorrent because it disturbs the existing order which, because it is "natural," is morally sanctioned.

The mere fact that individuals and groups profess certain beliefs is no assurance, however, that they will behave in consonance with their verbal expressions of norms. Beliefs and actions can be coherent only when the existing institutions, the ruling groups, and the dominant culture together certify the acceptability of given behavior patterns. To continue this line of reasoning, therefore, we are obliged at least to indicate what institutional organizations would be appropriate for the modern and traditional belief patterns indicated above.

A modern institutional structure is differentiated in order to permit the adjustment of limited means to limited ends. Mediating institutions exist to settle differences arising in the complex, differentiated situation. These institutions, particularly the government of the nation-state, must themselves be contained or limited in power in order to permit the sustained interplay of tempered decision, validation, and further tempered decision required to build pragmatic process into the situation. The pluralistic structure, then, is not without its order, the state being the ultimate arbiter of secular conflict, with procedures built into the system to change those "ultimate" decisions as society itself changes.

The institutional structure of the traditional society strives to contain pluralism within hierarchical form, so that a *single line* of authority connects each individual and group with higher social institutions and eventually with the instruments of divine sanction. This organic, or totally coherent and planned, approach to human relations is classical in Iberian political thought. The following quotation discusses the thinking of Diego Tovar de Valderrama, expressed in his *Instituciones políticas,* published in 1645:[4]

> ... the republic is an aggregation of many *families* forming a civil body with different members.... The families are the material or parts of which is formed this corpus ... vast congregations of individuals characterized by diverse occupations or employments.... Tovar limits these to eight: the clergy, the magistracy ... , the army, the nobility, agriculture, commerce, the liberal and industrial professions, and above all as principal member, the supreme power....

In traditional society, then, to know one major social characteristic of an individual is to know all. Mixing across class lines, sharing equally in some functions with all members of the society, aspiring to upward mobility—these are denied to the individual. Iberian society has grown much more specialized in economic matters since the beginning of this century, but the attempt is invariably made to see that the changes do not disrupt the social pecking order, the conditions of immobility, and the distribution of economic, social, and political power which characterized the traditional order. Corporatism is, of course, the Mediterranean attempt to change without changing.

It is now possible to attempt an identification of leadership with followership, relating the level of development of individual countries to the power potential as it is derived from the social structure and to power as it is directed by the value systems involved. No

[4]As cited in José Antonio Maravell, *La philosophie politique espagnole au XVIIe siècle* (Paris, 1955), pp. 91–92.

attempt will be made at a complete categorization of types of Latin American political leadership at the national level, the following being suggested only as indicative of major types.

The Caudillo.   In its broadest political sense, *caudillismo* in Latin America has popularly come to refer to any highly personalistic and quasimilitary regime whose party mechanisms, administrative procedures, and legislative functions are subject to the intimate and immediate control of a charismatic leader and his cadre of mediating officials. Historically the *caudillo* was usually a self-proclaimed military officer, although some have been civilians, and in either case *caudillos* were supported by irregular or otherwise nonprofessional armies. *Caudillos* have been liberal as well as conservative, urban as well as rural in orientation, modernizing in net influence as well as traditional. In short, the only common denominator of the *caudillo* is that he is personalistic and rules over a situation which is truly primitive, or one which he and his constituency *see* as primitive and simple. Only the least developed countries in Latin America still have national leaders of the *caudillo* stripe. Such recent cases as Anastasio Somoza in Nicaragua and Rafael Trujillo in the Dominican Republic come easily to mind.

Caudillistic governments should be subdivided at least by their effect, as the previous paragraph suggests. Very often such regimes encourage particular types of social change, especially through economic channels. Because, in contemporary times, such economic change is a peculiar combination of familistic enterprise and highly professional, small military organization, the result is a reincarnation of the mercantilist state. Cuba under Batista, Paraguay under Stroessner, and the Dominican Republic under Trujillo all exhibit these characteristics.

The "Oligarch."   Even rightist Latin Americans popularly refer to class-bound governments identified with upper groups alone as "oligarchies." Again, such governors are now found only in the less developed countries but, as in the case of the *caudillos,* were present everywhere during the last century and the opening years of this one. When Latin American societies indeed were composed of small upper groups divided according to rural or urban occupation, with the remainder of the population far outside the national continuum except for nascent middle groups involved in service undertakings, government could be little else but oligarchical in the narrow sense of that term. The oligarchies, however, split into Liberals and Conservatives throughout Latin America. Although the division is often attributed merely to a clash between urban and rural interests, each with its own ideological veneer, reality is more complex. The European-oriented anticlericalism and Social Darwinism of the Liberal was more than a cloak for naked interest, as the conservatism of his opponents was and is a deeply held conviction. Their clashes involved more than mere changing of the guard, despite their cohabitation within one social class. Most "oligarchs" were civilians, and in the more developed countries (Chile, Argentina, and Uruguay, most specifically) the Liberal oligarch paved the way for the accession of middle groups to power by his firm belief in the rule of law and the extension of democratic process.

The Middle-Class Professional. The growth in complexity of the Latin American states has given rise almost everywhere to stable, professional party organization, most commonly based in middle-class elements. Many contemporary presidents of major Latin American countries have come up through the ranks of this kind of party organization. Chile's Gabriel González Videla, Argentina's Arturo Frondizi, all of Uruguay's recent presidents, and the last five Mexican presidents all represent this tendency. Transitional leaders guiding their countries into this type of political life are also to be seen; Rómulo Betancourt in Venezuela is the most visible contemporary example. Again, these men have varying ideological bents, but most are members of Radical or Social Democratic parties. Eduardo Frei of Chile is the first of this type whose views embrace Christian Democracy, although a growing number of aspiring leaders in other countries are attempting to emulate him.

The Ad Hoc Military Amateur. Distinct from the traditional *caudillo,* the military leaders who ally themselves with significant civilian interest groups to attain complex, institutional, and partially impersonal ends comprise a category of increasing significance. They often alternate with the middle-class professionals, especially when standard political mechanisms cannot cope with the more acute crises of development. Rojas Pinilla in Colombia, Pérez Jiménez in Venezuela, Castelo Branco in Brazil, Pedro Aramburu in Argentina, and Castillo Armas in Guatemala are all examples of this type. They sometimes represent the interests only of elite groups, but that is not always the case. More commonly they are supported by a coalition of certain upper and middle elements, as is so obviously true in Brazil today and was in Argentina under Aramburu. The ideology of the military amateur ranges from middle-class radicalism to classical Latin liberalism, with a few cases of conservatism on the record. Whether or not some of the individuals concerned may have had dynastic ambitions, their regimes have usually been buffer operations designed to buy time for realignment of the conventional political machinery in directions more favorable to the interests and values which the *ad hoc* military governor represents.

The Populist Conservative or Falangist. The more developed Latin countries have large masses of urban dwellers, unabsorbed into the national community. Broken from their traditional culture, they are "mobilized" for further social interaction, but not yet integrated into the national community which is their only alternative. Mexico, Brazil, Venezuela, Chile, Argentina, and Uruguay have successfully weathered storms of integration of middle elements into national life, but the process is not yet completed for lower social groups. One of the most misunderstood of recent Latin political phenomena has been the emergence of the rightist populist movements personalized in the figures of Getulio Vargas in Brazil and Juan Domingo Perón in Argentina. They are often called leftist merely because they sought popular support in unintegrated but available groups; but their social origins, their military relations, and their ideologies have as often led them to be labeled rightist. They are not socialist, but corporatist; they are not democratic, but authoritarian; they are not relativists, but dogmatic absolutists. In short, they are in the Mediterranean falangist tradition.

The Totalitarian of the Left. Totalitarianism is a "modern" phenomenon in the sense that the all-embracing political control involved demands a high order of technology and a complex social structure. It is not "modern" in the sense of being self-sustaining, for not only are difficulties in arranging political succession inherent to such systems, but also totalitarianism specifically rejects the mechanisms designed to build the checks and balances of rational decision-making into the political process. The government of Castro's Cuba fits this category. Cuba was susceptible to totalitarianism because of its high degree of urbanization and its high rating on almost all other indices of development relative to its Latin American sister republics. As in all the rest of Latin America where Marxist parties are well established, the Cuban leadership is middle- and upper-class in origin, and most of the activist followership is in the middle group. Extended peasant support came only after Castro's victory in Cuba; elsewhere, Marxist parties have little success with lower-class elements, either in city or country. This situation is obviously not immutable. In the meantime, however, there is nothing to prevent quasi-totalitarian *manipulation* of prenational populations through the use of the appropriate symbols and force.

    The Totalitarian of the Right.   Little attention has been paid to this type of leader, perhaps because no one of them has as yet been successful in his search for presidential office in Latin America. Extreme right nationalists exist in all the more developed countries and have been very active in recent years in Argentina. Recruiting always from the same middle and upper classes used by other national leaders, they too have had little or no success with lower groups.

    This list could obviously be extended. Just as obviously, it mixes structural with ideological criteria. When the ideological label appears in the title, it is because such groups give weight to normative factors. When the structural label appears, it is because the groups are pragmatic in their search for the satisfaction of their value-interests and felt needs.

    It is also possible to discuss leadership elements according to their position in the scale of power and influence. Middle-level leadership is clearly of great importance in promoting political stability. Such leaders impersonalize the party as well as governmental and interest group structures. They give day-to-day continuity to public affairs. They can, of course, be fitted as subgroups into the above scheme. But, as a rule of thumb, it should be remembered that the more traditional and more personalistic a leadership structure, the fewer intermediate-level persons are involved, the fewer are the mediating functions, and the less important the institution as such.

    The preceding analysis has suggested, then, that simple left-to-right categorization of Latin American political ideologies is insufficient. At the national political level a double scale is possible. One scale, ranking the traditionalist elements, would run from the conservative right to the Falangist left. The other, including the modernizing elements, would start with Liberals on the right, run through Radicals, Christian Democrats, Social Democrats, and end on the left with certain of the Marxist parties. This simple scheme should, however, be adjusted to the conditions of each country. Certain center and left party groups are deeply traditionalist in their behavior, although many of their avowed attitudes may be modern. Just as behavior cannot be directly inferred from class position, it cannot be directly correlated with avowed beliefs.

CONCLUSIONS

It should now be obvious that the full range of ideological conviction is expressed by Latin America's national leaders. It has also been stated, but not so far supported by evidence, that these leaders almost invariably come from middle- and upper-class groups. Some summary statements about very generalized characteristics of Latin American leaders will not in themselves provide hard data, but may indicate the nature of the inferences which have been used here.

1. Almost all overt national leaders have a university education or its equivalent in military instruction. The Latin American university caters almost exclusively to persons from higher social brackets, if for no reason other than that only such persons can afford to stay off the labor market long enough to go through the university. In Mexico, for example, of every thousand children who enter the first grade, only one is graduated from a university.

2. It is probable that a very high percentage of Latin American leaders retain an interest in educational matters. To be an intellectual in Latin America is a mark of prestige often sought by the politician. Even many military leaders write occasional journal articles.

3. Leaders normally share the culture of the capital city. Even populist leaders rarely address the "masses" in a language other than Spanish or Portuguese.

4. Multilingualism has been a traditional mark of Latin America's elites. It remains a common characteristic of today's middle- and upper-class leaders that they usually speak French and English as well as Spanish or Portuguese. This statement is true also of military officers, many of whom learn foreign languages in military missions abroad. Perón, for example, was reputed to be fluent in Italian and German and reasonably proficient in French and English. Incidentally, he also prided himself on being a military historian, and he published several academic studies in the field of military history.

5. Extensive foreign travel is another classical proof of upper-class status widely imitated by middle groups. Doing the Grand Tour remains in vogue throughout Latin America's more favored social sectors. Political leaders very commonly have either studied for short periods abroad or have traveled reasonably widely.

This list indicates some important elements of the life-style of Latin America's leaders: they are cosmopolitan, marked with the formal aspects of high culture, participant in elite patterns, sensitive to international currents of thought, and evidently convinced that their appeal is enhanced and not inhibited by these characteristics.

These qualities serve to explain a basic Latin American political phenomenon: the mimetic quality of political organization or, to put it more positively, the intimacy of the reaction in Latin America to ideational change in the Western world. It is widely remarked that Latin America's constitutions have been but poorly adjusted imitations of American and French examples. We know, also, that the French Enlightenment immediately affected Latin America's elites, that Positivism in Europe became a Latin political creed, and that Marxism and its derivates served as a primary stimulus to political change. Plainly such immediacy of reaction must be related to the peculiarities of the leadership structure within Latin America. As we have seen, the value system and the social structure combine to reinforce the role of the Latin American leader as the importer and adapter of ideas from abroad.

In a very important fashion, then, the effectiveness of leadership is a combined function of the power system and the value system within a Latin American country, as well as the nature of the universe of stimuli to which these systems are subjected from without. It is at this point that the Spanish meaning of the word "formation" becomes meaningful. In this article we have taken "formation" to mean the relationship between the social origins of leader and follower and their ideological and value connections. In Spanish the word *formación* refers to the education and personality of a person— literally, to the way in which he is formed or fashioned. To the extent that the Latin leader is "formed" with a hypersensitivity to international currents of thought, an opportunity is opened to the United States and European nations to contribute with immediacy and directness to the politics of change in Latin America.

That this opportunity has been almost totally neglected in fact, although at times touted in diplomacy, would suggest that a study of Latin American leadership is in some essential part also a study of American and European leadership.

1966

The Unwitting Prototypes:
Latin American Students

FOR YEARS the question was "Why are Latin American students different from all other students?" Besides its wording, it smacked of the Passover service in its emotional context of comfort, the smug satisfaction in our having "made it," while those underdeveloped people wallowed in their backward emotionality and instability. Once Berkeley, Columbia, and even Dartmouth hosted student political activism, the question changed: "Why are North American students becoming Latin Americanized?"

Although facile, this equation of North and Latin American student politics is not totally erroneous. But I doubt that the persons who draw the analogy know the Latin American situation in sufficient detail to have any idea of where the verity of the analogy really lies. In any event, merely seeing the resemblance may be a momentous intellectual breakthrough in the United States, the beginning of understanding the real similarities as well as the dissimilarities between "modern" and the many kinds of "traditional" societies, an empathic capacity that might assist us to a foreign policy bearing some relevance to the internal social situations of the countries with which we deal.

The *latinoamericanización* of elements of American student movements should give us pause, for by any vulgarization of our rather weak theories of development, it should not have occurred. After all, academics and politicians alike have for long been telling Latin Americans that they need what we have, so that their universities can become professionalized service agencies. In the meantime, they should reduce the degree of student political involvement, get students out of policy-making "co-governments," professionalize

31

their administrative and fiscal policies, and turn academic policy over to full-time faculty members. The fact that such prescriptions were and are ideologically, politically, and economically impossible was no reason for not making them, of course. And since that recipe for betterment could be followed only by a few private universities in Latin America, most of them church-affiliated, in the early 1960s American governmental agencies began to turn their attention away from trouble-making state universities to the private institutions. The returns from this policy are now coming in: Catholic universities, as they have developed, are becoming increasingly similar to public institutions in the degree and direction of their student activism. In sum, we have helped to expand the institutional base of university political activity in Latin America, and we have not stopped to consider that the very processes we push may be at the heart of student unrest in the United States as well as Latin America. Our own problems "should not" have occurred if one assumes that economic well-being is the wellspring of all other welfare. But if the premises are that economic development answers only one set of questions and that it adds a set of muscles for effectively posing other important questions, then we may begin to understand some of the resemblances among recent manifestations of student unrest, whether in Latin America or elsewhere.

Certainly the similarities are felt by the students themselves. Although I have no hard proof, I suspect that the popularity of facial hair dates from Fidel Castro's 1960 visit. The cult of "Ché" Guevara mystifies many older persons, who saw in his useless and clumsy Bolivian death his failure to understand the very reasons for the success of leftist revolution in Cuba. But, as a student of mine put it, Guevara was admirable in death "because he didn't have to do it." *Quijotismo,* the romance of the *gauchada* (the spontaneous gesture of generosity), and the unveiling of naked personality are among the happier Latin American traits, although when applied to public doings they make pragmatic North Americans desperate. Perhaps students here feel some kinship with the Latin American style as they understand it because it seems to negate the careful, cautious, self-protective egotism they see as the instrument betraying the guts and heat of positive, national, libertarian American purpose.

It is the posing of the existential question in East, West, and South that has linked recent leftist student movements. *L'Express,* even with its conservative bent, summed up French student queries as being "To learn? But what? To make money and be useful for something? But to be useful for whom?" Such plaints are traditional in the literature of Latin American student polemics. A modern version is:

We are training men for the previous century, not for today, and least of all for the future. On the pretext of educating men who are not educated also in their high schools, with their fraudulent liberal arts curricula and their backward mathematics and physical science training, we are neglecting the formation of responsible producers and citizens.[1]

In the search for the purpose of being, and the purpose of being intellectuals, generosity of spirit is on the side of the student dissidents. In Latin America they have persistently argued that education should serve to reduce the weight of privilege and to turn their societies toward making merit selection a reality. They have favored national development and dignity together with aspirations for access to the wider world of ideas and aesthetics. They have opposed retrograde dictatorships and have propagated the rhetoric of freedom and social decency. Their opponents have consistently used the same mean-spirited arguments that one now hears in the United States. If society endows students with a free education, why complain? The university is a place to learn, not to think of politics. The implication is that political life is low and dirty, not a high humanistic expression of civic man. Notions of class responsibility and feelings of resentment are also important in the opposition to student activism. The better-placed antagonists argue that students are betraying their class. Their envious lower-status partners in enmity wonder why the advantaged students are rebelling against the very system that favors them. The students' rejection of the aspirations that hotly prod lower-middle-class and upper-lower-class persons makes headbreaking by police as joyous a celebration in Latin America as in the United States.

To carry this understanding of Latin American students further, and to distinguish them from their North American counterparts, we must now begin to place some limitations on our generalizations. Even though Latin American student movements have been reasonably well studied, creating a feeling for the total situation requires some delineation of categories, for the variety of experience is very broad. So far I have followed the modish practice of equating all student activism with ideological leftism. And I have spoken of "students" as a single lump. Let us now be more precise.

As in the United States, the politicized Latin student leader tends to find his followers in the better universities of national stature and among those students with high promise of career suc-

---

[1]Gregorio Weinberg, "Anacronismos en la educación argentina del presente," in Norberto Rodríguez Bustamente, ed., *Los intelectuales argentinos y su sociedad* (Buenos Aires: Ediciones Libera, 1967), pp. 151–52.

cess. In practice, then, we are speaking of national state universities, almost invariably situated in capital cities. Specific institutions, to name almost all of them, are the University of Chile, the University of Buenos Aires, the universities of Rio de Janeiro and São Paulo, the Central University of Venezuela, the National University of Colombia, the University of San Marcos in Lima, the National Autonomous University of Mexico, and, in the past, the University of Havana. A few smaller national universities, provincial public universities, and now Catholic universities also are beginning to become involved. Some of these are the Catholic University of Chile, the University of Concepción (also in Chile), the University of Córdoba in Argentina, and the University of San Carlos in Guatemala. To provide an idea of magnitude: student enrollments in the major national universities range between 20,000 and 75,000—and estimates are that the National Autonomous University of Mexico will have 150,000 students within the next decade. The provincial and private universities that are of political importance tend to have between 5,000 and 12,000 students apiece.

Size is relevant to activism in that the larger the university enrollment, the greater the tendency to teach a full array of subjects. To expand the curriculum beyond law, medicine, and engineering is to introduce social science and thus to heighten the chances for student political involvement. To enlarge the student body is also to broaden its social base and its felt interests, although very few university students anywhere in Latin America come from blue-collar families. Students consistently active in political matters always comprise a very small percentage of any student body. And always half or more than half of the students are politically inert. The critical statistic is how many of the remainder can be recruited to political activity in moments of stress. It is reasonable to suppose that in the politicized universities a quarter to a third of the students are sometimes "available"—a very high figure indeed.

By no means are leftist political ideas the only ones in currency. Organized groups of ultra-rightists can be found everywhere, from the practitioners of armed violence among neo-fascist groups in the University of Buenos Aires to the Guatemalan students who engage in right-wing terrorism. There are young Conservatives and young Liberals (something like followers of the late Senator Taft in this country), and Christian Democrats are very strong in many universities. In the University of Chile and the Catholic University of Chile, the Christian Democratic students have been in control of student government for a decade. They are also powerful in Venezuela, El Salvador, Colombia, and elsewhere; they and more radical Catholic student groups are a strong force for revolutionary change or profound reform in Brazil. Marxist groups—most recently *fidelista* and still including the traditional orthodox Communists, Trotskyists, and neo-Marxist democratic socialists—have been consistently the most interested in organized student activities during this century. But they have always had to share their participation with persons of other persuasions, and in recent years they have often been outvoted by more centrist groups and by the growing Catholic reform movements.

On balance, student interest in the internal organization of university life has probably promoted rather than lessened academic quality. Latin American universities are run by elected officials, except when the governments "intervene" and appoint the deans and rectors. Faculty members are usually part-time teachers, appointments are determined by competition, tenure is uncertain, and pay is very low except for a few full-time professors (rarely more than one percent of the faculty). In addition, for reasons of class and other kinds of group identification, and because initiation into adulthood comes at earlier ages in Latin America than in the United States, student participation in university affairs is neither strange nor unfitting. Besides, education as training only for specialization is not much approved in Latin norms, where the man of general culture, the "intellectual," is still highly valued. Thus, the notion that the professor knows best is patently untenable when applied to political and social goals defining the meaning of life and the role of the university in propagating ideas of life-styles.

Student influence on academic policy is usually exercised through sympathetic faculty members, whether the initiative comes from scholars seeking support for their ideas or from the students themselves. Student demands, however, sometimes run directly counter to professorial interest. Tenure is an important case in point. Student definitions of "relevance," for instance, usually boil down to a simplistic notion that universities must become directly involved in the processes of social change. Extension courses for underprivileged persons, social service activities, slum clearance and urban renewal, and other examples of "the university at the service of the people" imply a curriculum that is entirely applied in content. Correlatively, engaged students think that professors should not pursue classically "academic" paths and should be responsive to changing public needs. Thus, the tendencies of older scholars to become "pure" and specialized in their work must be combated by making appointments for only very limited time periods—usually five to seven years at most—after which the professorial slots should be opened up once more for competitive recruitment.

The fatal flaw in this approach is that it tries to hold the logically untenable position that higher education must be protected from political interference and yet that it must influence politics. In short, students arguing this kind of relevance ask that the university be activist from the inside in its effect on the outside, but that the outside must refrain from meddling within the university structure. The Central University of Venezuela was invaded by government forces in 1967 because it had literally become a site for the stockpiling of arms and a sanctuary for political refugees and guerrillas resting from their labors in the mountains. The same ambivalence was evident in Latin American reactions to North American scholars studying political processes abroad with the support of the U.S. Department of Defense. The heart of the complaint was not that the dividing line between academic and political endeavor was being breached, but rather that working for the *American* government was shameful. Few Latin American scholars see any conflict between their academic roles and their working for their own governments. (North American New Left groups sometimes share this confusion between political activity and university autonomy. I have heard one American professor propose that until students can elect guerrilla techniques in lieu of gym, it cannot really be said that academic freedom exists in the United States.)

Despite these logical difficulties in their policy positions, reformist and other kinds of leftist students in Latin America are also usually strongly developmentalist. Thus, they tend to favor curricular innovation and the introduction of new disciplines, especially in the social sciences. They are alert to foreign ideological and intellectual currents, and often prod their professors to the freshening of course content. Their fight for free university education for all qualified persons sometimes means that truly unqualified students matriculate. But the leftist students have also lent support to such equalizing devices as pre-matriculation preparation, and slowly they have come to accept the necessity for qualifying examinations. Maintaining the idea of a free university is a blow against class privilege and, in its way, not only democratic but also important in recruiting new elements to the labor force. Students, more than any other single force, have made public universities in Latin America as accessible as they are. Of course, the poor find it very difficult to keep their children off the labor force long enough for them to enjoy free higher instruction. However, Latin American societies are usually not closed to upward mobility, if persons somehow manage to acquire the necessary educational backgrounds for such movement. There is an overwhelming belief, in almost all sectors of national Latin American life, that education is the prime channel for movement out of misery. Student response to this attitude helps to make it real, even if only in very limited ways.

As a practical matter, then, student activism has its positive academic and libertarian points, particularly in those matters where the social position of the entire institution is not at issue. In national political life, however, in their looking outward from their temporary status as students, the effect of the activists has been highly varied. A fairly reliable rule of thumb is that the firmer the national institutional situation, the less effective is student activism. The firmness or strength of institutions is the important factor, not the degree of development of the society. The backward, personalistic authoritarianism of Paraguay is accompanied by as little effective student action as is the rapidly modernizing Mexican "soft dictatorship" (*dictablanda*—a pun on *dictadura*, "dictatorship," with *dura* meaning "hard" and *blanda* meaning "soft"). In moments of national weakness and disarray, however, students have often contributed to turmoil and have sometimes been instrumental in toppling governments and installing new ones. Then, if the process leads to political strength, the universities are pushed back into their academic roles.

Such cases are legion in the history of every Latin American republic, and their meaning for the political process is considerable. Student groups can muster the power for important political change because they are often far more highly organized than are other social groups. More important, they are obviously employing their class power: they are the sons and daughters of members of middle and elite groups. And, I would suspect as even more important, they employ their class and institutional positions toward the ends of national development—that is, they push against traditional privilege and in the direction most reasonable people would in any event like to go. Despite the presence of many centrist and rightist student groups, it is the center-left and left that manage to mobilize sufficient force to use students as political shock troops. Since most recognized Latin American intellectuals are on the left, most *effective* student activism is from that side, too. (There are some exceptions, as in Argentina, but they are truly exceptions.)

This phenomenon is complex. I do not think we should be satisfied with conspiratorial explanations, or such simplistic ideas as that the left knows how to organize and the right does not, and that the left commands dedication and the right does not. We must ask why the left can, and the right cannot, or at least does not. An easy way out is to say that, since most Latin American governments are rightist, that ideological sector of student opinion has no need to organize. And we might add that rightist ideology frowns on student (and thus elite) organization for the purpose of popular mobilization and national integration. And there, of course, may be the very point. Most of the left (including the new Catholic groups) either pays lip service to popular democracy, and now to "participatory" democracy, or really believes in it. In any event, the left taken as a whole wants supra-class national organization, economic development, sovereignty, and national "dignity," while some parts of it add that they would eventually like individual freedom, too. These goals are an expression of the political mythology of Latin America, as in the United States and the European democracies. There is now sufficient development of all kinds in Latin America to make such ideas more than a hollow promise for coming generations. Half of all Latin Americans live in towns and cities. Radio and television stations abound, and literacy rates are going up rapidly in some countries. Per capita consumption rates show only slow rises because of the population explosions of most countries, but the absolute increase in productivity and in economic plant is most impressive in at least ten or twelve of the twenty republics.

The students, where they have been effective, are talking, then, in the name of nation, and not of interest group or class. Their aura is not a romantic, unreal one: what they espouse is what many of their countrymen want, and what their societies must have if they are to become developed, national, and socially decent. The usefulness of the students is in raising real issues, and their effectiveness appears when the opposition is not so strong as to co-opt, kill, or otherwise render them powerless. But, once political change has occurred, students cannot administer into being the solutions to their complaints. Their cry is from the heart, not the head. And why should one expect them to provide an organized, administratively skillful blueprint for national development? After all, what students are doing is expressing the basic right of any citizen, the right to make an effective statement concerning what should be the nature of the society to which he lends obedience and pays taxes. To ask more of students is to ask the voter to decide what the Federal Reserve discount rate should be, to pose the asinine question "And just what would you do, exactly, if you had power and could get us out of Vietnam?" or "If you're so smart, how would you keep order on the streets?"

To assume that all public decisions must be based on expertness, on absolute knowledge of facts and procedures, is to fall prey to vulgar Platonism; it is a surrender to the politician and the administrator because the citizen on the outside cannot have access to the "facts," which are in any event classified, at least in part precisely so that he cannot have access to them. Because expertise is still a rare commodity in many Latin American countries, however, student revolutionaries have sometimes seen their successes crowned with their own appointments to high political office. The results are usually poor—no poorer, perhaps, than those of previous regimes, but not good enough to bring about the massive changes promised. Bolivia, Guatemala, Venezuela, and Mexico are living testimonials that the revolutionary can indeed cause change but that it rarely comes out the way he believes it will.

Cuba during the last decade does not belie this interpretation. Students had much to do with revealing the brutality and venality of the Batista regime and with contributing ideology and manpower to its overthrow. Many students paid with their lives for their nationalistic and democratic convictions. The installation of the Castro regime brought with it an enormous wave of initial enthusiasm and wholesale dedication to nation-building tasks, the mass educational portions of which were eminently successful. But economic and administrative troubles multiplied in the hands of persons who were essentially amateurs and guided more by ideology than by the necessary technical knowledge. At the same time, the political skill of the regime, propped up by external enmity, created a true social nation-state backed by the apparatus of a modern polity. Whatever the enormous economic troubles of contemporary Cuba, the political machine has managed to withstand blockade, invasion, its own economic ignorance, a violent change in the international economy, drought, hurricane, and the standard political troubles of the Communist bloc.

The wholesale emigration of professionals, however, denuded the teaching staffs of the universities. That weakening, together with the strength of the government as well as a determination to put education at the direct service of the state, has of course removed any vestige of independent student activism such as we have been describing in the rest of Latin America and the United States.

The standard answer of the *fidelista,* of course, is that such student activities are no longer necessary or desirable, for the Cuban government represents the "people," and past political activities were directed against the state as the enemy of the people. This argument, hoary as it is, raises two primary questions without confronting which any article on Latin American student movements would make little sense in the real world of politics. The first concerns the truly radical student, convinced that the present situation permits of no compromise and therefore of no reform. He defines the opposition as intransigent, entirely corrupt, and intellectually despicable. In short, he thinks his world is at the Hobbesian point at which man's ultimate natural rights are being threatened, and he feels therefore that one must work entirely outside the "system" toward its destruction. This view cannot be dismissed out of hand. Its proof or disproof is not up to such students, but rather is in the hands of those who can and do make effective choices inside the polity. Should they care to show that privilege, power, and capacity are not incompatible with libertarian reform, they will disprove the radical. Should they care to use their privilege, power, and capacity to deny the democratic development on which their true national growth depends, then they will have to use whatever force is required to put down their opposition. If the imposition of "order" requires totalitarian organization because of the very strength of the opposition, it would appear strangely foolish to blame that growing neo-fascism on the simple presence of dissidence. It is like saying that without the existence of the Jews there would have been no gas ovens, and therefore the Holocaust was their own fault.

The second grave problem raised by some of the truly radical students is that they have little meaningful respect for academic freedom and autonomy, as has already been noted. They seek to make the university relevant to "life." But if in so doing they destroy the integrity of the institution by denying its freedom of inquiry and dissent, then they invite the development of sciences of conformity. That path leads to incompetence, which creates the ultimate irrelevancy.

Total denial of the system and a lack of respect for the peculiar requirements of the academic life invariably combine to weaken the position of the far left student dissident, not least because few students will long follow such leadership. The intransigence demands a satisfaction far beyond the limits most students are prepared to set. And the anti-intellectualism offends the basic aspirations and notions of respect held by the center and center-left nationalist groups that make up most Latin American student bodies. In opposition they can join. In partial victory and consolidation they must split.

Thus, when Latin American students become active in national and university politics, they tend to make mistakes. They fight among themselves. They engage in verbal excess. They do not really know how to get what they want. They speak with massive ignorance of the intricacies of the political and the academic processes. They are young, inexpert, hot-headed, involved, brave, and foolhardy. After all, what should they be—old, wise, mature, intelligent, informed, temperate, and merciful?

Let it be enough that they have the generosity of spirit to cry out against misery and exploitation and falsehood. And let the rest of us try to help them "operationalize" that generosity, if we have it within us to remember that honesty and freedom are colleagues, the bases for both democracy and academic freedom. Latin American student dissidents are no experts, but they are better men than their fathers and, unhappily, better citizens now than they are likely to be twenty years from now. To turn the pessimism of that last sentence into a falsehood is at least as much our responsibility as it is theirs.

1968

Ethics and Programmatic Thinking
About Rural Welfare

THIS ESSAY about how to regard "rural welfare" in Latin America will address itself in particular to officials of agencies or foundations that sponsor developmental programs in that field. The points I make should also be of interest to researchers in the social sciences and to other readers concerned with what is, in fact, a crucial question in the evolution of Latin America. I have three basic arguments to advance:

1. "Rural welfare" is whatever we say it is. The words are entirely ideological, and thus imply only preferences, whether idiosyncratically held or firmly rooted in the conventional wisdom.

2. An ideology that is even loosely related to a belief in scientific procedures should lead us to prefer definitions of rural welfare that are tied as intimately as possible to propositions about society that have been or can be validated. Those propositions should also be as parsimonious as possible. Thus, they should be both as simple as can be derived, and as unobtrusive in staining social research as we can devise them.

3. Programs designed to promote our view of rural reform must take into account total social situations and their workings, but must attempt to influence only carefully selected portions of that totality. Those statements are not contradictory. They argue that our diagnoses may and should be synthetic, but our actions must be (and, therefore, should consciously be designed to be) only partial.

Obviously, to state the matter in this way is itself an ideological act. I shall not attempt to search out those value-roots, however, for that way lies madness—the lunacy of opposing two mirrors and

43

counting down the receding images. Instead, I shall stay on one level and, when appropriate, frankly state my own convictions concerning the matters at hand.

One problem with those three arguments is their complexity and the consequent difficulty of explicating them within the confines of this essay. Each of them taps one or more large bodies of social thought, none of which has been definitively mapped. For instance, the argument about ideologies raises questions concerning possibly differing levels of beliefs and about belief-systems and their measurement and the relationship of ascertained beliefs to other aspects of behavior. The second postulate, concerning ideology and the social sciences, invites us into the long-standing dispute about the possibility of a value-free social science, as well as into questions of relevance and commitment and similar concerns given new urgency by events of the past five or six years. However, I am convinced that we cannot *ethically* discuss rural welfare without considering these subjects, for my own convictions include a very heavy dose of rationalism and the concomitant belief that we should plumb our self-understanding as deeply as we can in order to allow the freest possible play to the testing of those thoughts in civic as well as scientific marketplaces, by the devices appropriate to each. That belief, however, does not make the expression of the arguments either shorter or easier—it just makes it necessary, in one form or another.

I suggest that we need to know what we prefer and how we see social change as being caused. Thinking about some of the standard ways in which causality is seen will help us to know ourselves. The following are some possible ways of going about defining rural welfare—or any other human kind, for that matter.

(a) One view of rural welfare is based on notions of "natural hierarchy" in human and animal affairs, a reflection of biological man sacredly created. "To know one's place" is thus a good thing, because it prevents persons from knocking themselves out by trying to change the immutable. "Welfare" thus implies working within the existing power order, making it function and seeking satisfactions fitting to one's station. Conservatives from the southern United States are by no means the only persons who hold variants of these ideas. Christian Democrats do, too, as does anyone who believes in a corporate system. Catholic natural-law theorists tend to fall into this class.

(b) Protestant natural-law theorists, proponents of a liberal view, argue that "welfare" is pursued by seeking to live in accord with natural order. They believe that individual and social welfare is served by differentiation established on a personal basis through the operation of egalitarian social mechanisms. The classical liberal school, then, seeks to serve the "good" by establishing the *processes* by which one attains the "good." Thus, (a) describes a static notion of welfare, (b) a dynamic one.

(c) Utilitarian ethics provide a third definitional system. Here the idea is to maximize values, whatever they may be, on the presumption that man is a naturally rationalizing and maximizing beast. The rational, modal man is the judge of the values and what is to maximized. Once values are socially set, realizing them becomes merely a technical task. This approach is the implicit one employed by most development advisors. Unwilling or unable to assume policy responsibility, and eschewing overt ideology, they accept the notion that everybody wants still more of whatever he wants, and that he wants to get it through the most efficient means—and off they go. The easiest solution, this one begs the most questions.

(d) A fourth way of defining welfare is to see it as the satisfaction of man's nature, taken as only a mundane, secular assumption, lacking sacred origins and discoverable through worldly techniques. It is in this way of looking at human progress that all Kantians and some Marxists come together. Ernst Cassirer, who belongs to the Kantian school, sees man as a symbol-creating and -manipulating entity and argues that whatever satisfies that unique ability of man is what contributes to his welfare. Marx argued that the reduction of alienation is the ultimate measure of welfare, which he saw as the ability of men in society to be able immediately to create their own situations and their own lives. The Kantians emphasize individual measures, the Marxists social ones, but both seek a reconciliation of social and individual criteria of the good—as, indeed, did their predecessors such as Adam Smith. As will be seen, Kantians and Marxists also tend to diverge in matters concerning social causality.

These explanations provide functional measures of welfare. In the first, welfare is found by serving God's given social order. In the second, it is found by organizing ourselves to find that order and, in the third, by defining wants as psychological tensions and defining welfare as their most efficient satisfaction. The fourth school sees welfare as the realization of a secularly defined "humanness." Another way of getting into the question of the meaning of welfare is through theories of causality, the ways that partisans of various theories see social change as coming about. For example, some persons see voluntarism—effective human decisions—as the only cause of social change; others think societies are caught in the grip of immutable historical forces; still others posit "great man" theories. The major instrumental and causal schools of thought we have to deal with are:

(a) Vulgar economic determinism. (Welfare rests primarily on an economic infrastructure.)

(b) Technological determinism—a school that includes many self-professed Marxists as well as North American businessmen and advisors. (Changes in techniques are a prime cause, forcing all other change.)

(c) Historical determinism—encompassing many Marxists of certain persuasion, all Hegelians, and dependence thinkers in Latin America. (Welfare is promoted by being in tune with historical "necessities" or even destinies.)

(d) "Great man" theory—propounded by leadership schools, including many practicing politicians who think leaders are the critical variable. (Welfare is served by empowering and following the "proper"—usually undefined, but always "strong"—leaders.)

(e) Voluntarism—including Kantians, certain Marxists, orthodox classical liberals, persons who think man makes his own world within the historical situation given to him. (The criteria of *what* should be done vary widely among Kantians, Marxists, and Liberals, of course. But they all agree that the area of "may do" is wide, that of "must do" is narrow.)

(f) Dialectical interpretations—given by all Hegelians and sophisticated Marxists, some Talmudists, persons who share the notion that man makes his own world within the historical situation given him, but who also emphasize the forms and processes through which change occurs. (The inevitability of contradiction reveals itself in processes of change that are ineluctably conflictual—though not necessarily violent—and which thus act as a *functional* limitation on the ways man can make his world for himself.)

(g) Functional determinism—everything that occurs is designed to answer a "functional necessity." This reasoning is narrowly circular, and is employed by many social scientists as a way to avoid entering into causal explanation with seriousness.

(h) Biological determinism—espoused by the "man as ape" thinkers, who assume that our biological natures determine cultural patterns, and that welfare comes about through welding cultural variables to biological constants.

The second of my original propositions, of course, introduced the skeletal idea that whatever notion of welfare we may adopt, and whatever the theory of social change to which we may wish to append it, we should allow room for the scientific study of society. Before I pursue that notion, however, let me underscore the sensitivity of any decision by introducing the partisan labels attached to varying mixes of the criteria for judging welfare we have listed, and the ways seen as efficacious for achieving it. The following are some common examples of the ways in which given clusters of parties take their stands with respect to welfare and its realization:

(a) Corporate parties believe in natural hierarchies, and thus assume that institutional changes can and should take place without disturbing the essential nature of class. Falangists, the *Opus Dei,* and all kinds of fascist organizations comprise the right wing of this group. Christian Democrats make up the left wing of the corporate spectrum, for they espouse maximum participation and mobility within a system of classes which as a totality are moving upward in terms of material welfare, levels of participation, and access to learning—but which remain hierarchically ordered through all social time.

(b) Among utilitarian parties are military technocracies, *técnico* groups in general, the Radical parties by and large, segments of the old Liberals, Chilean and Cuban orthodox Communists. The incumbent Brazilian and Peruvian governments are good cases in point.

(c) Voluntaristic parties include secular and nationalizing liberals, some Socialists, some *fidelistas,* and sectors of the PRI in Mexico.

The point should now be clear that this way of approaching the question of welfare and how to get it gives us perspectives on right and left that are somewhat different from the stereotypical views, and even different from the perceptions of the political actors themselves. We can begin to see the sharp differences between kinds of rights and kinds of lefts and to understand how some right–left alliances—even though they may be only tacit—come into being.

In any event, the time has come for U.S. agencies and foundations to make a choice. Not to seem to make one is to opt for hidden utilitarian premises. Obviously, my personal preference is for a voluntaristic approach governed by rationality and effectively hooked to appropriate institutional structures and procedures. That sentence is instrumental, however: it says nothing about what the routinized employment of effective reason is designed to gain. It is a great temptation to duck that ultimate question, not only for reasons of scientific method but also in order to achieve as much agreement as is possible. Still, I think we can go a bit further and still avoid the disaster of asking that we peer into the Great Void and turn around, having all seen the same vision. Let me suggest that social welfare be gauged by the ability effectively to employ reason in such a way as to increase the social ability effectively to employ reason. The statement is not solecistic; it holds not that reason is a good in itself, but that its employment *in a certain way* is the desirable. Let us work out a few examples.

It is usually argued by persons of democratic persuasion, for example, that participation is good *per se*. Certainly storm troopers and Blackshirts were participants in the social processes of their land, but it could scarcely be held that their participation increased their own ability and others' to continue to participate. In short, participation can be employed to reduce effectiveness. To take another example, social mobility is also often seen as desirable in itself. But it may well occur in such manner as to reinforce the power of persons who want to stop further mobility. Combat among ethnic groups within the United States and the heat of the school busing issue are related to this phenomenon. Clearly, the quantitative fact of mobility is not enough to assure the process a given qualitative effect. Similarly, *técnicos* may work in the service of a state that destroys or damages the intellectuals and the academic institutions which produced the technicians in the first place, and which give them the very ideological frames within which they operate. Societies may then develop that can boast of industrial techniques and technicians but not of science and scientists. The institutional structure needed to support technology is vastly different from that required to support a scientific establishment.

In other words, form and quantity are *necessary* aspects of welfare concepts, but substance and quality provide the components of *sufficiency*. The points I have been trying to make are that the fact of a situation does not dictate its quality and that without the fact there can be *no* quality. Forgetting these obvious statements has confounded much thinking about development in general, and particularly about material changes in the conditions of life. So let us continue with banalities for a bit longer.

On the side heavily weighted toward purely quantitative considerations come the subsistence facts of life: enough food for at least reproduction of the species, habitation and clothing and socialization experiences that permit the group to survive. Much "developmental" work in agriculture has so far been largely justified in terms of the population–food nexus, and has included survival questions not only for rural persons but for urban ones as well. Though it may appear obviously "good" in itself to help societies to satisfy these basic needs, cases are rare in which "welfare" can be so rudimentarily defined as to involve only questions of physical subsistence. Thus, the quantity of food becomes immediately enmeshed with its taste, its texture, the food habits of the population, status, and so forth. Habitation becomes measured by such relational words as "minimally decent"; clothing involves ceremonies and cleanliness as well as warmth; and, of course, "minimal socialization" turns out to be a function of the kinds of ideological choices we have been considering. Even when dealing with such seemingly obvious "good things" as feeding, clothing, sheltering, and teaching people, we do not escape a qualitative judgment, though it be no more sophisticated than the innocent belief that it is better to keep people alive than to allow them to perish or actively to kill them off.

In the matter of connecting the forms and facts of our social life with the meaning and uses of it, I wish to state a clear and crisp preference: it is desirable that all persons be as well prepared, activist, and self-aware as possible when infusing events and things with meaning, provided that the dominant culture loads the dice in such a way as to ensure that the significances ascribed to events and things lean toward ever-increasing openness in the ascriptions of future meanings. That sentence is not as obscure as it may seem on first reading. I am implying only that some groups and some persons are unable to make social meaning for themselves in such a way as to remain free themselves or to permit others to continue to exercise that freedom. If powerful groups themselves impose uniformity of thought in this basic respect, we should abhor them. If weak groups and persons can "see" the lives of all in only one narrow and rigid way, then to increase their structural power without concomitantly working on their ways of infusing life with meaning courts the creation of more powerful authoritarianisms or the overturn of partially open societies. Latin America teems with examples of both kinds of groups. The Brazilian government permits less play in value ascription than the Brazilian society as a whole is able to create; thus, that country is limiting itself in the generation of rational alternatives to problems they can define and diagnose, and it is also limiting itself in the amount of power that it can mobilize through broad skeins of consensual acceptance of public authority. For their part, major segments of the Argentine labor movement would impose an authoritarian rigidity on their land if they were able to substitute their traditionalism for that of their military government.

So, I make two ethical judgments about welfare, whether in the city or the countryside: first, it is better to keep persons alive than otherwise and, as a general proposition (not an individual one), one should do so without asking other normative questions; and, second, beyond ensuring physical survival, we should always ask the qualitative question whether what *we* do increases the ability of persons to understand what *they* do and to act in such a way as to increase their own abilities to expand such understanding and to act on their perceptions. Such criteria are not mystical; they are adjustable to the situations of individual countries and so they are relativistic; and they are susceptible to measurement. Also, and not least, they are not intellectually demeaning: they do not demand that we blindly infer quality from quantity, or posit long causal chains when social life is clearly netlike and not ropelike.

I am of the opinion that any further narrowing of preferences would raise questions of ultimate values that we could not resolve peacefully and without courting the irrationalities we are rejecting. It may be easier to say what we cannot believe, rather than what we must believe. That is, this general measure of the "good" can serve to tell us that we cannot accept any view that denies areas of meaningful choice, and that we must also reject lineal determinisms, whether narrowly utilitarian or broadly economic, whether reflecting a search for charismatic leaders or faith in a blindly operating *force majeure*. These denials will be more painful for some than for others, but they will entail some discomfort for everybody, since we all sometimes like to relax into the innocent irresponsibility of one simplism or another. I suggest we assume the following as common presumptions:

(a) That change is not lineal; it is caused by combinations of circumstances and some element of will made effective by power in some form, and it eventuates in changes in designs, in the configurations of variables.

(b) That even to posit the possibility of enlarging social welfare is an ideological act.

(c) *That to have a definition of welfare that can be tested independently of the initial value judgment itself,* we must employ a concept that allows room for scientific procedures.

(d) That to adopt such a testable concept of welfare necessarily implies placing some positive value on rationalism itself.

(e) That the previous commitments necessarily carry with them some recognition, if not approval, of secularism, social voluntarism, and the value of social life as a good in itself for at least certain purposes.

Past this point, each of us will wish to adopt his own more complete normative and explanatory system. If we could really agree on the foregoing, some of the corollaries which would seem to follow are:

(a) Rural welfare cannot be discussed in isolation from urban and national welfare—if only because the criteria for all of them must somehow fuse.

(b) Beyond matters affecting physical and group survival, rural welfare must have something to do with the distributional facts of life—with how much individuals and social groupings think they need, with how much they actually get, with how much they should get by applying independent criteria of judgment.

(c) Rural welfare must also have something to do with *how* values are allocated—with the degrees and instruments of coercion, with the kinds of participation, types of decision-making, and the normative measures (that is, with how values are valued).

(d) Rural welfare must also be seen as a process evolving through time, and thus involving mixes of habit and of fresh reasoning, in turn influenced by the considerations of power, hierarchy, selectivity, and motivations mentioned above.

As a general rule, I suggest that welfare anywhere should be measured, beyond survival, by the increasing ability of a maximum number of capable persons in each society to find personal satisfaction in social action—part habitual and part consciously rational— that creates, ascribes, and allocates values in such a way as to increase future possibilities for such activities. This statement goes beyond my previous notion of expanding rationality by adding the idea that social action should be seen as an expressive good in itself, as well as by taking into account social structure, participation, and economic functions. This way of putting the matter also begins to make it more easily applicable to the cases of individual countries.

The third major argument I advanced in the beginning of this essay was that we should think about whole situations and plan for particular, partial action in light of the general view. If I am to think in an ordered way, then I should now turn to the first major, analytical cuts we might want to consider in order to organize thinking about specific actions. With my criteria of the "good" in mind, I suggest the following:

(a) We should think of rural welfare in the same normative terms as national and even international welfare, adjusting only the *tactics* of our activities to the specific rural scene or scenes with which we may be concerned. Rural welfare is not served by developing rural areas in isolation from the national cultural scene, although sometimes "separatist" economic and political measures would seem temporarily desirable to defend a rural area against depredations from without that may threaten even physical survival, let alone the ability to preserve selected elements of rural life as national cohesion grows. In the long haul, however, rural welfare is served by helping persons who live in the countryside to become both urbane and rural, connected with central authority and yet partially self-determining. If the price of keeping people on the farm is also to make it impossible for them to share in the products of cosmopolitan culture should they wish to do so, a poverty of the spirit is forced upon them.

(b) If rural people are to be able to seek ways of continuously expanding their options, then they must have the power to make effective a reasonable array of their choices. Power is generated on a day-to-day basis through obvious institutional mechanisms: ownership patterns, cooperatives, access to credit, party mechanisms, and the necessary educational supports. Power potential is transmitted through time as a function of class and race. We should not deal in such areas unless we clearly recognize that we are affecting power distributions immediately, as well as through social time. And unless we attempt to increase the social effectiveness of rural persons, we shall be acting only manipulatively and possibly paternalistically.

(c) Openness to national and international culture, as well as the ability to create and apply social power, can be the attribute of the many or the few. Equality before society's institutional and cultural opportunities is a critical part of any welfare concept. It is through such equality that the intergenerational effects of social class and race are muted, and the society is put into a posture of predisposition for selection and self-selection. Education may well be the most important single institution in its potential for assisting persons to demand and make use of equalities before the laws, the state, the marketplace, and even social ideas of the metaphysical.

For readers engaged in development programs, or for researchers whose work has direct developmental relevance, the programmatic implications of the above statements should be fairly clear; and the necessity for being entirely country-specific is obvious. In other words, we need to begin to think about how institutions are related to each other in given cases, about the costs and benefits of attempting to change one or another part of the total structure, and about how change in one area may relate to changes in other portions.

1972

II. Traditions of Thought

In Search of
Theoretical Room for Freedom

THE CONCERN of some North Americans for Latin American victims of political disorder has a long if spotty history. The part played by the United States as a haven for political exiles and refugees should not be minimized in its significance, even though until recently the government and the universities had little to do with directly easing the pains of such displaced persons. José Martí rolled cigars for a living. Rómulo Betancourt, José Figueres, and many other social democratic refugees of the 1950s had difficulties extracting visas from the government, but once in the United States became honored members of the faculties of prestigious universities. Behind the few major figures, however, the United States has played host to many lesser luminaries, who have completed their higher educations here, found professional niches for themselves, and often have just as discreetly returned home, frequently to assume positions of importance. Little scholarly attention has been paid to this persistent and sometimes large-scale social phenomenon. Without doubt ideological understanding, organizational skills, and party-building have been directly influenced within Latin America by the historical period in which members of the elite sought political asylum, and the countries in which they took refuge. The opposite is, of course, also true: political refugees from abroad have importantly affected North American politics, from the beginnings of the republic.

Amorphous feelings about this country's tradition have been the major normative dimension in debate and action concerning the proper role of the United States in issues of human rights and civil liberties. Racism, fear of the unknown, recurrent Red scares, and

protection against cheap labor have been the motivating forces behind exclusionist measures. On the other hand, the vision of America as a land of the free and a host to the oppressed has guided those
who favor hospitality to the politically harassed. The zigzags of
policy have benefited refugees of both rightist and leftist ideological
persuasion. The former, if they are of favored social groups, need
no economic assistance; if not, they are often helped by the government, as in the recent cases of Cuban and South Vietnamese refugees. The leftist groups earlier in American history came to this
country in large blocs, providing labor for the rapidly expanding
country. In more recent times, overt political refugees of left persuasion have usually been assisted by academic groups, if they are
scholars, or else by organizations of formal religious affiliation.
Their numbers are small.

The matter has been assuming urgency in recent years because
of the qualitative changes that have been occurring in Latin American politics, fueled by the new weaponry and other instruments of
political control that have been made possible by the technology of
"postindustrial" society—a grotesque term. These changes are certainly part and parcel of growing social uncertainty throughout the
European culture-world, an uncertainty which may well involve the
very nature of our social orders. The Latin American political
changes of interest to this discussion have to do with the emergence
of states which, in the ferocity of their dedication to social control,
can be termed totalitarian. That is, they are able to brush aside
ascriptive protections of age, sex, race, class, and even institutional
position in clergy, military, or economy, and impose control directly
upon individuals. The lack of mediatory and meliorative agencies
between state and person and the lack of a quotidian system of
political accountability together define the essence of totalitarianism,
as distinct from the institutionally constrained and class-bound traditional authoritarianisms to which we have been so accustomed in
Latin America. Totalitarianism, by this definition, is not only a latent
property of more "developed"—differentiated, specialized, urbanized, industrialized—populations, but also of some of Latin America's least developed states. Specifically, Chile and Uruguay are not
the only two nations whose states possess the ability directly to
constrain individuals. A small, highly trained, and well-equipped
police force in Nicaragua, for example, also has the ability to put its
finger on almost all potentially oppositionist individuals. The formal
terror of the state far overshadows the terrorism of revolutionary
groups. It should not be forgotten that a heavy helicopter gunship
can, for a short time, unleash as much firepower over a city street as

that possessed by a World War II destroyer. The overthrow of such governments may be cued by *guerrillismo,* but the sufficient condition for their removal involves foreign intervention, self-destructive tensions within the state itself, or a general withdrawal of tacit consent by the civil population.

The nature of the crisis that has generated such regimes is a matter of widespread debate, of course. I cannot evade that diagnostic problem entirely, for one major reason: the human-rights and civil-liberties issues must involve the larger problem of democracy, which brings with it the entire question of democratic freedoms in a world of high technology, economic conflict, increasing social demands, and international tensions involving the possible use of weapons of at least massive and possibly genocidal destructiveness. An ancillary reason, but one of particular interest here, is that the political confusions of our age are attended by an equally great intellectual confusion. As citizens, we have a general concern with democracy. But those of us who are scholars have a particular responsibility for the state of knowledge.

When it comes to our citizenship, most Latin Americanists have acted reasonably well, without overweening partisanship. Beginning with the Onganía administration's actions in 1966 against the universities in Argentina, and continuing through the present crises of academic freedom in Chile and Argentina, the Latin American Studies Association, many scholars, church groups, universities, certain foundations, and members of both the executive and legislative branches of the national government have cooperated to ameliorate the politically inspired oppression of intellectuals and academic persons. The faceless ones in less favored occupations have received no help from academic people in the United States, although church and European governmental agencies have been effective in both Chile and Uruguay in recent years in aiding blue-collar refugees.

The record could be much better, but it is not dismal. The discomfiting aspect of the matter is that we have given because other Americans have assisted in taking away. The sympathy of the American diplomatic and international economic communities for the incumbent Chilean and Uruguayan regimes is no secret. The scholarly world, however, is also not without blame. Whatever our overt expressions of assistance may be in the cases of violations of academic freedom, we have neglected to think about the relationship between academia and its needs and the rest of the society caught in the processes of profound transformation. We have not assisted in the task of asking whether freedom is merely for the academic and thus academic for everyone else, or whether relativistic, rationalistic, and effective action is not, in itself, both the pre-condition for and the fruit of "development." In other words, our sentiments about our colleagues in Latin America have not been disciplined or intellectualized, turned into a significant element in the explanations we generate and the research we pursue in Latin America or, for that matter, in the United States. As an academic community, we have been at best ademocratic, and at worst—in the majority of cases—antidemocratic. We have not provided room in our theories for democracy.

The very word *democracy* has a negative ring to it among most Latin American social scientists and, by reflection, North American Latin Americanists. It has come to symbolize hypocrisy. Democracy is only for those who can afford it; it is a luxury that comes at the end of a long process of economic development. The world's democratic countries may be partially democratic for themselves— "bourgeois" democracies—but for the poorer parts of the world, they are only the extractors of surplus value, the imposers of colon-ialism, the buyers of local elites, the prompters of worldwide dislo-cation, as they move about in the ceaseless search for economic advantage and military security. *Democracy*, like *liberalism*, is there-fore a right-wing word in Latin America, connoting authoritarian-ism and economic exploitation. Rejecting the international practices of democracies is one thing, but rejecting the *concept* of democracy is quite another. To equate democracy with capitalism is a historical accuracy; but to see all present democratic-capitalisms as early ver-sions of Nazi Germany—"the last stage of capitalist oppression"—is a historical falsification and a political absurdity. It is false because two of the most important phenomena of our time are the *avoid-ance* of fascism in Western Europe and the decreasing impact of authoritarian ideologies. Western Europe may not know where to go, but it seems to have decided for the moment where it will not go. And the construction is absurd because the future is neither history nor actuality—what a country may become is not what it is. To label "civil liberties" as a solely "bourgeois" phenomenon is to deny that one constructs the future out of the present, to throw out the best of the Enlightenment and of classical Liberalism with the corruptions of its historical maturation, and—worst of all—to leave oneself without a theory of freedom, institutional accountability, and the relationship between a generalized social ethic and per-sonal dignity.

The preceding paragraph has about it a polemical ring. Nev-ertheless, it is meant to be a synthetic statement about theoretical fact. Its implications will be pursued in the remainder of this essay.

First, however, another step should be taken in wringing the polemicism out of that paragraph. The practical, everyday political importance of distinguishing among types of capitalistic societies and of respecting even a Liberal rule-of-law concept has come home to many Latin Americans in the last few years. The destruction of partial democracies (classbound ones) in Chile and Uruguay, the crumbling of the Argentine system and its built-in restraints, and the atrocities of Brazil reveal not only the cruelties which profound value-clash invites but also the critical importance of thinking about accountability, constraint, respect for individual rights—about human rights and civil rights in general—as goals in themselves. In other words, the loss of "bourgeois" civil liberties, even though they were always fragile and of partial application even in Chile and Uruguay, is a phenomenon that must be thought about in itself alone, as well as with respect to the general "system" in which the loss has occurred. Otherwise, one emerges from prison, if at all, with burns and psychoses that have no reason, that are the result only of some persons having had a taste for one political way instead of another. The victim of torture needs to be honored with more than mere personal sympathy or the even grimmer admonition that he shouldn't take the matter personally—it wasn't he that was hated but his politics. The mechanistic and anethical social science we employ leads precisely to such shredding of personal and human experience, to impersonalizing pain or to rendering it asocial. As it is, we have done very well in the social sciences in ridding ourselves of the notion that the bell really does toll for all of us. For that reason, our lending a helping hand to refugees is only an expression of sentimentality, not of an ethical sentiment given intellectual muscles by its placement inside a theory of society. Our reigning social theories can leave us with no other conclusion.

Most American social scientists see the social process as linear, homeostatic, and agglutinatively comprised of individuals responding to similar "drives." The motor force, the "drive" is usually some derivative of the Utilitarian pleasure-pain calculus, whether we are talking of rewards and punishments, or of gains and losses, or of burnt hands and cicatrices. As each individual reacts to this inherent psychological "programming," so moves the whole society—in and out of adjustment, always in search of the happy mean, the state of equilibrium, the automatic self-adjustment, and survival. Thus, change proceeds essentially in a wavy line, which may be "up" or "down" depending on the measures in use, and "stability," "dynamic stability," "dynamic equilibrium," or some such term becomes the criterion of a society working "normally." Many variants of these views exist, especially as each discipline has adopted the model for its own purposes. Common in one or another degree to all the variations, however, are the following elements:

1. The homeostatic "paradigm" (the current fad-word) does not contain any guides to understanding social structure and institutional organization. Those manifestations of the social order, when treated at all, must be grafted on top of the theory as epiphenomena.

2. Reason, when considered in any way, is secondary to what can only be called "instinct," or some other word to refer to inherent factors. A derivation of this secondary placement of the intellect can be seen in the evolution during the late 1940s and early 1950s of the idea of "management of crisis"—intervention into the self-adjusting system by administrators, leaders, managers, or other authoritative actors to help the mechanism get itself back on track.

3. The insistence on subcortical causality in social events and the explicit slighting of the consciously working mind also depersonalize the social sciences. Responsibility declines with the diminution of reason; what has happened has had to happen. Concepts of morality and ethics enter as themes to be investigated, but not as affecting the investigator in other than potentially antiscientific ways.

Utilitarian theoretical derivations have dominated American social science for years. Marxist and neo-Marxist streams of thought have only recently become strong; earlier they were trickles, not streams. Because of the overriding cultural influence of psychological reductionism and its attendant "automatism," North American Marxists have tended to emphasize the analogous part of Marxism—the workings of the dialect. At least, however, Marxists have for long debated as to whether or not history is "inexorable," while there can be no room for such doubt among those departing from an instinctual basis for their social science. Still, if one adds a mechanistic view of the dialectic to a crude lacing of the material "infrastructure" to the "superstructure," again one is left with a social science in which blind "forces" are all too busily at work, and in which persons (as distinct from individuals) have little part to play. The mechanistic uses of Marxism, usually and with good reason called "vulgar," are by far the most common in Latin America as well as in the United States.

A more "humanistic" understanding of Marx—an understanding of the "young" Marx, in the current vogue—would start from his theory of alienation. The loss of control over the effects of one's labor is alienating, a ripping away of man from his nature as social being, a deprivation of that which he creates by his labor. Capitalism, based as it is on "surplus-value," is precisely a system which *requires* alienation, the "denaturalization" and thus dehumanization of man. This unnatural relationship is built into the fabric of society, made necessary by the class system. The state, in this construction, is but the arm of the bourgeoisie to force the extraction of surplus-value from the proletariat. Civil liberties and human rights were invented to further the growth of capitalism—to free labor from serfdom and ascriptively based isolation from the marketplace, and thus to make labor mobile and recruitable to industrial capitalistic tasks. "Bourgeois" civil liberties were primary characteristics of the growth of industrial capitalism but have never truly been extended to the "masses." And when the stage of monopoly capitalism begins, the need for a "reserve" labor army signals the desirability of decreasing or perhaps even doing entirely away with limited democratic rights in order to maintain sufficient oppressive control over the permanently marginalized population.

Although Marxism is, above all, an institutionalist theory—unlike Utilitarianism—it gives no room in its foundations to intellectualism (usually reduced to the manufacture of ideology, the concretization of false consciousness, the attempt to persuade one class to act in the interests of another), and sees creativity and invention as "superstructural," epiphenomenal. More important for the purposes of this discussion, the Marxist theory of the state, such as it is, is anemic. The presumption that the capitalist state is merely an instrument of oppression of one class by another extends itself into an inadequate discussion of the role of the state in successor, "socialist" regimes. The presumption is that only the proletariat can be the universalizing class, the only one without the ability or need to oppress lower ones when it arrives at power. The "dictatorship of the proletariat," then, is the use of coercive force to achieve the nonalienated society, the society of universal membership. The problem is made evident, however, in those states now calling themselves "socialist" and "Marxist" in inspiration. What is their politics of transition? How does the proletarian state make itself immune from bureaucratization, how does it render itself accountable to the "masses," how does it avoid the construction of a Gulag? This eminently institutionalist theory, then, is of little use when the moment of payoff arrives, when men actually begin to employ organized power in the name of achieving their avowed ideal state.

A third general view of the nature of the social world has been lurking in the corners for many years, and is slowly beginning to assume shape. In shorthand, this approach has to do with the structuralism of Lévi-Strauss, the linguistic structuralism of Chomsky, or, in more classically philosophical terms, with the phenomenological school derived from Kant and given its most rounded contemporary expression in the works of Ernst Cassirer. These views are related at their roots in the sense that they assume the universality of the human condition to lie within the capacity of each person to construct understandings in determinate *ways* and, to some extent, with given commonality of content. If this assumption is employed in its neo-Kantian derivatives, then a theory of freedom inevitably accompanies it. That is, the nature of man is that he is a symbolizing entity; the realization of this nature is desirable; only through freedom to interact, to communicate, to create community and individuality simultaneously, can this fulfillment proceed. The process is also never-ending; man never ceases to be able to symbolize or to work out the ramifications of the basic structures of meaning and being. In other words, he never ceases to create himself. Such a view of man obviously emphasizes as basic what Utilitarianism and Marxism put as secondary: choice, the personal creation of meaning, the ethic of these matters, and, consequently, the linkage among dignity, freedom, and social interaction as the bases of a society adjusted to the "human condition."

However, as I have said, these neo-Kantian views have gained little currency in the social sciences as a whole, and virtually none outside linguistics and anthropology. They are no part of standard sociology, economics, demography, political science, or even social psychology. Perhaps more to the point, phenomenological views have not been translated into institutional theory: we know no better what to do with them with respect to modern politics, for example, than do the Marxists with their "politics of transition." But it should not be forgotten that Rousseau was the prime inspirer of Kant, and that therefore some of the classical Liberal- and Enlightenment-derived American views of governance and the rule-of-law are primitive social evocations of what came to philosophical bloom only later.

Latin Americanists within the United States have had no choice but to use one or another of these three generalized schools of thought in constructing their particular understandings of Latin America. The exposure to Latin America has often modified concepts for North Americans, but usually within the Utilitarian–Marxist spectrum. The reason is clear, of course: in theoretical matters, the Latin Americans are as squarely set in the Western philosophical tradition as we. They may tap the pot from different spigots, and add different spices, but the basic brew is the same for all of us. Consequently, scholars as well as intellectuals and others in both hemispheres are without structured, fundamentally established ideas about the place in our thought of human rights, civil liberties, and democratic processes. Formal democratic theory itself seems old-fashioned, rooted in the eighteenth century, or else denied by Utilitarian practice, labeled hypocritical by Marxist thought, and essentially unexamined in its contemporary manifestations by most phenomenological reasoning. (There is an ongoing attempt in Europe by a few Marxists to pick up the early Sartrist attempt to wed Marxism to phenomenology, notably in the writings of Lucio Colletti, but as yet there is little understanding of—though there is increasing acquaintance with—this trend in European thought in Latin America and the United States.) It is not to be wondered at, then, that Latin Americanists in this country have contributed little to an understanding of the relationship between democracy and other social occurrences in Latin America. Let me be as specific as I can in this highly condensed discussion.

Mainstream American economists are, *par excellence,* Utilitarians. They have so abstracted and universalized their "laws" that most of them seriously pretend to being apolitical, technical men—the "pure" scientist of the social sciences. Some of them feel entirely uninhibited by the nature of the political regimes to which they lend their services. Aside from moral questions, there is an ethical one: to the extent that economists help to reinforce extremely harsh governments, they tend to banish their social-scientific brethren from the ability to work in those countries. As we have seen in Chile and Uruguay, and to some extent in many other countries, the only social "science" respected by harshly authoritarian governments is economics.

To the extent to which demographers share the professional aspirations of economists, they enter the same ethical thickets. Because the demographers are fewer in numbers and less influential and less attractive to the technocratic aspirations of authoritarian governments, they do not materially affect the picture.

Most political scientists during the past twenty years have been caught up in the positivistic framework of what that discipline calls "functionalism." They employ a loose systems-analogy with which to organize their materials, leaving themselves without a secure theoretical footing for discussions of democracy. In the nature of the discipline, however, questions must be raised concerning the several types of authoritarianism that prevail in Latin America, and of course there have been many works on formal democracy in Latin America, especially concerning Uruguay, Chile, Costa Rica, and more recently Venezuela and even Colombia. The historicist bent of the discipline also has been conducive to studies looking retrospectively at the ebbs and flows of "free" and "dictatorial" regimes in

Latin America. This body of writing, in its essayistic as well as more formal empirical manifestations, is the one that has most concerned democracy, naturally. But the point I am making is that even political scientists have not devised a way of *theoretically* seating the idea of democracy, or the possible centrality or marginality of civil liberties and respect for human rights, in the processes of contemporary social change in Latin America. Pluralist theories of competing interest groups are but a variant of homeostatic theorizing; "civic culture" approaches are usually and justifiably accused of American ethnocentrism, but they also do not treat of democracy as more than a convenience for the better lubrication of a system; political-party studies simply beg the democratic question; and some political scientists bluntly assume the inevitability or even the desirability of authoritarianism in developing states, and leave the matter at that.

Anthropologists do not, by and large, deal with themes of civil liberties, justice, and human rights as they refer to European-derived nations and states. Their work, thus, is generally peripheral to this theme, although Richard Adams, Anthony Leeds, Oscar Lewis, and others have provided understandings and information directly consumable by anyone who may be interested in such questions at the level of the nation-state. It should also be added that anthropologists have been more concerned with the ethics of research abroad than has any other disciplinary group. Economists and demographers do not wish to discuss the issue; political scientists have worried about it but have gone nowhere in any organizational sense. But the sociologists have attempted to join their concern with that of the anthropologists, although they have not been as successful in achieving consensus, for it is perhaps the most conflictful of all the social scientific disciplines in Latin America.

The large numbers of Latin American sociologists far overshadow the relatively few North Americans who have taken their sociological skills to Latin America. And, as is well known, much of what we call political science in the United States is carried out by political sociologists in Latin America. In addition, subfields have proliferated: Latin Americans are involved in everything from the sociology of knowledge to the sociology of education, and from market research to migration studies. They have also been theoretically innovative. By joining a neo-Marxist outlook to the structural economics of persons revolving about the Economic Commission for Latin America, they have contributed dependence concepts to the world. Our own sociologists, then, must have at least a working knowledge of Marxist or Marxist-related views to be able to interact with their Latin American compeers across any broad spectrum of institutions or countries. Dependence theory, however, is even more silent on issues of freedom and democracy than most other Marxist-derived analysis, for it is a theory that addresses itself to the *absence* of power, rather than to its creation and uses; to the patterns of dominance, rather than to paths toward liberation.

Clearly, this discussion could proceed through social psychology and history, and even some archaeology, were we to attempt to complete the inventory. But the point is sufficiently made: the classical concepts of tyranny, human rights, civil liberties, democracy *in its ethical sense,* and justice have not been on the social science agenda. To change the metaphor, when they have come to the plate at all, it is as condiment, not as meat.

This essay is no place for proposing a new theory of democracy and its relationship to development, or for attempting to resuscitate and renovate old ones. Still, it is worth recalling some of the classical elements in democratic theory:

- The labor theory of value informed classical Liberalism.

- Hobbes, Locke, and the Encyclopedists were empiricists in their epistemology, providing a comfortable basis for the Utilitarianism that claimed the classical Liberal heritage. But Rousseau was convinced that reality was first constructed within man, providing the springboard for Kant and his followers. The two ideas have been in conflict ever since.

- Classical theories were institutional in nature, not based on the individual, and concerned the relations between whole *persons* and the institutional order.

- The institutions were vested with an ethic by their being counter-posed against an ideal-type, the "natural" institution, thus suggesting an ethical North Star for everyday life.

- State-of-nature notions were secular in the sense that nature (though perhaps God-given) was equal for all men, regardless of their particular sacred beliefs.

We would also do well to remember that, as historical occurrences, Protestantism, capitalism, democracy, science, and nationalism grew together in patterns that for many years were mutually reinforcing. It is obvious, however, that the nature of each of these bodies of thought and behavior has been changing. The conjunction is no longer harmonious. Therefore, like it or not, be comfortable or not in the moment in which we are forced to live, the problem of the total construction of our society is before us. The position of scientists in this conjuncture is especially poignant, in that the constraints of the acceptance of the scientific task imply a coeval acceptance of free institutions. My point is not merely the obvious one that academic freedom is required for experimentation, replication, and cumulation of knowledge. Even more important, the essential scientific premise is the same as the essential democratic premise. Both must depart from the conviction that ultimate certainty must escape us but that we must at any given moment act as though our premises were constant. This is the heart of relativism, which impregnates the scientific process as much as the democratic process. In science, we must accept our conceptual parameters at the same time that we always attempt to change them. And in democracy, we must accept the paramountcy of law at the same time that we know that laws are temporal and temporary. We must give to science our absolute respect for its canons and expect from our scientific colleagues no sanctions other than those of *scientific* failure—not partisan denial. We must give a democratic order our absolute support of its laws and expect in turn absolute equality before them. We cannot have freedom to be scientists unless we establish the institutional conditions for such freedom and allow absolute equality before the procedural and substantive mandates of our intellectual task. And we cannot have freedom as citizens unless we also establish the institutional conditions for such freedon and allow absolute equality before the procedural and substantive mandates of the public task.

In this sense, good science and good politics demand the same preconditions. A practical application of this historical parallelism would make us better practitioners in Latin American or any other social research. And it would give us better grounds than *gremialismo* or sentimentality to be concerned with the violations of human and civil rights in Latin America and elsewhere in the world.

1976

Some Long-Term Effects
of Industrialization

A DISCUSSION of the long-term effects of industrialization will be of
no more than technical interest if we speak only of industrialization
and capital accumulation, or industrialization and technological
change. Rather, I judge that consideration of the long-term effects
of industrialization is designed to reveal what a change in the techniques of production may do for people and their ways of social life.
After all, the very reason for expanding our time horizons is to
remind us that industrialization is implementation, a means to an
end and not a good *per se*, as is aesthetic satisfaction or sensate
pleasure.

The intellectual and ideological confusions of today's world
make the developmental optimism of the late 1940s and early 1950s
seem naive, and the opposing views of those days appear to be in
semiagreement. Many Latin American governments of twenty and
thirty years ago had become entirely convinced that national industrial development was the key to effective sovereignty and to cultural
independence. The view was also widely accepted that major investments could be underwritten only by the state, within a context of
general economic planning. This mild form of *étatisme*, a "mixed
economy" designed to industrialize and to provide for a simultaneous measure of social welfare, was looked upon with grave suspicion by many North Americans as a form of "creeping socialism."
Still, the availability to Latin American states of monetary reserves
accumulated during World War II, and the need for governmental
guarantees of loans made by such entities as the Export-Import
Bank and the World Bank, laid the grudging basis for the kind of

67

national economic planning later made official and respectable under the Alliance for Progress. Developmental agencies such as the Chilean Development Corporation, founded in 1938, were established in many different Latin American countries, invariably in all the more economically advanced ones. Though their styles of operation and their political coloration varied widely from setting to setting, they provided the essential institutional basis for the kind of "structuralist" economic reasoning advanced by the Economic Commission for Latin America from its earliest days.

Despite ideological bickering, a common innocence linked purist *laissez-faire* economists in the United States with welfare-oriented structuralists in Latin America, as it also linked the more extreme oppositions of socialist and capitalist thinkers. It was widely thought then—and still is—that the economic system of a society is infrastructural and that economic change is the precondition for all other substantive social change. Even though North American statesmen railed against "Marxist materialists," they pursued their own materialism through the simplistic belief that a privately owned and managed economy must eventuate in the establishment of democratic political regimes. Vulgar Marxists, for their part, advanced an argument of similar design, although its component parts were different: a popular democratic order could be erected only upon the foundation of a collectively owned and managed economic system, whose establishment necessarily had to antedate the promised political order.

These discussions were not sterile; they established working views of the world that affected political action and the lives of people. From the left, for example, the Arbenz regime in Guatemala argued that land reform was necessary in order to establish a landed bourgeoisie, for in the absence of a middle class the preconditions for eventual socialism could not be established. The "stages" of growth toward socialism must be respected. Examples on the right are more bountiful. For instance, economists of "monetarist" persuasion went to country after country in Latin America, insisting that "austerity packages" be imposed in order to control the inflations that broke out to accompany postwar economic development in such countries as Peru, Chile, and Brazil. These programs involved credit restrictions, a reduction of governmental subsidies and welfare programs, and wage controls in the absence of price controls. Often the results were that illegal strikes occurred and that persons were killed as a direct consequence of these "technical" prescriptions. And rarely was inflation more than temporarily halted, for Latin America's governments lacked the participant and consensual polity that makes possible a relatively leakproof austerity package. There are countless other examples in national economic development and in international economic relations of the power of the idea sets that informed developmental thinking only a short generation ago.

By the late 1950s, however, it had become apparent that industrialization, the preferred form of economic development because it was the easiest and threatened the fewest established interests, was not producing the automatic results its proponents had so easily assumed. First of all, it was learned that industries are inorganic: to put two of them together is not necessarily to spawn a third. Then, it was found that, by establishing a local factory whose finished product would substitute for an import, one created a rigid necessity to import raw materials in place of the greater flexibility of importing finished goods. Simultaneously it was learned that the wage structures of industries tend to spread through all urban occupations and then to stain out to rural ones, affecting the prices of raw materials. Also quickly learned were other lessons of an entirely economic sort about tax bases, the growing spread of world prices between finished and raw materials, the difficulties of exporting industrial products, and the effects of monopoly ownership on market conditions, income distribution, the nature of products, and the orderliness of supply.

These economic happenings did not occur in isolation, nor were they simply extensions or historical extrapolations of previous periods in the growth of industry and trade in Latin America. Instead, they came at a time when the advanced world was moving from one kind of technique to another kind, from "industrial society" to "postindustrial" society, to use the inadequate terms of the contemporary lexicon. More aptly, the advanced countries were moving from specialized production and management (with an emphasis on *specific* techniques and on production as totally distinct *functionally* from distribution and consumption, and a correlative emphasis on the inevitability of scarcity) to universalized management and self-supervising production techniques (with an emphasis on the *generality* of skills and the functional links among production, distribution, and consumption, and a correlative emphasis on the possibility of abundance and the related issues of power, influence, and social questions). Thus, the kind of industrial development that began to occur in Latin America a quarter of a century ago was both the last of the old and the first of the new. The old demanded a series of narrowly related happenings that nurtured the deterministic ideas of certain benefits flowing from industrialization: education to support the new cadres of managers and workers, cities to house the new laborers of all stations, road and rail networks that would open the hinterland and blend city with country, and a political structure that would permit the mobilization of the people and their organization into new tasks that would permit them to consume differently, thus enlarging their sense of investment in community. The new, however, introduced an element of freedom into the social context; today's industrialization, "postindustrialization," does not "demand" masses of skilled and semiskilled labor, terrestrial communications nets, the creation of urbane populations to live in the city, or a politics of encouragement to belong to a community. As we shall see, the new industrialization may *permit* those happenings to take place with greater efficacy than does the old, but it does not *require* them. We are no longer empirically permitted the easy romanticism of the old determinism. The new reminds us that industrialization does not make industrial, "modern" man. Instead, we are forced back to the uncomfortable truism that men—modern or otherwise—make industries.

The implications of the differences between old and new patterns of industrialization have been only dimly perceived, but they intrude themselves willy-nilly on our awareness. There are subtle as well as obvious reasons for our intellectual restlessness. Within Latin America one reason is most salient: industrialization simply has not brought in its train expected consequences. Social equity did not automatically increase, unemployment often grew rather than diminished, increased national sovereignty and autonomy were not palpable phenomena, and political institutions did not, by and large, become stronger and more impersonal. Rapid population growth contributed to disappointing figures when read on a *per capita* basis, and the conditions of the international economic order began to be felt more intimately inside Latin America, and across more social groups, than ever before. Still, there was massive, undeniable absolute change, and an urgent need to explain it. That is, whatever was happening in terms of anticipated results, gigantic urban metropolises grew, masses of persons became involved in the total industrial process, university populations expanded dizzyingly, a wide array of consumer goods became available to middle- and upper-class persons and to the skilled among blue-collar workers, trade union organization became more robust in many countries, literacy rates began a steady climb, and communications systems rather slowly but consistently ramified themselves. The specific part that industrial organization has played in all these changes is not easy to discriminate. But changes there are, and a desire for an explanation of them has grown among professionals, intellectuals, entrepreneurs, and the varieties of men in public service.

Explanations have usually taken one of two forms: one has insisted on the primacy of economic factors in social change, and thus sought to examine social impediments to the "proper" and "appropriate" working of the economic institution; and another, only slowly and hesitantly developing in Latin America, as elsewhere, is attempting to understand social change as shifts in a multidimensional tapestry of social occurrences. As is to be expected, the traditional explanations had their day first, even though the analyses were made by persons institutionally new to the Latin American scene, the modern, empirical social scientists whose numbers expanded rapidly past the mid-1950s. The post–World War II economic changes of Latin America did not burst on a region that had no prior experience of industries. Neither did the empirical social sciences appear in cultures without a previous history of respect for intellectuals, *pensadores,* gentlemen historians, and lawyers, who had created a large and respectable body of speculative and descriptive writings and who had often contributed to political leadership. The new social scientists were, however, qualitatively different—concerned with methodological rigor, replicability, and those other aspects of scientific endeavor that imply stable institutional bases and the development of a social science community. Until the early 1960s, the new apparatus lent itself to two old tasks, the examination of "impediments to growth" and the production of *técnicos,* men dedicated to the proposition that expertise can somehow be practiced in politically antiseptic ways. Both endeavors—in research and in training—were relatively unwitting adjustments to the idea of the blindness of forces, to the notion that given stimuli must eventuate in determinate reactions. By the mid-1960s, however, these ideas were under strong attack by social scientists and other concerned persons in the United States and Europe, as well as in Latin America. The new thinking was beginning to catch up with the new technology.

I have written these retrospective opening pages in the attempt to demonstrate, even if loosely and subjectively, that we are in a time of qualitative change, and that therefore extrapolations from past experience to future behavior may well be a dangerous exercise. It is usually, and often justifiably, said that the best predictor of future comportment is past comportment. When the actors are essentially the same, and when they are behaving in only a slightly changed systemic pattern, then that predictive probability is warranted. When, however, we are in a period of intersystemic change, and when the configurations of significant actors are also shifting in composition and quality, then the routinization of prediction and diagnosis is highly suspect. I should like to turn at this point to the consideration of a series of flawed causal links which were part of our conventional wisdom only a few years ago. My purpose, of course, is not only to discuss the proposition that our immediate past is an uncertain guide to our future but also to lay the bases for a fresh look at the possibilities inherent in contemporary industrialization patterns.

It is commonplace now to state that the social sciences throughout the world are in a state of crisis caused by the gap between what is postulated to occur and what has actually happened with such rapidity in today's world. Clearly, something is wrong with the causal sequences and linkages social scientists have been using. The following are examples of the ways in which knowledge and behavior combine to confound lineal and narrowly deterministic causality:

1. For several centuries it was held that industrial growth demanded concomitant educational systems in order to promote *production*. Now the transfer of capital goods and a few skilled persons can permit massive industrial plants to be built in the entire absence of local engineering schools, accountancy schools, or even trade schools. The demand for expertness is shifting to the distributional and consumption sides of the economic institution. To put it another way, a causal link between education and production has been weakened, if not entirely severed.

2. For even longer the view has been common that cities create the prime condition for their effective functioning: the urbane man. At least in the short run, we now know that cities can be and are inhabited by villagers. City air need no longer make man free, as the medieval prescription had it. Rather, the demographic and ecological facts of city life are now increasingly being divorced from the qualitative styles of life followed by city dwellers. Urbanity can now be fostered in demographically rural settings. Orwell's *1984* posited the possibility of cities that included walled areas in which deviants, misfits, and the noncivil could be physically and politically isolated. A disquietingly analogous situation has been growing in some of North America's more important urban settlements, such as New York, Detroit, and Newark. The link between the quantitative facts of density and the qualitative facts of social life has been weakened.

3. Again in the United States, the connection between occupational success and the educational experience of the individual has become so severely eroded as to be statistically invisible for major sectors of the population. (See the well-known Jencks and Coleman reports.[1]) That is, the occupational consequences of type of school,

---

[1]The James Coleman report was published as *Equality of Educational Opportunity* (Washington, D.C.: Government Printing Office, 1966). The Jencks report is Christopher Jencks *et al.*, *Inequality: A Reassessment of the Family and Schooling in America* (New York: Harper Colophon, 1973).

nature of pedagogical techniques employed, ancillary equipment employed in teaching, and even neighborhood seem to have little bearing on occupational success. The result has been wholesale questioning of one of the most cherished causal chains in the entire Western cultural heritage: the expectation that education can serve to overcome the socially debilitating effects of class, race, and occupational family situation. Although similar findings certainly cannot come out of the Latin American experience as yet, this disjunction is worth pondering when considering the possible long-term effects of any major institutional change.

4. Economic modernization has long been presumed not only to foster upward social mobility but also to promote attitudinal change among the mobile population, making people more receptive to the rationalistic, pragmatic, changeful biases of the "modern" man. We now know that much industrialization can take place in the absence of upward mobility, although lateral mobility is almost always promoted. In addition, we are also learning that in itself the experience of mobility does not foster the acceptance of modern attitudes. On the contrary, it seems that in Latin America upwardly mobile persons tend to assume the value stance of the groups into which they have moved, whether those groups are predominantly "traditional" or "modern" in their views. We have long known that class position does not correlate with a single cluster of interests and worldviews that we can call "class consciousness." That failure of relationship should have alerted us to a similar lack of correlation between movement from one social level to another and the clustering of beliefs.

The extension of this list is easily made, for the prime characteristic of development is that it increasingly puts under potential social control the effects of actions or, conversely, that it reduces the "necessity" of given consequences of behavior. Indeed, what else could we mean when we say that development enhances man's control over his social and physical environments? The operationalization of that concept of control means that areas of effective options are opened, which in turn implies—but does not make *necessary*—the possibility that those options can be exercised with a growing quotient of reason. What this view does not allow, however, is the extraction from causality of group and individual decision-making and the responsibility attendant upon it. Development implies a decreasing dependence on "forces" as an excuse for behavior, and consequently an increasing appreciation of the degree to which collectivities and individuals make events happen. A false construction of the causal factors in social reality, however, leads to a procession of mistaken policies whose consequences are now widely seen in the betrayal of the interests even of those who promulgate them and push them to implementation. I have already suggested the many betrayed promises that have come from an incorrect estimate of the relationship between the economic institution and general social change. Let me now refer to several other examples that have beset the already industrial world.

Perhaps the best-known failure of contemporary prediction revolves about the Vietnam war. From the theoretical perspective of most social scientists, it was inconceivable that a lightly industrialized, rural, apparently folk culture could fight a modern war, even without aircraft, electronic gear, and the other highly sophisticated weaponry of fully industrialized states. It is usually considered the mark of the modern "citizen-soldier" that he fights well far from home, and that his propensity to pull the trigger in combat is high, for he has the conceptual tools to understand the relationship between an individual act performed at high personal risk in foreign lands and the protection of his community. Also, because of his acceptance of individual participation and responsibility, he can continue to act as a soldier despite the loss of his immediate field commanders. These characteristics were generally true of the North American soldier in Vietnam. But they were also generally true of his North Vietnamese antagonist. No standard social theory based on an "automatic" view of the consequences of industrialization, urbanization, institutional differentiation, and free-enterprise economies can explain these equal talents of citizen-soldiers from countries whose institutional structures could hardly be more dissimilar. The inability to understand North Vietnamese reactions included even the imputed psychological effects of North American bombing, which was designed to force the opponent to the conference table in the belief that the prospects of physical destruction would be a sufficiently powerful stimulus to produce that end.

Other examples concern the failure in the United States to foresee the racial disturbances of the last decade, or the student activism that followed closely on the heels of race, class, and international troubles. It must sadly be reported that, instead of maintaining silence on these matters, most among the best known of American social scientists dismissed the possibility of student upheaval as an absurdity. At the moment, the country is beset by inflation, whose course was little diagnosed or controlled by economists, by international monetary crises similarly out of intellectual hand, and even by changing birth rates that promise to bring about Zero Population Growth at a time when demographers were gloomily predicting continued expansion.

The major conclusion of this essay should now be obvious. If by "effects" we refer to concrete macrosocial situations, such as social organization in the nation-state form, or variants of democratic or authoritarian polities, or even cities and slums or sacred and secular organization, then it is obvious that there are *no* long-term "effects" that flow ineluctably from the simple physical fact of industrialism undertaken in the new mode. The real long-term effects are both more subtle and more significant. The new style of industrialization makes it *possible,* not *necessary,* to raise and to have the power to answer an array of significant questions about societies that far transcend mere subsistence and survival, going beyond to the *purposes* and *styles* of subsistence and survival.

I am certain that, by this point, many readers will have long since become restless with this construction. Some will be protesting that the ratio between population and resources is far from stabilized on a global basis, that cruel starvation afflicts massive portions of the people of the world, and that the classical trials of drought, pestilence, and war continue to be the lot of all too many men. But this essay is about the long-term, not the immediate, situation. And in departing from the immediate to talk about the future, I have chosen not to write in terms of averages, but rather of the more meaningful facts of dissonance and disharmony, of the coexistence not merely of natural and social disasters, but of the "good" and "bad" of war and peace, famine and glut, subsistence agriculture and automated factories, as well as generosity and selfishness, murder and self-sacrifice, and empathic understanding and fanaticism. These are the real terms in which asynchronous, disjunctive, inharmonious social orders are perceived and lived by all of us. In the midst of this scene there have appeared harbingers of new possibilities, among them the uniquely new techniques of industrial production. And, to repeat, the social import of this uniqueness is that the new industrialization *demands* little in the way of accompanying and ancillary support, and thus it provides new power at the same time that it constrains options very little, rather opening them. Thus, the long-term effect of industrialization is both to widen choice and to increase the amount of power—or effective demand—that can be used when choice is exercised. What the new industrialization does not do is to suggest implicitly which options *should* be chosen. That ethical task is left for men, as it has always been our lot to make such judgments. The new industrialization simply makes it more obvious than ever that the making of a decision is an entirely human act.

Viewed in this perspective, then, a fully mature industrialization in the new style, which must include agricultural production, would transcend the satisfaction of needs in narrow and even mean senses. Instead, it would carry to a qualitatively different level the generation of "need" that supply has already accomplished to some extent. That is, an ideal type of new industrial establishment makes it possible to define as needs whatever it is that the ethos of a society may decide is essential to the nature of man, and not to his mere survival, as said above. It is in this fashion that production, distribution, and consumption become one with each other in a unified process and are linked to the ethical values that may inform a given society. In this situation there will no longer be room for the *técnico*, but only for mechanics who operate the rationalized instrument, and for those who establish policy (that is, define "needs")—whether they are philosopher-kings or a participant citizenry. The new industry makes either extreme possible, neither necessary.

1973

Fate, Chance, and Faith: Some Ideas Suggested by a Recent Trip to Cuba

Written with FRIEDA M. SILVERT

THE TWO AUTHORS of this essay spent the first fifteen days of July 1974 in Cuba. Since then, the questions most often asked of us are how we got in and why we went. A recent article in the *Washington Post* (August 24, 1974) refers to our visit, among others, as though it formed part of a pattern. "Quiet but significant initiatives are under way toward ending the 13 years of hostile relations between the United States and Cuba," begins the article. "Conciliatory signals are being flashed between Washington and Havana through a variety of intermediaries. Although these probes have been unofficial in nature, they are being monitored and evaluated at the highest levels in both capitals."

That, at least in part, is what our visit is being made out to be. The way it came about, however, and what we thought it was while we were on it, are quite otherwise. The affair started about two years ago, after one of us had participated in a two-day conference in the Senate Office Building to discuss Cuban-American relations. That involvement happened because the organizer of the meeting, which had been sponsored by almost a score of senators, is a friend and thought it would be pleasant to have good company. That person and we also share a friend in the United Nations. In turn, that friend—a Chilean of Christian Democratic persuasion—had occa-

77

sion to visit Cuba on official business soon after the Senate sessions, and he returned with the notion that it might be worthwhile for someone talking about Cuba to see what the place was like. We did not follow up on the idea at that time, in order to avoid any muggings in the alleyways of international politics. But about five months ago, after a long evening in New York, the Chilean friend convivially asked whether we were ready yet to go to Cuba. At that time of night, and at that distance from the Washington meeting, it seemed like a good idea. So a letter was written, a response was received, we replied, appropriate permissions from governments and places of work were obtained, and off we went for Mexico and Havana.

On our departure, we had no idea that Pat M. Holt, of the staff of the Senate Foreign Relations Committee, was to overlap with our visit for a week. Nor did we know, until we read it in the papers, that Frank Mankiewicz, former director of the Peace Corps, was in Cuba with two colleagues during the latter half of July. We had been asked by the Cuban authorities what we wished to see; we replied that we were interested in the university situation, the role of intellectuals, and the national health program as an example of public administrative procedure. Naturally, we also expected to talk politics, because that is an avidly pursued avocation of all Latin American buffs like us. In conversation, however, we were very explicit that we did not wish to serve as political carrier pigeons.

We went to Cuba because we were curious and because we thought that reporting our observations might help to inform American thinking about that country during a time of international political change in the hemisphere. The Cubans probably invited us because a distinguished Latin American asked them to. We were treated graciously and well, but we received little evidence that the Cubans knew much about us, our professional interests, or our degree of knowledgeability about Latin America in general, or that they had any especially pointed motives. This amorphous attitude on the part of our hosts showed itself in a schedule that for several days became actively boring in a country that should be intellectually fascinating for any social scientist. When the nature of our entirely personal and private status on the trip finally was understood, relations became clearer and easier. In Cuban terminology, we were visiting in a manner that was *oficioso* (*ex officio*, in function of our roles), and not *oficial*. Like so much else about the trip, reaching that happy definition of status was a matter of chance.

It took faith for the chance to work. We arrived in Havana on a lumbering Ilyushin-18 at 4:15 A.M. on the second of July. We knew no one in Cuba, had no hotel reservations, did not know whether we were to be met, had never before been in a country calling itself socialist, and had no past experience of long residence in Cuba on which to fall back for clues. We were two middle-aged academic tourists, the only American citizens on a plane loaded with Chinese, Koreans, Canadians, Australian Salvation Army people, Argentines, Mexicans, Peruvians, Frenchmen, Dutchmen, and nationals of at least half a dozen other countries—all of whose passports marched before us in Mexico as our own papers were given very special attention by immigration and police authorities. (The legal blocks to the travel of North American scholars and journalists to Cuba are not formidable, but they are *very* bureaucratic.)

Our faith that we would be adequately swaddled on arrival was shaken a little as we waited in the usual lines watching others being picked out for greeting. When a Panamanian UN official whom we knew went off with a welcoming committee and the round of ceremonial greetings of others seemed stopped, we resigned ourselves to finishing the process and then talking around to learn where to find a bed from which to greet the dawn. A pleasant touch was added by the immigration officer, however. When he asked my occupation, I [Kalman H. Silvert] reached for the title of "foundation official," being somewhat sleepy and thus careless. (The Ford Foundation, for which I work, is commonly denounced as an agency of imperialism by many Latin American leftists.) The official looked at me gently, and then asked, "But you are also a university professor, no?" I nodded yes, and he said, "Well, let's put that down." As we moved away from that thoughtful man and toward customs, at 4:50 A.M., we were approached by a man who identified himself as being with the University of Havana, in charge of international relations "with capitalist countries." We were taken to a modest but comfortable receiving lounge, where we found waiting—at that terrible hour—a dean of the university, a professor, and the chauffeur and guide who were to facilitate every step of our stay. The greetings were warm and gracious, with curiosity strong on both sides. The ride through the still dark and deserted streets of Havana was pleasant—especially so because it was very good to come in out of the cold of insecurity. One should not become so accustomed to precast arrangements.

The Attempt to Understand

The social and political feel of Cuba as it reached us subjectively was one of relaxation. It is not merely that we were told, in so many words, that the worst of the economic troubles are past, that Cuba feels no sense of urgency in opening relations with other hemispheric countries although she would like to do so, that both the ration lines and lists are considerably shorter than in the past twelve years, and that moves toward political opening have begun. Our observations strongly suggest that the people are not "uptight." Perhaps the best evidence we have is that we engaged in many political discussions, some of them in direct disagreement with Cubans, and incurred no open hostility nor any hint of impatience. Of course, it was generally assumed that we were stereotypical American liberals and that probably nothing much ideologically or theoretically could be expected from us. When we drove past this barrier, and raised questions of political liberty, relativism, civil liberties, and democratic participation within a context that fully recognized Cuba's right to its political sovereignty and its desires for socialism, discussions often broke down—but they never became unpleasant.

Very early we were told that criticism was welcome, but only within the frame of a general sympathy with the goals of Cuba's revolution. From one point of view, this request is legitimate and understandable. Why should Cubans have to defend themselves against attitudes that question the very fundamentals of their national being and ideological premises? But, from the point of view of our present understandings of social theory (including Marxism in its many forms), the request is most difficult to honor. The reason is that the very determination of the frame within which Cuba fits is a harshly troublesome theoretical problem. We discussed no question more exhaustively, for nothing seemed to us more important than to determine the *nature* of what we were seeing, the kind of victory that Cuba has won and is now beginning to enjoy. Is it truly a socialist victory, or one of another kind? For, let there be no doubt, the Cubans have won something. That is why the air of relaxation.

The intellectual baggage we took with us to Cuba led us to questions and emphases that, in combination, are not common. First, our professional experience fills us with the daily fare of the ordinary development specialist—problems of the Green Revolution, population, urbanization, and the like. Second, our political life experience pushes us toward placing primary valuation on social dignity, personal freedom, and due process. That is the residue left in us by war, Nazism, a general disgust with arid technocracy and corporatism, and the conviction we carry about the essential role of intellectualism in making for a decent life. Third, our long and varied Latin American experience has exposed us to all the important currents of Marxist thought of the last fifty years. Thus, we went to Cuba with a working knowledge of the writings of Lukács,

Gramsci, Sartre, Marcuse, and those many others who have debated the meaning and sense of Marxism in contemporary life. We have been thoroughly exposed to the two Cold Wars that have raged in our times: that between "capitalists" and "socialists" and that among the many brands of Marxists. We find both conflicts inevitable, but tiresome because so little seems to be learned. Lastly, we went to Cuba with the presumption that the *structure* of political society underlying all modernizing countries is the nation-state, whether the countries concerned are capitalistic or socialistic in their ideologies, democratic or authoritarian in their practices. Obviously, we do not expect others to agree with a mélange of prejudices, information, and theoretical precepts that reflect our own crystallized idiosyncrasies and life-accidents. Conversely, we cannot shed this pattern of thought in understanding others. Our question to ourselves could only be whether these views are useful in explaining what we saw in Cuba. In any event, these ideas necessarily conditioned the diagnosis we now advance.

Cuba has either already solved or is well on the way to solving every standard "problem" whose solutions development specialists seek in their work.

Population.   There is no population explosion in Cuba. In the early years of this century, the annual rate of population increase was 3.31 percent. In the years of depression and political turbulence of the 1930s, the annual rate went down to 1.59 percent and has stayed low until the present. From 1964 to 1970 the rate is given officially as 1.91 percent, one of the lowest in Latin America.[1] Thus, the Cuban population has had a manageable birthrate since before the revolution. Present practice is to wrap family planning into general health care.

Health.   Cuba's health coverage has been widely and favorably observed. It is said to be a truly national system, reaching to all portions of the country and of equal quality for all. We have no firsthand knowledge, but were told many glowing stories by foreigners resident in Cuba. Official statistics support the anecdotes. Studies by the Economic Commission for Latin America (ECLA) and

[1] All figures are from the *Anuario estadístico de Cuba 1972,* published by the Junta Central de Planificación of the Dirección Central de Estadística in Havana, and from *La esperanza o expectativa de vida,* 1974, *Análisis de las características demográficas de la población cubana,* 1974, and *Análisis de las características laborales de la población cubana,* 1973, all published by the same agency cited above. Government statistics pertaining to economic matters are always published at least a year out-of-date as protection against economic harassment by the United States.

TABLE 1   *Shifts in the Economically Active Population (over 10 Years of Age) in Cuba, 1953–1970*

Economic Sector	1953	1970
Farming	41.5%	30.1%
Industry	17.4	20.0
Construction	3.3	5.7
Transportation and communications	4.9	6.4
Commerce[a]	20.3	12.0
Services	11.0	23.1
Others	1.6	2.7

[a]The drop in the figure for commerce is the only atypical change. It reflects Cuba's state collectivism, of course.

by the Latin American Demography Center (CELADE) put life expectancy at the turn of the century at 35 and 33 years of age, respectively. By 1956, the same sources put the figure at about 60 years. At present life expectancy for men is 71 years, and for women almost 74 years. The Cuban statistical studies permit themselves a touch of boastfulness in reporting these findings, stating that Cubans are almost at the limits of biological possibility. However that may be, comparable figures for Argentina are 67.1 for both sexes, and 52.3 for Ecuador. In 1970 in the United States, life expectancy for both sexes was 70.8 years. More important from a social standpoint, health care has been taken out of the money economy: it has become an inalienable right for all.

Employment.   Cuba has only fractional unemployment. Even though the population is young (a third of all Cubans have been born since 1959, the date of the revolution), 47.3 percent are economically active, a very high figure. The unemployment rate in 1970 was 1.3 percent, as contrasted with 8.4 percent in 1953, a year when a military coup installed Fulgencio Batista as president, and a reasonably good year economically. Unemployment, underemployment, and sporadic employment were endemic problems in Cuba in the past, given the nature of seasonal work in the fields. There is now a labor shortage in Cuba. But, as is often pointed out by foreign critics as well as in the public speeches of Cuban officials, inexpertness and low productivity characterize much work that is done in Cuba.[2] A popular recent Cuban film dedicates itself to revealing inexperience and bureaucracy in the countryside in the early years

[2]René Dumont, in his controversial book *Is Cuba Socialist?* makes much of this point. The book was published in English by Viking Press in 1974.

of the revolution, and their effects on productivity. Whatever the varying quality of work, which we are not able to judge, the occupational profile (see Table 1) is showing a change toward employment patterns typical of fully developed lands.

Education.   Like health care, the educational system has been widely hailed abroad as a striking victory of the present Cuban government. The first great push was for literacy. The literacy rate now could scarcely be raised. The second great push was in primary education. From 1958–59 to 1971–72, the number of schools has been doubled (from 7,567 to 15,364), as has enrollment (from 629,877 to 1,267,322). The number of urban primary schools has remained constant (2,678 in 1958–59, 2,638 in 1971–72), while the great expansion has occurred in the countryside—from 4,889 schools to 12,731 in the years being cited. The third big effort is now being made in the secondary schools, the level of education which, in Latin America, has traditionally separated lower- from middle-class students. That class-related bottleneck is now being mitigated: the number of secondary schools rose from 184 to 478 between 1958 and 1973, while the number of teachers increased from 3,612 to 15,966, and enrollments soared from 59,582 to 201,810. The announced desire of the Cuban government is to do away with the idea of an educational pyramid—that is, to turn Cuba into a modern evocation of the old French rationalists' dream of a teaching society, in which education proceeds at all levels, ages, and walks of life. This ideal is mixed with a Marxist vision of creating a truly universal man, one who is equally at home in intellectual pursuits, farm work, industry, and in the fruitful pursuit of leisure.

The marriage of these two ideas, made into a triangle by the labor shortage, results in the work-study plans that characterize all education from primary school up. For example, most of the new secondary schools are *secundarios en el campo*—"in the country." Students are resident, and in addition to taking an academic curriculum, work in the fields three hours a day. Truck farming and the production of citrus and other specialized export crops are already making important use of this student labor. At the university level, all students are expected to spend twenty hours a week in paid work. The first year is usually dedicated to unskilled tasks, after which the work duties are increasingly related to the career being followed by the student. Obviously, this system works better for students of engineering or medicine than it does for those in the social sciences and humanities.

Except for engineering, medicine, and related skills, the universities have so far been generally neglected. There are three universities, with a total enrollment of about 70,000: La Habana (45,000), Las Villas (10,000), and Santiago de Cuba (between 15,000 and 18,000). The Faculty of Humanities in Havana (which includes journalism, history, political science, legal sciences, arts and letters, modern languages, library science, and sociology) has some 1,600 students, plus 5,000 workers and others in extension programs of various sorts. Its latest school, sociology, was founded in 1968 and this year had only 18 regular students, plus 70 worker enrollees. In the coming semester the same number of workers will be admitted, but student enrollment should go up to 45.

The more important questions about the university concern academic freedom, university autonomy, and the role of the intellectual in society. We shall touch again on these matters later.

Urbanization. It may wryly be said that pollution is no problem of Cuba's cities. There are very few cars. There is also little problem of crowding, even though the urban population of the island has gone from 51 percent of the total in 1953 to about 60 percent now. Despite the decrease in rural occupations and the increase in typically urban service and industrial undertakings, population flow to the cities has been absorbed by building towns in the countryside and by the construction of large, integrated townlike housing developments in areas surrounding the three major cities. Like the matter of higher education, however, the subtlety of the problem is not suggested by numbers. Havana has been visibly neglected, for example. It is drab and unpainted; many buildings in its once elegant suburbs have been misused by occupants (often students) with little knowledge of how to preserve a house. Informal governmental estimates have it that merely putting Havana back into its prerevolutionary physical condition will cost some US$300,000,000. For the usual town planner, Cuba's urban problems are not great. For the social thinker, though, they are massive. We shall return to this theme.

Food and Agriculture. Rural affairs have been the subject of the most intense ideological debate and confusion of any aspect of Cuban governmental activity since 1959. Dependence on sugar, attempts to diversify, food shortages, the vagaries of the international market, and the ruralist romanticism of the revolution's leaders have played themselves out around questions of how to organize the national economy and, within it, the place of country people. In this process, the star of Ernesto "Ché" Guevara rose and fell. Whatever was in the past, even here a turning point has been reached. The world price of sugar has risen markedly. Water storage facilities are being increased dramatically throughout the island, promising stability in the cultivation of such diverse crops as rice and cotton. The citrus crop is beginning to be profitable in the export market, although little is available for consumption at home. Truck farming is improving, and vegetables and fruits are not in such short supply as even two years ago—although the variety of the Cuban diet leaves much to be desired. Fish and seafood are plentiful; beef, chicken, and pork are not. In short, there is enough to eat for everyone, but much remains to be done in the foreign-exchange scene as well as the domestic one, and the satisfaction of national food tastes is yet to be achieved.

These accomplishments of the Cuban government are relatively easy to measure. Much more difficult is the matter of participation. A universal theme is the need for and desirability of total participation. Almost everyone with whom we spoke took participation to be a good in itself. Organizations are legion, and organization is universal. There are the Civil Defense organization (the *cederistas*—CDRists), women's organizations, trade unions, the Communist Party, block and neighborhood associations, and all other manner of cells, collectives, and institutions. A basic reason for continuing voluntary labor in the fields is to further this organized mixing of the population. The subject need not be belabored. The point is that organization is complex, based on cement sidewalks as well as grass roots, and open to all. Participation is real and effective at this level: justice is dispensed at the bottom for minor crimes and misdemeanors; university curricula are affected by these activities; even the slowly evolving legal codes are checked with organized groups in neighborhoods and provincial villages. Whether this universality of belonging and publicly doing is "good" or "bad" is not our question at this moment: it exists and serves to complete this summary of the dream of the routine developmentalist. In the material aspects of life and in the basic social organization of the local community, Cuba has met the prescriptions of the hortatory statements about development one finds in the reports of the World Bank, the Inter-American Development Bank, the Agency for International Development (AID), the Agricultural Development Council (ADC), and all the rest of our grand gamut of assistance agencies. But,

- Participation is not democracy.
- The *quantitative* facts of development do not assure the *qualitative* essence of a good social life.

• Egalitarianism is not *equity*.

• Increasing the number of urban persons does not increase the number of *urbane* ones.

• The *indicators* of development are not development.

These matters are worrying Cuba's leaders, as they worried us throughout our trip. They did not seem to worry anyone else with whom we spoke, however, and it is for that reason that we occasionally argued so strenuously. It is to these matters we now turn.

THE CITY OF SOCIALISM

We were feeling rather depressed about Cuba after four or five days. Certainly we were seeing much to admire. Certainly we continued to be treated with consummate consideration. Certainly we were very busy meeting social scientists and others in the university for extended and entirely free discussions. But our minds insisted on interpreting, extrapolating, wrestling with what we saw. Also, we were fresh from the last stages of Watergate and from the noise, color, and pollution of Mexico City. The elements of our sadness were as follows:

1. We were offended by Cuba's two newspapers, *Granma* and *Juventud rebelde*. Those papers may serve party functions, but they do not give the news. Crudely, almost naively, propagandistic, they must insult any mind that wishes to reach some conclusions for itself. Television is no better. And, obviously, no foreign papers or magazines are available. Thus, we felt ourselves isolated from a world in which we had recently been so intensively involved. Our breakfast *Granma* was a daily put-down.

2. Status position made an enormous difference among the university persons with whom we were speaking. The higher the position, the more we felt intellectual relativity to be present. At the level of the working-stiff professor, we found little adjustment to our own state of knowledge or sophistication. (We do not know the reason for this woodenness. We guess it to be a reflection of genuine naiveté, and no sign of ill will.) Thus, many of our interviews were repetitive. History began in 1959. Quantities were emphasized; qualities were evaded. No Marxist ever lived after Lenin. Participation is a good *per se*. Cuba is in a state of the dictatorship of the proletariat, and matters will march along inevitably through the stages prescribed in the historically sanctified writ. Questioning of the Soviet Union or of any other Eastern European country evoked

only silence. The low point of this mutual incomprehension came when we were told that there could be no intellectual meeting ground at all between us as North American social scientists and Cuban social scientists pursuing Marxist ideas. And this comment came as we painstakingly tried to explain that a survey of industrial workers' attitudes being carried out was technically and operationally exactly like a multitude already done in the United States over the past twenty-five years.

Our sadness had two aspects: we regretted a closing down of the ability to talk; and we regretted a status-related ability to be open and relativistic in thought. Still, we did appreciate the many sparkling minds we found among the deans, assistant deans, and directors of schools. This observation prompted what we have come to believe is one of our more significant insights: the higher one goes in the social scale, the more intellectual merit one finds. This conclusion was roundly denied by those to whom we advanced it, but we continue to think it valid.

3. For someone fresh from Greenwich Village, Havana is a shock. It is not the traffic jams that one misses, but rather milling on the streets and sidewalks. Window dressing is not an art in Havana as in Buenos Aires; therefore window shopping is not a social sport. Random clabbering does not occur. There is no whey in which social curds can form. A demographic concentration does not a city make. And we like cities.

4. A fourth and last reason for our depression was that we had little solid information on which to bite. Although we requested written material and statistics, they were not forthcoming until late in the visit. We had no course outlines to mull over, no texts to read with professional tongue-clucking, no research-in-progress to savor. So, we were forced back to the evanescence of the interviews and our pointillist impressions.

Sitting on the wall overlooking Havana's scalloped bay, we joined our pasts with the moment, coming up with several working explanations which we had little occasion to amend in our second week.

The fundamental breakthrough came with a puckish grin from the female, sociological member of the duo, when she said, "You know, Cuba is a great big open-admissions system." This statement was informed by some years of teaching experience at New York's City College during its trauma of the late 1960s and early 1970s. Open admissions, meaning that anyone who has a high school degree can enter the free city system, has critical political and educational dimensions, especially in a population that has been economically and culturally deprived and is rent by ethnic divisions. Clearly, the good that is so evident in Cuba has to do with an opening of all social institutions to persons from all of life's stations. But there are obvious costs. Because poverty is a cultural as well as an economic and a class phenomenon, the transition toward a society of universal membership implies that many persons will be doing jobs and occupying institutional roles without the polish, conditioning, and apperceptive knowledge one takes for granted when recruiting from middle-class bases. Lower-class secretaries will not spell well. Physicians recruited from the lower classes will not understand the diseases of the rich. Provincial persons will find it hard to empathize with people of foreign cultures. Cuba is engaged in a massive digestion of its own people, turning the entire populace into a truly national citizenry. The result, at least temporarily, must be provincialism.

This self-absorption and accompanying sense of isolation are not an effect alone of the fifteen-year economic and cultural blockade of Cuba; they are also consciously planned, and related to the mythology of the revolution. The emigration of half a million Cubans, many of them urban, professional, cosmopolitan persons, has contributed importantly to reducing the stock of intellectual refinement available at middle and lower levels in Cuba. Further, the Cubans have been doing the very best they can to work out their own destiny and are troubled by ideological racket made by those who do not understand their historical uniqueness. C. Wright Mills, in his early book on Cuba called *Listen, Yankee!* made the point that Cuba's leaders had not been scarred by the Marxist ideological wars of the 1930s and 1940s. But no European or North American political person, whether of leftist or rightist persuasion, can cross out of his mind Stalinism, Central European totalitarianisms, Tito and the national question in socialist development, or even the widespread student disorders of the 1960s and their evanescent and shifting ideological components. The Cubans have not been immune, either. The radical "liberationism" of Guevara has been discarded, and Cuba's "new man" will bear many marks of the old one. Some material incentives are back, and attempts are being made to get away from artificial pricing and into some mechanism that will permit demand to affect supply through ordered market mechanisms. Withal, the Cuban leadership has its own vision, heavily influenced by Cuban history and, after all, the obvious fact that Cuba is a part of the Americas. Therefore, its culture contains a certain set of attitudes about functional democracy and the role of man in society.

In the midst of trial and error, a fight for survival, the necessity to learn how to make everything from toothpaste to new laws, and an attempt to conceptualize its situation, the Cuban government has understandably insulated the country to some extent. *Granma* demonstrates that fact every day. Ultrasensitivity to foreign criticism also reveals it. Perhaps all countries undergoing total social integration need to look to themselves for a while, and to see *cosmopolitanism* as a dirty word. Certainly Burma, China, and several other examples support that thesis. But, whatever the needs of the past—real or imagined—the future will be different, for the isolation is about to break.

Another, related catchphrase helped us understand our depression. It had to do with understanding what had happened to Havana as something more than replacing the urbane by the provincial. What, after all, is a city to do if it is stripped of its capitalist functions? Take away the shopping areas, the eating places, and the sense of variety that commercial competition brings with it, and style must suffer, as must the ebb and flow of individual movement. The city is reduced to its classical colonial functions: it becomes a political and bureaucratic center, an educational focus, a transportation hub, and a place to sleep. Theatrical spectaculars may be offered, but where is off-off-Broadway? Cabarets and nightclubs may flourish (as they still do in Havana, where the Tropicana is alive and well), but where is the site of that scrabbling, constant social rubbing which permits fad to blend into movement and movement to melt into national style? There may be some official newspapers and magazines, but where are the offbeat experiments which can grow and enrich the lives of the nonelite?

We are not engaging in a mindless, habit-inspired plea for the urban style as a counterpart prejudice to equally mindless redpecked ruralism. Rather, our argument is that a truly urbane city permits the accomplishment of the idea popularized by Richard Sennett, the "positive uses of disorder." We are talking about the positive qualitative consequences of physical milling, the serendipitous emergence of varied ways of looking at the world, or at problems, or at Herblock's cartoons. We think such variety to be of inestimable use to rationality in public matters; we also think it an ultimate good, for it is an enrichment of personal life. When this purposeful disorder exists, then city air does indeed make man free. Otherwise, we have only *campesinos* suffering demographic density.

Socialists seem to have trouble thinking about cities. At issue is not only the question of whether there is a functional substitute for the play of competition, whether economic or artistic or ideational, but also the effects of the emphasis placed in most socialisms on the accomplishment of economic tasks. Because socialism has appeared in developing countries, as in the Cuban case, much worth is obviously given to discipline in work and in social interaction. However, to plan only for order and increasing rationalization is to invite only technical responses to a situation that touches on the core of national style. Cuban urban planners seem much like their counterparts in the United States. Their worries are literally only concrete.

The Cubans have a particular difficulty in thinking about the city. Almost all the revolutionary leaders were born outside Havana and came to the capital for their higher education. Despite the fact that their success was made possible by city people, both in Cuba and abroad, they have practiced a revolution based on the rapid underwriting of social change in rural areas and small towns. This process has a fundamental justification: it is a major step on the way to reducing urban-rural differences, to carrying communications and services equally to all parts of the relatively small and manageable land that is Cuba. Thus, the relative *physical* neglect of Havana has been balanced by the educational, health, and organizational integration of all the other Cubans into participant local communities. As in the indicators of development listed in the previous section of this essay, the absolute task is well on its way to accomplishment. What is left is the quality of the task, what kind of community is to be the one or the ones that Cubans have now joined.

The third tentative understanding at which we arrived on the wall overlooking the bay was that Cuba's resounding victory was in the construction of a nation-state, the basis of participant national community. Any truly socialist victory still lies ahead. This view needs explanation. We wish to say, first, that we do not pose the issue this way in order to sneer at Cuba's accomplishments, or to share in the snotty attitudes of such writers as René Dumont, whose romanticized, allegedly Chinese, bias in favor of rural cooperatives leads him to misunderstand the Cuban situation entirely. Cuba is the first Latin American country to become a true nation-state—secular, partially egalitarian, aiming toward total participation, able to call on its people to show ultimate loyalty to fellow Cubans despite status-derived differences. It is this accomplishment that evokes admiration—but not without worry. As we have said before, we view national community as a precondition for socially despicable as well as admirable societies. With the accomplishment of national community, Cuba has joined the modern world. Indeed, because it has become national with what amounts at least to a temporary erasure of iron-bound class lines, it may avoid the crises of some of its categorical peers, which have not yet fully resolved their class-nation conflict. (The United States, unhappily, is one of the countries that have been unable to settle, once and for all, racial and class oppositions to the accomplishment of full equality before the institutions of the nation.) As of this moment, we see no reason to fault Cuba for not having created a socialist paradise. It is quite enough that it has built a social nation, the tool for the realization of more difficult dreams—for *gulag* or true equality before the laws, for heedless obedience to the will of the state or the real submission of an accountable government to the periodic expression of informed public choices.

For us, then, the essential clash of our time is only vulgarly put as being between socialism and capitalism. Rather, we see it as between democracy and totalitarianism. An economy that is unaccountable because it is controlled by a state apparatus is no better than one that is unaccountable because it is run by privately owned combinations. The essential *political* issue of both states and economies is the same: their control, their forced accountability, through mechanisms responsive to rationally formed and expressed desires of a citizenry embracing all willing and competent persons within the relevant political area. The idea is a classical one, as reading Montesquieu demonstrates, but it has become extraordinarily muddled in recent years. Thus, to repeat, the creation of national community is an unavoidable step in the process of generating the power to contain public institutions. However, national community is double-edged, creating the legitimacy and consensual acceptance of authority that may produce the unaccountable totalitarian state.

With this mixture of feelings, we left to spend the weekend on Varadero Beach, which we are happy to report is as lovely as ever. Our schedule promised a coming week similar to the one we had just spent. Although we had enjoyed many small encounters with diverse persons, and continued to be grateful for the tasteful and unobtrusive courtesies extended us, we did not look forward to a repetition, so we promised ourselves to desist from thorny discussions, for after all we had not traveled to Cuba to grind personal partisan axes, to perturb, or to throw sand in gears. But chance intervened again. A member of the Cuban diplomatic mission to Allende's Chile had fallen in with some of our friends working in UN offices there. They had requested that we say hello to him but had warned that he would probably be traveling in Europe. Without much hope, then, we asked that our host transmit greetings to him, if he could be found. On our return from Varadero, we learned that indeed he was in Havana, that he would come round as soon as possible to see us, and that he worked in the same agency as the person who had originally extended us the invitation through the New York offices of the United Nations. The world isn't so small; it's just a place full of accidents.

With the assistance of our intelligent and worldly new host, the continued support of our university acquaintances, and the experience we had accumulated during the first week, we were able rapidly to add complexity and some depth to our knowledge of Cuba. The high points of this time were an illuminating discussion with the dean of the law school, a long talk with Vice Premier Carlos Rafael Rodríguez, and a morning with two old and experienced ideologists of the Communist Party. There is no point in summarizing the content of these discussions, for much of what we learned has infused what we have so far written. A few notes concerning the flavor of the encounters may well be more revealing than a recitation of questions, answers, and debates.

The afternoon we met with the dean of law, the graduating students were giving themselves a party. As our talk began, we did not know of the impending party. Nor did we know how symbolically important it was until we later reflected on the afternoon. The dean, with an impressively organized mind, took us through an intensely interesting discussion of the evolving mix of new and old law in revolutionary Cuba. Many of the revolutionary leaders, including Premier Castro, were trained as lawyers but despised the uses to which law was put. Therefore, the university reform of 1962 reflected a desire to improve technical training and to downgrade the law. Legal studies received such a bad name that in 1969 only 11 students were enrolled in the law school of the University of Havana, the only one in the country. As the dean remarked, Cuba was getting to the stage "of being all revolution and no law." The notion was that the revolutionary spirit would provide justice. It was only in 1969, after seven years of experience with the Popular Tribunals and with the beginning of the concept of "institutionalizing the revolution," that the need for an ordered new set of laws began keenly to be felt. The dean was the first to tell us that, because Cuba was not yet a socialist society, law remained necessary. After some two hours of tightly packed discussion of laws, procedures, the provincial elections taking place in Matanzas during our visit, and university affairs, two students shyly but firmly interrupted and affectionately insisted that it was time to go to the party. We were invited, too. The occasion was to celebrate the first graduating class of respectable size and capacity in many years. The party was fun, characterized by the enthusiasm and the anticipatory nostalgia that accompany all such gatherings anywhere.

The meeting with Carlos Rafael Rodríguez was the only one

attended by K. H. Silvert alone. It was supposed that straight politics
would be talked, and that one-to-one and man-to-man would be
more fitting than a triangular discussion. Don Carlos Rafael has the
reputation of being a man of warmth, intelligence, and sophistication. I [Kalman H. Silvert] found him to have all those attributes in
abundance. We spoke for well over two hours, and I left with a sense
of having talked with someone of intellectual delicacy and consummate good taste.

Our discussion was both rambling and pointed—a very positive
use of disorder. We talked a bit about published materials, and then
chatted about some of the experiences shaping the political minds of
young people today, and their relation to our own youths. I made
mention that the Vietnam War seemed to play the same part—even
though a more intense one—for many young Americans that the
Spanish Civil War had played for me during my own college days.
Don Carlos Rafael said that the Spanish Civil War and the Mexican oil
expropriations had been the two key, symbolic events of his own
college days. He then said that the Spaniards seemed to be on the
brink of truly integrating their civil war in their awareness. A short
time ago he had been in Madrid, where he saw a movie that mentioned the war in its opening passages, and there had been no reaction in the theater—that is, the mention was taken as a normal event,
and was not censored. He then recommended that I see the picture. It
was *The Way We Were*, with Streisand and Redford. My wife and I had
both seen the film and had been struck by the generational differences between those who liked it and those who did not. We thought it
accurately evocative of the period, while many of our younger friends
thought it actively boring and without meaning. Once we had established some equivalence of taste and experience, we launched into
questions of international relations, the hemisphere, and Cuban-
European relations. And from there we roamed through the Matanzas elections and other aspects of Cuban planning. When I was sure I
would not be misinterpreted, I felt free to test our idea about open
admissions and the notion that Cuba's resounding success was its
nationalist revolution. When I found understanding (I do not know if
there was agreement), I was emboldened directly to ask when socialism would begin in Cuba. The response was a hearty laugh of understanding, and the statement that now, truly, Cuba was in condition to
begin the job. What others called "institutionalizing the revolution,"
C. R. Rodríguez was willing to call "building socialism." As had been
implied earlier by the dean of law, the job involves connecting the
present patterns of local participation with effective national participation. It is for that reason that the Matanzas elections, the first to be

held since 1959, are being followed with such intense interest. It is hoped that they will be the first step in a process that will end with elections of a national government.

We will not discuss the Matanzas elections further, for it is obvious that they are of such importance that they need particular study of the kind we were not able to carry out for lack of time.

Our last formal meeting was supposed to be something of a private debate with the two Communist Party ideologists. Instead, we found them to be old and tried enough to view their own thinking with detachment and humor. They were invaluable sources of information about events of the 1920s, 30s, and 40s, and we learned much from them, but two matters stand out. One is the sense of closeness to the colony many Cubans still have. The historical fact that Cuba was (in 1898) the last Latin American country to gain independence from Spain is a textbook datum until two such men wrap that quite recent event into the thinking of the three generations of Cubans of the independence period. The second element of their comments that will long remain with us concerns the question of totalitarianism. As we gently circled around the point of personal freedom, civil liberties, and the other pitfalls of modern countries both capitalistic and socialistic, we found that we were able to speak openly about Eastern Europe with these two gentlemen, as we had not with others. Certainly they were not going to show ingratitude or engage in Red War rhetoric, but also they were not going to deny the problem. They expressed faith that Cuba would not fall into a repressive personalistic dictatorship because "the Cuban people would not permit it, because of their idiosyncrasy as Cubans." A narrow ideologue of the Left would dismiss such talk as anti-Marxist. Many a dogmatic empirical social scientist would dismiss it as "soft" and undemonstrable. We found it a touching expression of faith and an intellectual recognition of the importance of culture in social action. They could not have learned as much from us as we did from them.

By the end of our second week, our depression had become diluted with even greater respect for Cuba's past accomplishments and reason to hope for future ones. Obviously, dangers are far from over, and many mistakes will be made. The Cubans have intelligent leadership, but followership remains varied, uncertain, and insufficiently equipped with skill, understanding, and civic initiative. Further, the international situation remains murky in intellectual and economic matters, although Cuba's particular international strain is certainly soon to be eased.

THE INTERNATIONAL SITUATION

Even before we made our trip, rumors began to fly that a break in Cuba's hemispheric position was about to occur. Mexican President Luis Echeverría was openly seeking to rally Latin American support for a general move toward recognition. (Mexico never broke relations with Cuba, despite the OAS resolution calling on all member states to do so. Chile reestablished relations in 1970, and broke them again after the military coup of 1973. Trinidad and Tobago, Jamaica, Barbados, and Guyana opened diplomatic relations in 1972.) The Mexican initiatives proposed that Cuba be invited to the next meeting of the Latin American foreign ministers, to take place in Buenos Aires later in 1974. Secretary of State Kissinger let it be known in the spring in Mexico that he would not oppose such a move. The rightist Brazilian government said the same. As matters seemed to be shaping up in July, only Chile, Bolivia, Uruguay, and Nicaragua would continue to oppose opening either full diplomatic or commercial relations with Cuba. In June the Argentines had inaugurated a large trade fair in Havana, sending some six hundred Argentines to the undertaking. Affairs speeded up after July. Rumors were widespread that it was former President Nixon who personally opposed a move toward normalization. With his departure from office, that personal element was removed, and in August Mexican foreign minister Emilio G. Rabasa spoke with Messrs. Ford and Kissinger about convoking an OAS meeting to lift sanctions against Cuba and to open the way for that nation's full return to the hemisphere. In the same month Panama recognized Cuba, and Venezuela, Colombia, and Costa Rica were using the threat of immediate recognition to put pressure behind the move for rapid OAS action. By the time this essay appears, certainly more details of this wide-ranging set of moves will have emerged.

Many questions attend these events. They concern Cuba directly, of course, but they also have much to do with Latin American diplomacy in general, and with the role of the United States in the hemisphere. Outsiders cannot know the full story, or the entire range of motives impelling these moves. A reasonable guess would certainly be that the Mexican, Argentine, and Colombian and Venezuelan moves are related to a desire to establish some mechanism for international collective bargaining. Because the Organization of American States is not an appropriate vehicle for expressing purely Latin American interests, the periodic meetings of Latin America's foreign ministers (attended also by the United States) are being proposed as the germ of what may well become a regional political organization, in addition to the OAS. If this postulation is correct, then the moves toward the recognition of Cuba are symbolic of a declaration of independence from the strictures of North American views of what is proper in the hemisphere. It is obvious that the United States cannot stubbornly refuse to change its Cuban policy in the face of this concerted attack, for to do so would be to admit the death of the OAS. Such recalcitrance would also signify public advertisement of the United States' weakness in the hemisphere, for we probably can only delay but not stop the trend.

Cuba's inevitable reemergence into the hemisphere will, nevertheless, pose important problems both for Cuba and the United States. In the case of our country, the difficulty will not stem from a loss of our often repeated position that Cuba must eschew armed intervention in her neighbors' affairs before readmission to the family. The wholesale willingness of neighboring Caribbean countries and of other Latin American nations to recognize Cuba must be taken as *prima facie* demonstration that those countries no longer fear Cuban interventionism. The remaining issue is global: normalization of relations with Cuba implies that the United States recognizes and tolerates the Soviet presence in the Western Hemisphere. It also legitimizes Marxism in the hemisphere. The effect may be more subtly significant than most North Americans imagine, because for us Marxism is indelibly alien, while for Latin Americans it is not an unimaginable way of thinking. The problem, then, is more psychological than military. It involves a recognition that some Latin American nations, at least, are beginning to emerge on the world scene as relatively independent actors, nations of the second class in their symbolic significance, even if of the third or fourth class in terms of military might. From a "special relationship" characterized by marked subordination and superordination, we are faced with the need to evolve a special relationship somewhat in the Western European style—with nations sharing many common cultural elements, with interests that are complementary as well as competitive. We will have to negotiate on conditions of relative intellectual equality. Cuba itself is incidental to this trend, but for the moment the symbolic meaning of Cuba expresses the essence of the movement.

Reentry will be traumatic for Cuba also. The overt diplomatic moves will be simple. Havana will not return to the OAS but will participate fully in the foreign ministerial sessions and in other inter-American agencies. The difficulties lie elsewhere. Is Cuba ready to break her isolation? Can she control the ideological buffeting she is likely to suffer, especially at the hands of Latin America's litigious, divided, and wrangling leftists? Can she find common cause with states of such opposed persuasion as Brazil and Bolivia? Will the appeal of superbly trained North American technicians be so strong as to fortify technocratic tendencies in Cuba and inhibit the growth of democratic socialism?

Interesting times are coming in the hemisphere. After ten years of decay and listlessness, hemispheric diplomacy is unmistakably astir. Cuba as symbol is important to the present mix. But Cuba as problematic society is of longer duration and deeper fascination.

The lingering aftertaste of our visit is very pleasant. The UN official who arranged the trip repeatedly told us that his dominant impression of Cuba was "cleanliness"—*limpieza*. We now know what he meant. He was referring not only to a physical characteristic but to an approach. One should admire a people that has faced up to a materially and intellectually difficult situation, and has emerged with a victory of which it is proud. We found patriotism, but not arrogance, and honesty and straightforwardness of thought and behavior. We also found that Cubans think their way is the correct one for the rest of the Latin hemisphere. Certainly an American has no cause to criticize the nationalistic *hubris* of others. We liked what we saw because the Cubans have opened new possibilities for themselves and have created the ability to make their own future. If we worry about that future, it is because we worry about our own, too, and for essentially the same reasons.

We wish the Cubans well.

1974

III. Ways of Knowing

Politics, Political Science,
and the Study of Latin America

PROBING THE RELATIONSHIPS between the disciplines and area studies is a theme with a long and drab history. I have no intention of weaving my way through the extensive literature on the subject. Anybody curious about such matters may begin by consulting the omnibus note whose number is given at the end of this sentence.[1] Furthermore, I have an equal disinclination to defend myself and my fellow political scientists who write on Latin America from chronic charges that we are somehow not up to the task, or at least not as "good" as our colleagues who labor in other geographical vineyards. Herewith I am providing another footnote number to satisfy any prurient curiosity you may have about such gossip.[2] The discussion has some redeeming social value, but very little academic worth. Instead of treating area studies and political science as essentially different

---

[1]See Fred W. Riggs, ed., *International Studies: Present Status and Future Prospects* (Philadelphia: The American Academy of Political and Social Science, 1971); Allan A. Michie, *Higher Education and World Affairs* (New York: Education and World Affairs, 1968); Robert F. Byrnes, "The Future of Area Studies," *ACLS Newsletter,* Volume 19, Number 7 (1968); Hugh Borton *et al., Report of the Committee on the College and World Affairs* (New Haven: The Hazen Foundation, 1964); the numerous issues of *Far Horizons;* many issues of the SSRC's *Items,* and so on and on.

[2]Charles Wagley, ed., *Social Science Research on Latin America* (New York: Columbia University Press, 1964); Manuel Diégues Júnior and Bryce Wood, eds., *Social Science in Latin America* (New York: Columbia University Press, 1967); Howard F. Cline, ed., *Latin American History: Essays on Its Study and Teaching, 1898–1965* (Austin: University of Texas Press, 1967), 2 vols.; Richard M. Morse, "The Strange Career of 'Latin American Studies,' " *Annals of the American Academy of Political and Social Science,* Number 356 (November 1964); many issues of the *Latin American Research Review,* and particularly Peter Ranis, "Trends in Research on Latin American Politics: 1961–1967," *LARR,* Number 3 (1968); and so on.

enterprises, I wish to suggest that the latter had better ingest the former if it is to prosper and not continue to languish in its present state—as a discipline that has creditably managed to discredit most of its recently popular theories but has not summoned itself to the general and scientifically transient acceptance of more useful constructions of reality.

The reasoning I will pursue has little documentary backing, for the historical separateness of area studies and the social science disciplines is the stereotypical strain throughout the available literature. The commonly accepted view is summed up in the following résumé by a leading student and impresario of area studies:

> there have been four stages in the development of relationships between area studies and the social sciences; that is to say—naming the extremes—between the gathering of data and their ordering by theoretical constructs. In the first stage, data about foreign areas were collected through field research by area specialists. A second stage saw the comparison of similar problems in different areas through the broadening of training of area specialists. In the third stage, data from several areas were used by social scientists to develop new theories and to overcome the parochial basis of much existing theory in the social sciences. In the present, fourth stage, the development of theory begins to influence the types of problems area specialists investigate and the kinds of questions they begin to ask as they undertake field research, in part because, more than ever before, the training of area specialists is becoming assimilated to the training of social scientists. This is bound to have effects on both. . . .[3]

On its surface, the process as described appears ideal: an inductive gathering of data by area specialists leads to theoretical, disciplinary interpretations that permit the deductive approach to begin.[4] Area studies are "prescientific," while the discipline provides the science, which then impregnates the continuance of area analysis, which in its turn moves ever closer to the disciplines. Would that life so ordered itself. This view of "natural" process is highly reminiscent of the "trickle-down" theory in economics, the belief that a well-primed pump will be made to continue to shower some water on everybody, for reasonable and rational men will see the personal advantage in keeping consumers alive. The trickle-down theory

[3]Bryce Wood, "Area Studies," *International Encyclopedia of the Social Sciences* (New York: Macmillan and Free Press, 1968), Volume I, p. 405.

[4]I am using "induction" and "deduction" vulgarly. We all know that data cannot be "gathered" in the absence of previously extant notions of order and significance. Thus, the "induction" of initial area data-gatherers in truth describes searching around without explicit recognition of the guideposts actually being employed.

breaks down, partly because unequal power distribution all too often prevents the flow from permeating the entire society, even most inequitably. Analogously, the flow of data from "areas" to the disciplinary mills and back out to the "areas" dries up because the mill is unable to process the raw material; it cannot convert "information" into "data" without changing its own nature, without grappling with the fact that area studies came into existence because of the very ethnocentric limitations of the disciplines. Political science is a weak sister. Area studies are her crutch.

Although standing the discipline–area relationship on its head is unusual, comments on the debilities of political science are not. Once again, I do not propose to summarize arguments about neo-positivism, quantification and "qualification," the meaning of "institutional approaches" in political science as distinct from sociology and economics, or the significance of "structuralism" in political science as distinct from anthropology. Whatever one's persuasion, it is a matter of fact that the discipline has not dealt *conceptually*, and hence *scientifically*, with some of the more astounding political developments of the past two decades. The failure is beyond debate. Joseph LaPalombara wrote in the inaugural issue of *Comparative Politics:*

> A less generous reaction to much of the recent whole-systems theoretical output of the discipline is the observation that we have returned to the ancient art of scholasticism, armed to be sure with new terminology, but not any more successful than were the ancients in narrowing the gap between abstract formulations and theoretical realities. It strikes me as enormously telling that at precisely that moment in the profession's development when methodological tools will permit the rigorous comparative testing of hypotheses the distance between hypotheses and general theory should be widening and that the linkage between hypotheses and macrotheory is either terribly obscure or of such problematical logical construction that theory itself cannot be falsified.[5]

The literature in all social science disciplines, both in the United States and abroad, is now rich in such observations, and in yearnings after a new "paradigm."[6] The area specialist has long known that he has had trouble with organizing concepts, but understanding precisely the nature of his trouble does not come easily to him. In the article from which the above quotation comes, LaPalombara

---

[5]Joseph LaPalombara, "Macrotheories and Microapplications in Comparative Politics: A Widening Chasm," *Comparative Politics*, Volume I, Number 1 (1968), p. 54.

[6]I am using the word *paradigm* in the same sense in which it is used by Thomas S. Kuhn, *The Structure of Scientific Revolutions* (Chicago: The University of Chicago Press, 1962).

condemns—rightly, to my mind—the search for "systems theory," "holistic theory," "general theory," or "grand theory." Perhaps the "systems" idea is in itself a major impediment to understanding how to generate hypotheses that will order our understandings. That is, maybe we should seek to know something about total *situations* but not beg the question by searching for the order, rationalization, self-contained "sense," and bias toward "system-maintenance" that is involved with the very word "system." Certainly, any student of Latin American politics would be hard pressed to describe national phenomena in the region in terms of a single coherent "system" or of a master "system" with its "subsystems." After all, the core of Latin American politics has to do with ambiguities, the interactions of different and often opposed views of desired social "systems," the asymmetry of rapid change, and sometimes grotesque adjustments among seemingly contradictory forms, ideas, and practices.

Behind systems theory, however, lie other North American cultural biases, which, by influencing the mainstream political scientist[7] in his choice of theoretical views, have also made it difficult for him to "see" Latin American politics and perhaps even his own. The rejection of "institutionalism" in comparative politics is an appropriate case in point. Turning away from legalistic descriptions of formal political structures was certainly justified. Not defensible, however, was a simultaneous withdrawal from concern with institutions as historically developed clusters of routinized behavior patterns, with their appropriate sets of sanctions. Abandoning the study of institutions in that sense, implying as it does abandonment of historical and cultural specificity, inhibits our ability to develop causal analyses and to create true syntheses, beyond merely adding up analytical statements and labeling the sum "holism." The result has been that we have developed great strength in deciding what is "necessary" to an occurrence (the individual elements that comprise a situation), but we have been woefully laggard in arriving at "sufficiency" (the configurations of the "necessary"—their *melding* into a social event or a social latency, an integrating task vastly different from a simple addition). What is more interesting, however, than the rejection of the richness of institutional, historically bound research and thought is what was adopted in its place.

The commonplace explanation for the abandonment of histori-

---

[7] I am specifically addressing myself not to the many competing schools of thought in the discipline, but rather to the principal figures and tendencies in the field of comparative politics. The principal omissions have to do with those political scientists working within Marxist ideas, or those others who, implicitly or otherwise, assume the "inevitability" of governments of force.

cally tied research is that the social sciences followed the rising star of the physical sciences, determined to find universals, an equally defensible set of "laws" to cover the entire human experience. Consequently, the idea developed that one must place primary emphasis not on clusters of historical uniqueness—institutional situations, ideological sets, social classes, families of social organization—but rather on whatever can be found everywhere, such as stratification, biological "determinants," functions, and allegedly common psychological motivations. That approach is antithetical to area studies, whose prime task is to establish the cultural parameters of social activity. Thus, political science and area studies could not converge; data from foreign fields could not be absorbed by a discipline so fixed on a search for the common that it had no idea frame for holding the different. Naturally, area-studies specialists and mainstream political scientists also diverged theoretically—for it was never true that the area man was without theory, or that the disciplinary person was especially gifted in theorizing. In brief, most American political scientists became modern-day Utilitarians,[8] with one or another variation. On the other hand, most political scientists concerned with the Third World, and particularly with Latin America, have been on a long search through the writings of Locke, Rousseau, Kant, Hegel, Marx, Weber, Mannheim, Durkheim, Lukács, Gramsci, and the like to find understanding of the partially Mediterranean, partially industrial, partially patrimonial, partially modern, partially traditional, and highly changeful and varied sets of occurrences with whose understanding we have been charged. Our colleagues in the United States, when they knew what they were doing, were adapting Bentham and Marshall and Parsons while remaining more than slightly contemptuous of anyone who thought that social class and race and ideology were "variables" worth worrying about. But the Latin Americanist had little choice in the matter, not least because the Latin American intelligentsia is tied to the European scene and the latter's interest in precisely what we were discarding. Thus, all of Weber was available in Spanish by the late 1940s, long before it was available in English. Generations before the MIT Press bestowed Lukács on American readers, he was the subject of wide discussion in Latin America, his works available in transla-

---

[8]See, of course, John Rawls, *A Theory of Justice* (Cambridge, Mass.: Harvard University Press, 1971). The great impact of Rawls' book, primarily because of its discrimination between Utilitarian and Liberal thought, is again somewhat surprising to a Latin Americanist, for in that part of the world the distinction has always been clearly recognized. Still, it is a pleasure to read such a painstaking attempt to disaggregate what has become in so many heads an undifferentiated mass.

tion through the good offices of Spanish publishing houses, which have published the writings of even esoteric Marxists and distributed them at relatively low cost.

Concern with such thinking is justified by much more than keeping up with the Sánchezes, however. What is happening in Latin America cannot be understood in light of the common ideas produced by positivistic neo-Utilitarianism—such ideas as that stability is *ipso facto* "good," that "ideologies" are important only when "things" are in crisis, that a mean is "happy," and that politics or anything else can be pursued in the absence of ethical and moral values. Neither political scientists nor political men can afford such luxuries in Latin America. Equilibrium theory looks strange to persons trying to change their political orders—whether for right-wing or left-wing "developmentalism," or revolution, or whatever. Amoral politics is a double-edged sword when losing can sometimes mean dying. And ideologies are the essential stuff of party politics when consensus is lacking concerning the definition of the good society. But Latin American social scientists and North American "Latinists" generally are either convinced or trending toward the conviction that neo-Utilitarianism is not only of little use for understanding Latin America but also inappropriate for the United States and not very good "science." Some of the reasoning is as follows:

1. Utilitarian equilibrium theory and its contemporary derivatives, the various forms of functionalism, presume that change occurs because of one or another reaction to "tension" created by deviation from harmony, balance, or the "functional" working of a "system." Even with the introduction of ideas of "tension management," the theory deals essentially in psychological reductionism. The exercise of reason is epiphenomenal, or at least of less theoretical importance than is an inherent striving for evenness. The major implications are two. First, such ideas depart from antecedent liberal views linking social action to a moral basis—a basis expressed by Locke and Smith, for example, in the notion of a "natural" *structure* the search for whose achievement *should*, ethically, motivate behavior. Thus, Utilitarianism discards a social ethic in favor of an inherent and essentially individual psychological calculus. Second, the downgrading of reason opens the door to technocratic thought, to the assumption that all social problems essentially involve manipulating tensions into their resolution. Hence, "crisis managers" appear, to replace political men, and social scientists are confused about the difference between "pure" and "applied" research, so that we blur the difference between a scientist and an

engineer. Rationalization becomes the principal function of the Utilitarian social scientist, even when he is putting in order an irrational or antirational structure. This kind of "social scientist" in Latin America is known as a *técnico*; the word connotes something more than a technician and something less than a freely inquiring scientific spirit.

2. Emphasis on the universality of motivation slights effectiveness of action as well as the possibility of a rational component in arriving at decisions. Consequently, social muscle and the exercise of intelligence are relegated to secondary positions and, indeed, given no comfortable place at all in Utilitarian thought or its derivatives. Class as a measure of potential access to manifest power and culture as the reservoir of justifications for the use of power are concepts critical to an understanding of historical continuities, of the ways in which societies get where they are and move themselves to where they are going. But theories derived from Utilitarianism have little to say about these matters. They are as inhospitable to the basic questions of political science as they are to an appreciation of the ethical bases that sustain the relativistic and rationalistic enterprise that characterizes science itself as an institutional social undertaking.

The Utilitarian structure of thought is "pure" in the sense that it is unsullied by data; rather, its design establishes data as being "out there," not an integral part of the theoretical structure itself. Hence, the complaint of LaPalombara and many others that "theory" and hypotheses are moving apart. Since hypotheses *must* refer directly to data and *should* be an application of a theoretical construct, a separation of theory and hypotheses makes of "systems theory" and its cousins mere ideology—or "normative theory"—the subject matter of what we usually call the history of political thought. Certainly such constructs are not empirical theory, an intellectual guide to research and to the particular methods appropriate to given research problems.

Latin American politics forces us to remember what we have been professionally taught to forget. To put it another way, the exercise of standard American professionalism is incompetence in explaining Latin American politics. Let me make this point by asking the reader to join me in a vicarious tour of Latin America. Become innocent—naively listen to what is being said, observe what is around you, and make a layman's decision on what is important, what is amusing, and what is ephemeral and casual. Here, in no particular order, are the most commonplace "variables" of Latin American politics:

- Class, power, and color. Words and phrases in common use are *aristocracy, bourgeoisie, proletariat, upper class, middle class, lower class, decent people, modest people,* the *jailaif, accommodated people, marginal populations, professionals, industrialists, workers, white-collar employees, elites,* and so forth. Similarly fine gradations are used to denote ethnic origins, and neighborhoods are carefully defined as to their status.

- Foreign companies. Dependence. The CIA. Imperialism and colonialism and feudalism and patrimonialism. Sharks and their sardines, and the powerless ones.

- Torture, force, the police and military plots, *guerrilleros,* military equipment, rumors and gossip of who is in jail and who is out, corruption, bribery, theft, and favoritism.

- At appropriate electoral moments, parties and candidates, and at all times ideologies, the persuasions of left, right, and center; Marxism, Communism, Falangism, corporatism, democracy, liberalism, conservatism, and the men who in partisan and ideological pleading embody views and parties.

- Nationalism, laws, patriotism, taxes, regulations, bureaucracy.

- Inflation, jobs, industrialization, economic policy, social security, strikes, health care.

- Salacious personal gossip—who is doing what to whom when, how, and how often, and with how much relish.

Now, let us translate these quotidian matters into more formally expressed concepts. To wit:

- Social class, social structure, stratification.

- The nature of community (national community, the relation between nation and the international political order, local-national tensions, the role of a secular state as opposed to or in conjunction with church, economy, and others of the major institutional spheres).

- The rule of law—its extent, the "ins" and the "outs" as a real type measured against the ideal type expressed in the formal body of rules.

- Overt values (ideology), the predication of approved behavior, and actual behavior.

- The illegality of the governors, the illegality of the governed, and legitimacy and consensus.

- The place of individual idiosyncrasy in grand and petty politics. The place of accident, taste, personality, and intelligence in political life.

Nothing is new about these lists. They contain the subject matter of all standard political discourse from that of the ancient Greeks to this morning's newspapers. But are such subjects studied in much of the literature of comparative politics? Let us discuss this question next and then turn to a more difficult matter concerning the nature of the idea sets required to discipline our thinking about the use of such information. It is not intellectually enough to point out that common subjects of discussion about Latin American politics are omitted, or little mentioned, in many scholarly books. We must also attempt to demonstrate that they *should* be mentioned in given ways for the purposes of more efficient diagnosis and, perhaps, prediction.

I will make no pretense to an exhaustive search of the literature. Instead, I have put my hand on four books sitting together on my shelves, all expressions of the functionalist school of comparative politics. They are the following very well known volumes: Almond and Verba, *The Civic Culture* (1963); Pye and Verba, eds., *Political Culture and Political Development* (1965); Fagen, *Politics and Communication* (1966); and LaPalombara, ed., *Bureaucracy and Political Development* (1963).[9] I mean nothing personal by selecting these volumes, and I am fully aware that all the listed authors have since changed their ideas, some of them profoundly. Still, the several indexes to those books should tell us what was not being discussed in this sampling of some of the leading books of the 1960s—which, perforce, continue to be assigned to our students to read in the 1970s.

- Class, stratification, etc. Fagen, one mention: "elites, separated from masses." Almond and Verba, one mention: "elites"; and perhaps one could stretch items concerning "political competence," "citizenship," and "participation." Pye and Verba: "class structure, in Mexico" (appropriately), "elite political culture" in India, Mexico, and Turkey, and "mass political culture" in India. LaPalombara: "political elites," with twelve page references. Note that there are no references at all to outcasts and others of the least privileged.

- Fascism, Nazism, corporatism, authoritarianism, dictatorship. LaPalombara, no mentions; Fagen, three mentions of authoritarianism "as a communications system," "stabilizations, communication changes," and "groups" in "authoritarian systems"; Pye and Verba, three page references to "fascists," another to "authoritar-

---

[9]The Fagen volume was published by Little, Brown in Boston, the other three by the Princeton University Press.

ian personality" in Italy, and five references to Nazism; Almond and Verba, no mentions!

- Ideology as explicitly mentioned concept. Almond and Verba, no listing; Pye and Verba, one reference under "ideologies"; Fagen, no listing; and LaPalombara, no listing.

- Nationalism. Almond and Verba: "national character" and "national pride" come as close to the idea as the volume offers; Pye and Verba provide six page references on "national identity" and four on "nationalism, Japanese"; Fagen has five page references on "national integration, and political development"; and LaPalombara has no mentions.

- Corruption, torture, terrorism, lying, etc. (strange index items, to be sure, but commonplace political practices). LaPalombara, no mentions; Fagen, no mentions; Pye and Verba, no mentions; Almond and Verba, no mentions.

- Power. Almond and Verba, no listing in the index; LaPalombara, no listing; Pye and Verba, no listing; and Fagen, one page reference ("power, as communication").

A summary glance through the indexes of two books on Latin America will show us how different is the tone to be inferred from the subjects mentioned. Both books are the products of persons sharing mainstream North American social science ideas. One volume is an edited work prepared by two scholars, one deeply involved in North American political sociology, the other in Latin American political sociology. It is *Elites in Latin America* (1967), edited by S. M. Lipset and Aldo Solari, and contains articles written by scholars from both Americas. The other is a so-called "country book," which attempted to study Colombia by applying some of the then reigning notions in comparative politics. Written by Robert H. Dix, *Colombia: The Political Dimensions of Change* was published in 1967.[10] I will not break down the index mentions as above, for there are too many. Instead, I will take each book and run alphabetically through some of the pertinent entries.

Lipset and Solari. The relevant items begin with "Alienation. *See* Class consciousness." Then: Apathy. Authoritarianism (two page references). Bandits (five page references covering nine pages). Bourgeoisie (six page references with cross-listings). Business executives. Capitalism. Class consciousness (six references). Social

[10]The Lipset and Solari book was published by Oxford Press, the Dix volume by Yale University Press.

classes (fourteen page references and an extended discussion). Corruption (five pages listed). Dictatorship (one reference). Elites and elitism (major entry, of course, given the title of the book). Equalitarianism (eleven page references, many to multiple-page discussions). Falangists (one entry). Ideology (two and a half inches of small index type). Integration (national and social) has seven entries. Labor (seven entries covering at least twenty-two pages). Left-wing ideology (nine references, many to multiple pages). Masses, materialism, middle classes (twenty-eight entries, most to multiple page discussions), nationalism (close to two inches), occupations (approximately an inch), terrorism (four entries), value-orientation (an inch and a half), value-system (six entries, and five pages for value-movements), and, penultimately, working classes (thirty page references, including one covering pages 256 to 296).

   Dix.   This volume is not as richly indexed as is the Lipset-Solari work, but the index reflects the same factual concerns. It starts off immediately with *abolengo,* the Colombian landed aristocracy (four page references). There are over two inches of entries for *campesinos* (peasants, poor farmers). References are made to workers' confederations and unions, corporatism (two page citations), corruption (two more), crises of integration and participation, dictatorship (as modernizing regime, one reference), education and social status. About two inches are given to elites. There are entries for electoral fraud and intimidation, falangism (four references), fascism (two references), guerrillas (eight page references, including two referring to extended discussions), intellectuals (and their social status, political role, and Communist Party affiliation). Extended discussions of the lower classes are indicated, with about two inches on the "middle sectors," and about a half column on various entries having to do with the military. Modernizing elites earn a separate heading; nationalism has eighteen page references, national integration another twelve, and so forth.

   The narrowest reasonable inference from this somewhat juvenile exercise is that Latin American politics is discussed in factual terms different from those applied in some of the best known works in the literature on comparative politics. There is more to the matter, for the choice of subjects for study in Latin America implies a way of looking at politics that, until very recently, has been alien to most North American political scientists. The past decade, however, has raised many Latin American questions for the United States. Assassinations, urban *guerrillismo,* racial disturbances, favoritism and

corruption and official illegality, debates on the subjects of meritoc-
racy and technocracy, the obviousness and persistence of differences
among major groups that can be called class divisions, ideological
confrontations, student disorders, the growing political involvement
of police and military groups, the downgrading of Congress in favor
of a strong and personalistic executive—what a different index Ogg
and Ray would have prepared for their text on American government had they (or any other writers of such standard texts) considered the full theoretical possibilities that became reality in this
"slum of a decade" just past.

Now that we must explain instability, disjunction, asymmetry,
intersystemic change, the creation and uses of power, ideologies and
behavior, violence, and so many other manifestations of a total
situation in rapid and wrenching change, most political scientists
find themselves stranded with values, theories, and methods dedicated to finding and measuring opposite phenomena. That is, our
bents, ideas, and techniques are designed to search out stability,
conjunction, symmetry, intrasystemic extrapolations, manipulations
of existing influence, the separation of ideas and action, and the
tameness of a citizenry led by an "elite." Almost our entire statistical
enterprise illustrates this point. We search diligently for scalar relationships, for we must have evenness, predictability along a single
line. If two macrophenomena do not correlate, then they are obviously not "related." One will not "control" or "explain" the other. It
may very well be, however, that linear relationships across the major
manifestations of any society are rare, and that they indicate either a
static "organic" society or one in such crisis that its individuals and
groups are forced to reconcile their values and their many different
sets of institutional behavior patterns. It may also be that only some
individuals hold political and social values in a scalar relationship,
and that others do not wish to do so, or cannot. That is, the very fact
of value coherence may be a critical indicator of the *kind* of value
posture being held. The f-scale provides a good case in point. One
of the most cogent criticisms leveled against this measure of fascist
attitudes was that similar scales could not be constructed for nonfas-
cists, libertarians, democrats, or whatever one may wish to call such
persons. Adorno and his associates long ago pointed out, however,
that it is entirely possible that a basic distinguishing characteristic of
the fascist is his inability to tolerate ambiguity, while his opposite
number demands it. That is, the nonfascist cannot maintain full
attitudinal consistency and consonant desires for behavioral conformity, because the world is not a consistent one for the person willing
to see its dissonance, disharmony, disjunction, or, to use less negative

words, its variety, cultural richness, and the special overarching synthetic stamps of particular peoples. Methodologically, then, in macrosocial studies the fascist can respond to a scale, the nonfascist only to a typology. Significantly, scales are usually constructed inductively, while typologies are almost always built deductively.

But let us not lose ourselves in examples. The point I wish to make, to repeat, is that the factual material pressing in on us from Latin America, and, indeed, from almost everywhere, demands theoretical, methodological, and technical change from us. The following are some generalizations out of the Latin American experience that contain implicit within them what I consider imperatives for the evaluation of current theories and their possible amendment in contemporary situations of profound and rapid change:

1. A lack of "fit" among elements within social situations is the usual case, and "harmony" is rare. Legal systems only loosely describe behavior, morality, and the power relationships within societies. Members of social classes do not share similar ideologies or even more basic values. Industries do not produce uniformly industrial men, and cities are not inhabited only by the urbane. We need a word other than the negatively weighted *disjunction* to describe our normal inconsistency.

2. Institutional differentiation does not occur evenly or uniformly as societies "develop"—or industrialize, urbanize, become literate, media-participant, empathic, or whatever other configuration of indicators one may wish to select. Specialization of function may occur within institutions, but overwhelming evidence indicates that certain interinstitutional attachments tend to become strengthened as modernization proceeds. It is notorious that economic and political interests become ever more tangled in many "modern" states. Also, as religious institutions are in many lands pushed out of politics, they become more strongly attached to family and education. When one institution is employed to perform some of the functions of another, and when the autonomous interest of one is sacrificed to the interest of another, then one is safe in saying that institutional differentiation is not increasing.

3. Latin American political events strongly suggest that the major interinstitutional differentiation is not among individual institutions, but between those serving an affective, immediately satisfying purpose (most importantly, the family and religion) and those seen as serving instrumental purposes (education and the economy). Affective attachments tend to be held unquestioningly, hence ritualistically, unchangingly, or "traditionally." Instrumentalism tends to be viewed as adjustable, changeful, hence as "modern."

4. A prime issue everywhere in Latin America, in varying ways and to different degrees, is not only how each institution will relate to the others, but what is the overall configuration of such relationships. That is, the question refers to the total social order, not only to the partialities of "free" or "collective" economies or to the separation of church and state. A major problem involves the nature of social synthesis, the ways in which a seeming lack of "fit" among major social elements is given sense within a synthetic ordering of the entire situation.

5. The role of the state and the polity is everywhere being seen increasingly as a key element in the establishment of total configurations; in some countries, it is seen as *the* key. I am not saying merely that states have much to do with economic development, population policy, health and welfare, and the like, although they certainly do; I am suggesting that critically different politics attend the conviction that a polity should be only instrumental in nature and the opposing view that it should be both instrumental and affective—that politics is something worth doing for itself alone, that influencing the course of one's communities of membership at all levels is essential to the reduction of personal and group alienation. Politics as instrumentalism is fatally authoritarian, while politics as an activity worth doing *per se* (as well as for the accomplishment of other goals) sets the foundation for meaningfully participatory systems.

6. The part played by the polity in establishing and sanctioning the overarching system of interinstitutional relationships defines the secular or sacred nature of any society. Purely instrumental politics are exercised to further sacred purposes and, often, the private purposes of family and individual within rigid status and class systems. Affective politics creates the conditions for secularism. Such activities and beliefs make possible some ultimate, mundane commitments to fellow citizens and the communities we inhabit. Secularism allows room for religious belief and the pursuit of some entirely private interests. Sacred society does not allow room for secular relativism. Again, to evoke an earlier argument, the sacred view demands coherence, the secular one does not merely tolerate but promotes ambiguity.

7. These observations drawn from Latin American societies suggest that an appropriately complete theoretical construction will dissolve the differences between micro- and macrotheory that now hobble our intellectual freedom. That is, they suggest that individual idiosyncrasy, institutional settings, social structure, and ethos can be reconciled within one intellectual frame.

A study of Latin America pushed me to such observations as those above. The development of comparative politics in the United States since the early 1950s has also given me something to hone myself against, provided me with a useful mental antagonist that sometimes confused me but usually sharpened me. I advance these ideas because they have been useful to me in explaining Latin America and, obviously, Watergate and its antecedents in the United States. What more can one ask of the social sciences? I did not say "political science," or "area studies," or a combination of the two. Not enough of us are genuine social scientists with a primary interest in politics. It is in that construction of our role that we will arrive at a reconciliation of interdisciplinary, multidisciplinary, policy-oriented, disciplinary, and area-studies endeavors.

1973

An Essay on Interdisciplinary and
International Collaboration
in Social Science Research
in Latin America

UNIVERSITY UNREST is a fascinating part of the recent world situation of great promise and threat. A certain mystery and romance inhere in Berkeley, the Católica of Chile, Columbia, Warsaw, and the Sorbonne that it would be shameful to cheapen with hasty judgment. There are some apparently common threads, however, not least among them the search for new definitions of academic-civic relations. I should like to explore one small corner of this problem area through an examination of certain implications of a recent move toward collaborative research between North American and Latin American scholars. The relationship between such research linkages and much more general social problems is not as attenuated as may at first seem the case, especially because any cross-cultural comparisons can suggest to us what kinds of social relationships are "necessary" and which ones are subject to conscious and thus—conceivably—rational choice. That choices can be and must be made in setting new national courses is an awareness impregnating many societies. Perhaps the broad effects of and extreme sensitivity to university commotion is a part of this awareness, a feeling that the disarray of the intellectuals can actually make a social difference. It is for this reason that I dare to stretch what could be a discussion of mechanics and procedures in United States–Latin American academic diplomacy to one about the larger substance of town-gown relations.

117

I strongly suspect that much of the current faddishness about collaborative research in Latin American social science and about interdisciplinary research and teaching approaches is a respectable political reaction to a real political problem, but that the reaction is little refined and often even less academic. The political reasons for our preoccupation with collaborative research are clear. The Camelot episode [described in the next essay] precipitated widespread United States reactions, long before all was obviously not well in United States–Latin American academic diplomacy.[1] Let us not labor the point: we all have heard much about saturation, untrained scholars, ideologically freighted studies, the failure to make research results available to Latin American scholars and concerned agencies, the inapplicability of certain alien techniques and theories to the Latin American "reality," covert intelligence connections, and so forth. Before this wave of recriminations, too, we all were well aware of the great shortage of scholars involved in Latin American studies, that quality was spotty across the disciplines, that some Latin American societies were (and still remain) almost totally unstudied in systematic ways by anyone (whether North or Latin American or European or Asian), and so on. We know that all these statements of the past decade remain true. But there also have been many profound changes. I should like to list some of those changes that appear to me most pertinent for the purposes of this discussion:

First, there has been a physical proliferation and qualitative upgrading of Latin American studies of significant proportions in the United States. The quantitative dimensions are perhaps best described in the study documents submitted to the Department of Health, Education and Welfare in connection with the still unfunded International Education Act, notably that prepared by Bryce Wood. Qualitative aspects are reviewed in *Social Science Research in Latin America*.[2] Greater academic prestige, more scholarships, more students, more articles and books and monographs, and more university-wide involvement have made Latin American studies an intellectually exciting and rewarding set of fields of study but have also exacerbated problems of collaboration with Latin Americans.

Second, Latin American social science has been undergoing a revolutionary elaboration in many senses. Empirical sociology was to all intents and purposes born only twenty years ago in Latin America, and already it has spawned world-famous professionals and

---

[1] I do not mean to say that Camelot began the move toward such collaboration. The SSRC-ACLS Joint Committee on Latin America, for instance, was discussing and working toward collaborative research at least a year before the Camelot episode.

[2] Charles Wagley, ed. (New York: Columbia University Press, 1964).

appreciable numbers of competent yeomen as well as camp followers from market surveyors to sociomilitary analysts. Latin American economists have tried valiantly (if so far probably vainly) to elaborate their own particular economic theories, while anthropologists and archaeologists have gone up and down in local and international esteem and professional competence for almost half a century. New waves are appearing in political science and social psychology, and even the historians are beginning to feel the pinches of their colleagues.[3] As a result, foreign scholars working in Latin America are finding that areas of theoretical, ideological, disciplinary, and institutional vested interest have been staked out where only a few years ago vast plains unmarred by enclosures waited to be grazed.

A third important change is in the institutional structure of Latin American higher education. Through one or another administrative procedure, major universities in many nations have begun to provide for research support and to make organizational room for the empirical social sciences. Semiprivate research institutes (sometimes with an allied training component) have also come into being; the Vargas Foundation (Brazil), the Di Tella Institute (Argentina), CENDES (Center for Economic and Social Development Studies, Venezuela), and El Colegio de México are among the better-known examples. This structural elaboration in higher education, making possible full-time research staffs, has been accompanied by a massive enlargement of student bodies. The combined result is that the recruitment base for scholars has been effectively broadened at the same time that institutional channels have been opened for their partial absorption.[4]

The extent of this institutional growth should not be overstated, of course, for the culture and the procedures of science are not as yet firmly established in Latin America—particularly in the politically sensitive social sciences. Florestan Fernandes, a distinguished Brazilian sociologist, has weighed the matter as follows:

> Before converting scientific and technological knowledge into permanent social and cultural influences, the social scientist must mold the inherited existing social institutions or help new ones to emerge, thereby laying the cultural foundations of science and scientific technology, and

---

[3]For a qualitative evaluation, see Manuel Diégues Júnior and Bryce Wood, eds., *Social Science Research in Latin America* (New York: Columbia University Press, 1967).

[4]There are no reliable statistical surveys at hand to indicate the full magnitude of these changes in size and structure. It would be extremely useful to have for every country such studies as OECD, *Education, Human Resources and Development in Argentina* (Paris, 1961). Incidentally, this survey shows that in Argentina university enrollments jumped from 84,000 to 175,000 between 1950 and 1960 (p. 38).

of education based on both. In some Latin American countries which are more advanced in the urban and industrial revolution, many of the principal conditions already exist for the normal operation and progressive specialization of the social institutions on which the growth of the scientific system depends. Nevertheless, even in these cases there are certain defects which impede the development of scientific research and of its educational and technological applications.[5]

Fourth, a similar growth—but inside a different institutional setup—is clearly discernible in the United States. The crisis of the private university and the correlative flowering of state institutions form part of a more generalized student, professorial, and research support explosion that reflects the expansion of knowledge as well as of population. All else being equal, we may expect continuing pressure for the use of Latin America as a research theater.

And, last in this list of major academic changes, we may mention the slow and hesitant growth of Latin American interests in Europe and Asia.[6] As a generalization, it is probably correct to say that European and Asian involvements will grow as a function of their social science sophistication; that is, the more developed the social sciences, the greater the tendency to reach for comparative approaches in order to reduce the ethnocentricity of theories derived from the data bases closest to the hands of the social scientists.

These changes, clustered within the post–World War II period, would in themselves have been sufficient to cause stress. However, added to complex political and other large-scale social transformations in the international community as well as within Latin America, their effects have been profound, in many senses far surpassing the relatively mechanistic questions of collaboration and disciplinary organization we are considering here. We cannot analyze the internal changes in Latin America either globally or in such a way as to take into account the many families of occurrences to be observed there. But I hope I will be forgiven some generalizations concerning the political stance of many parts of Latin America and the United States, as well as the role of scholars within that context.

Scholars involved in Latin American affairs have been buffeted by many emotional, intellectual, and ideological currents in the past

[5]Florestan Fernandes, "The Social Sciences in Latin America," in Manuel Diégues Júnior and Bryce Wood, eds., *op. cit.,* p. 22.

[6]Many bits and pieces of information about these developments are available in both published and manuscript form. The volumes of the Royal Institute of International Affairs, the reports of the Bellagio conference on European interest in Latin America, Dutch and German periodic inventories, the listings of research given in *Aportes,* and many others are all relevant.

twenty years. Between 1945 and 1950, as some Latin American countries began expanding their industrial bases within a political context that was carried on the democratic words of the war, there was general optimism that libertarian processes could be used for the purposes of modernization. As the Cold War settled over the world and conservative military-spawned regimes proliferated in Latin America (roughly to be dated from 1948 in Venezuela and Peru, and spreading to many other countries), some pessimism set in, broken by seemingly democratic reactions in Argentina, Brazil, Venezuela, and a few other places by the end of the decade. In the academic world, partial internationalization of Chilean social science, the rapid emergence of sociology in Argentina, and many similar happenings in other countries gave promise of variety and the strength of a dedication to some measure of freedom. The short-lived Kennedy period seemed to fortify these possibilities, at least for North Americans—skeptical as many were. But in the last three or four years a leaden pall seems to have descended on many Latin American intellectuals and their countries. Military dictatorships in Argentina and Brazil, the low and generally unexciting output of the Mexicans (surprisingly backward in the social sciences, in any event), the technocratic and applied political attitudes of the Chileans, and many similar situations add up to an uninspiring picture. In addition, no indigenously Latin American social theories have gained acceptance through the standard procedures of scientific validation. Thus, social science there has remained mimetic; it has not found its own confident self-identification.

I may be accused of allowing my own perceptions to tint, if not taint, the actualities of the matter. Perhaps even though I am attempting to avoid polemics, with this warning in mind I will permit myself to continue these generalizations by attempting to summarize some Latin American views. These attitudes are largely representative of leftist persuasions, for Latin American social science is not yet sufficiently developed to permit many persons of rightist political stance to become empirical social scientists. The most important drift toward conservatism can be noted in the appearance of "apolitical technicians"—in itself an ideological attitude, one that has been popular in Chile and Mexico for at least fifteen years and is now gaining ground rapidly among the affective refugees of Argentine and Brazilian social science who have remained corporeally at home. But in the main Latin American social scientists are in ideological camps that range from center to far left. These groups are in varying states of disarray. They do not know how to reconcile matters of freedom, civil liberties, and rational political organization

with the nature of their oppositions and the processes and procedures of modernization. Their ideologies have been confounded by
the subtleties and the crudities of events, and their institutional
homes have been invaded physically as well as spiritually.

This state of confusion has been compounded by the United
States. Indifference and intervention, pedantic words and development assistance, fellowships to scholars and support to governments
that "intervene" in universities, verbal attacks on dictatorship and
defense of the principles of noninterventionism as well as of the
adventures in the Dominican Republic and Viet Nam—all these
make for a bit of ideological racket. The most highly developed
nation in the hemisphere has become prone to abandon the politics
of diplomacy for the directness of military power. The most highly
developed countries of Latin America are under military or other
forms of authoritarian rule. *Freedom* and *liberty* and *democracy* are
words now used most easily by authoritarians in Latin America and,
when heard from the lips of Americans, are suspect as either the
ingenuous terms of children or the lies of tyrants' assistants.

It is now time for me to condition these statements. I am well
aware that countries like Chile, Uruguay, and Costa Rica exist. I
know, too, that no Latin American dictatorship is totalitarian in its
sweep. In all countries there are institutional nooks and crannies in
which intellectuals may hide and ways in which free academic inquiry, even on sensitive subjects, can be pursued. In addition, many
academic disciplines (law, medicine, agricultural sciences, and so
forth) are not practiced by individuals with strong ideological commitment or else are sufficiently specialized and thus encapsulated
that they react only weakly to strong political change. Even in Argentina, local social scientists can investigate a wide array of subjects
without inviting official sanction; discreet self-censorship permits
survival, even if its price is to file off the cutting edge of imaginative
innovation. In short, there are variables in the situation: the countries concerned, the nature of the academic community, and the
particular disciplines that have become advanced, the kind of government, the immediacy and nature of European and United States
ties, the scholarly associations and their relations with international
entities, and those many other factors describing the relationship
between the scholar and the public.

It is against this erratic background that the significance of the
moves toward both scholarly collaboration and interdisciplinary research need to be seen. The former can degenerate into a political
need rationalized as a scholarly good. The latter is an intellectual
and cultural necessity to satisfy the demands of scholarly compe-

tence and social relevance. Unless we carefully and cautiously define what it is we are about, we run a grave risk of squashing the necessary separateness of academic inquiry into the mélange of immediate social need. A rush to put academic freedom and autonomy to the unquestioned service of society as represented by the state is, of course, precisely the way to void the meaning of academic autonomy and freedom, and thus of academic usefulness. If modernization is a process of growing differentiation within growing patterns of social synthesis, then we had best be careful to keep our distinguishing marks and our social responsibilities in balance. Such distinctions are not simple to make when comparing societies of very different levels of institutional development.

The advantages in collaborative research between North and Latin Americans are easy to list: (1) the Latin American may be a distinguished scholar who can test complex theories with sophisticated techniques; (2) the Latin American can supply an institutional base and thus give identity and local sanction to the undertaking; (3) the Latin American can be counted on to supply linguistic help and point out areas needing research; (4) the Latin American component can help assure access to the publics and places to be researched; (5) the Latin American can reduce threats to research continuity; (6) the Latin American can recruit research assistants where needed; (7) the Latin American can point out areas of danger and of security; meanwhile, (8) the North American can supply his usually greater technical and perhaps theoretical competence; (9) the North American can more easily attract research funds; (10) the North American may bring international prestige to the undertaking; (11) the North American may be able to assist in the United States training of Latin American students before, during, and after the research period; (12) the North American may extend a measure of political protection to his Latin American colleagues by the symbolism attached to his mere presence in a collaborative arrangement; and (13) the North American may more easily assure publication of the research results.[7] This list does not exhaust the possible benefits. Visiting scholars may offer teaching services, there are gains potentially inherent in merely the facts of interchange, and so on.

Given all these positive elements, why should I counsel caution? Because, simply, the mutual advantages tend to hide substantive differences of viewpoint and interest that may well damage the

[7]This full list of mutual advantages applies most strongly to quantitative studies employing survey research techniques. But elements of this list pertain also to such inherently individual tasks as historical research, anthropological community studies, and so forth.

scholarly task in itself. Parsons, in commenting on the political involvements of American scholars, recently pleaded for "a primary commitment to the intellectual task" as the basic dedication no social scientist can afford to forget either in his academic or his citizenship role. The place of this dedication is not generally the same for North and Latin American scholars. Let us return to the Camelot episode for exemplification. The Chilean academicians who attacked the undertaking were not complaining because Americans work for a government. After all, they themseves recognize no firm distinction between their roles as professors and as aspiring or practicing members of their own state apparatus. Indeed, most of them would argue that it is the absolute duty of the academic to make his services available for the public good, and that the university must be activist in the pursuit of social ends. Their complaint against the Americans is that they were working for the *American* government, and it will not do to excuse their view because the Department of the Army was the particular agency concerned. The criticism is directed as well against the State Department or any other part of the United States government involved in sponsoring overseas research.

The reaction in the United States was quite different. Here we raised questions concerning the proper boundary between academic inquiry and government sponsorship.[8] Our reactions concerned university autonomy in its fullest sense; the Latin Americans, despite their historical interest in autonomy, raised only a procedural and political question. The differences boil down to two essential matters: how to create a *relevant* social science and how to be relevant and retain the integrity of the total academic enterprise. It is my opinion that the Latin Americans are not handling this issue well, and that any ideologically inspired surrender by North Americans to ingenuous Latin American decisions in this area will lead to a continuing second-rate social science. There are, however, some Latin American scholars who have thought clearly, incisively, and with intellectual elegance on these matters. Notable among them is Florestan Fernandes, whom I have already cited in this connection. He writes:

[8]See especially the Fascell and Harris subcommittee reports of both House and Senate, the recent collections edited by Irving Louis Horowitz, *The Life and Death of Project Camelot: Studies in the Relationship between Social Science and Practical Politics* (Cambridge, Mass.: MIT Press, 1967), and Gideon Sjoberg, *Ethics, Politics, and Social Research* (Cambridge, Mass.: Schenkman Publishing Co., 1967), and the special issue of the *American Behavioral Scientist,* Volume 10, Number 10 (1967) devoted to the proper role of the academic. The matter has been treated consistently in *The American Sociologist,* although no special issue has been given over to the subject.

Latin American social scientists are obviously striving to intensify scientific research. But so far as the results of such work are concerned, the direct results, which contribute to theoretical advances in the social sciences, and the indirect ones, which further the progress of the relevant educational and research institutions, it is the indirect results which attract the greatest interest and attention. This means that owing to the conditions under which they work, these scientists must give exceptional weight to results transforming scientific research into a means for achieving other ends. Although these ends are essential for the expansion of science and scientific technology in Latin America, their importance entails choices that may seem strange to the social scientists of the more advanced centers which are mainly or exclusively concerned with theoretical advances.

This fact must be faced with complete frankness if the different positions and evaluations of the foreign Americanist, and of the Latin American social scientists are to be understood. In one way or another, the latter is a conscious agent of social change. His approach to social objectives and activities is that of an innovator in the field of cultural dynamics. . . .[9]

Note however, that Professor Fernandes is careful to state that the applied aspects of the Latin American social scientist's work should be directed toward the development of the institutions in which his scholarly tasks are to be carried out, and that it is basically in this way that he becomes a responsible agent of social change.

I should like to align myself firmly with those persons who plead for a relevant social science. But let me indicate what I mean by that term—and perhaps my alliance with that group will be rejected by some of its members. It is my view that the integrity of academia *and* its relevance are not separable. The only authority academic commentary on sociopolitical matters can have comes precisely from the methods of study, of expression, and of replication peculiar to the several social disciplines. I trust the personal political views of my colleagues to be objective and "intelligent" no more than I unquestioningly trust the views of my local garbage collector or congressional representative. I do not believe that intellectuals should rush into government service, or that their presence therein guarantees good government. At least one reason is that all too many intellectuals convince themselves that they are possessed of "truth" instead of validity. Indeed, academicians in general and intellectuals in particular are peculiarly equipped to persuade themselves of their own merits. Certainly an inducement to self-delusion comes from the very protections the tenure system builds into academic life. What is

[9]Fernandes, "The Social Sciences in Latin America," p. 21.

supposed to guarantee the freedom of institutional inquiry through the guarantee of individual freedom can be turned to opposite ends by a sanctionless presence outside the academic world in the political one. Those colleagues who assist governmental policy-making as paid consultants or civil servants, and then defend those policies as members of faculties, are cases in point of a breakdown in institutional differentiation that can only make social science irrelevant under the guise of relevance. To have a policy investment in the consequences of political action is to make it difficult if not impossible to maintain research and teaching objectivity with respect to those policies. A relevant social science then necessarily must be an *academic* one based on *a primary commitment to the intellectual part of the task,* to repeat the phrase.

Latin American social scientists will find it very difficult to be as purist as the above prescription demands. Again to repeat, development implies that growing differentiation is partial: class situations, institutional maturation, and social expectations all demand multifunctionality from the more as well as the less educated. Latin American university professors work at many jobs by no mere accident. Societal demands and their own educations permit them to discharge many different functions. Thus, it is natural that they should take advantage of those seams in their societies that bind elevated prestige with academic attainment, political activism, high incomes, and the exercise of the many occupational positions fitting this talent-prestige-income-power construction. Latin American universities are not alone in the dilemma resulting from the universally jointed professor. Italian students are rioting because, among other complaints, they do not wish academic chairholders to appear once a year and spend the rest of their time in the national legislature, meanwhile drawing their full university pay, small as it may be.

Cross-national collaborative research must of necessity point up differing academic roles, particularly in the critical matter of the choice of research subject. For example, Latin Americans commonly complain that many North Americans' research matters are of no earthly use to them. And many North Americans complain that Latin Americans investigate matters either so abstruse or so applied that comparison and testing are severely hampered. The clash revolves around meaningfulness defined as applicability. And that problem raises the other one—applicability to what, and for what?

Research relevance, social commitment, and professionalism are, to my mind, inevitably linked. I am not of the school that thinks that to be "value-free" is to be socially irresponsible in the sense of abandonment of political outlook, activity, and of the politically (or more broadly socially) motivated choice of research subjects. But I would order the matter as follows: all social science inquiry is irrelevant if incompetently accomplished; all social commitment denying the particularity of the scientific enterprise in itself invites the incompetence that guarantees essential irrelevance; all politically motivated research that damages the autonomy and freedom of the professional task is also destructive of competence, and thus assures irrelevance. In short, the irreducible component in the entire game is the maintenance of the scientific commitment *per se.*

It is probably historically valid to say that in the past North American scholars sustained a narrow science-for-its-own-sake approach, while the Latin Americans by and large plumped for a science at the entire service of the public interest as variously defined. This relatively clear division has now become blurred. A growing school of American social scientists is trying to reconcile professionalism with social commitment, while a similarly increasing school of Latin Americans is going "technocratic," or "rising above politics," as many social scientists, military officers, and others are increasingly putting it in Latin America. The case for the changing North American view has recently been put as follows:

> In effect, thus . . . [I] recommend . . . two things: (1) that in some respects it is not only *logically* necessary to dispense with the Lundberg-ian idea of differentiating between citizen role and scientific role—it is *wise* to dispense with the idea; and (2) that we view the status "sociologist" as calling for a dual role involving interdependent (a) research-teaching activity, and (b) selected social action activity. Such a view of the sociologist role is simply an assertion that particular types of social action, in addition to other kinds of action, are as proper for the sociologist as is laboratory building for the chemist; neither activity is "pure science," but each is essential to its respective profession.[10]

The author of this quotation adds that public activities supporting the continuing ability of the social sciences to function *as a scientific activity* should be a legitimate area of professional concern. I concur. But what the article does not spell out, and what I consider crucial, is that over any reasonable stretch of time the political mechanisms permitting social science to operate must be libertarian in content. The tug and pull between North and Latin Americans over these points has been subterranean but intense; there is little reason to feel that the state of disarray in both groups will not contribute to continuing problems. The worry involved is also clear:

[10]Thomas Ford Hoult, ". . . Who Shall Prepare Himself to the Battle," *The American Sociologist,* Volume 3, Number 1 (1968): 3.

it is that research collaboration stemming from political necessity may well lead to permitting Latin Americans ultimately to judge the subjects to be researched. I find no *prima facie* evidence to indicate that those choices will necessarily fulfill the first condition—the competence condition—for social science activity. I also find no evidence to indicate that Latin Americans are particularly competent to define relevance in the more narrow sense, that they are peculiarly equipped to decide the subjects that public interest imbues with a high priority. For example, more Latin American governments are (and have been) rightist than leftist. Where are the studies of rightism? Again, many Latin American economists reject "monetarist" economic theory. Where is the "structuralist" theory that can compete with "monetarism" on an academic basis? Where are the political studies needed as an essential ingredient of structuralist economic thought? To take a third example, more than a few Latin Americans contend that in the last analysis the United States controls their destinies. Where is the academic study of the Dominican episode done by Latin Americans? Of the Guatemalan occurrences of 1954? Of the effects of the Vietnam War on Latin America? Indeed, to be even cruder, where are the courses taught in Latin American universities on "the United States as area study"?

Significance and relevance used to be handled more simply in the recent past. Then we told ourselves that economics was the key: industrialize, and then each country could adapt those particular political institutions and cultural idiosyncrasies it wished within a minimum level of animal comfort for all. So we deluded ourselves that we could intervene without interventionism, so to speak. Now that we know that the very quality of life is somehow involved with economic and all other kinds of development, we are left with no way of disentangling development-directed research from judgments concerning the meanings of given institutional patterns and cultural dispositions for social change. If research is to be relevant to development and modernization, then it cannot fail to take into some account such intimate matters as life-style and general ways of being. No matter how restricted the research, if it is to have applicability to problems of change, it will have implications in extraordinarily delicate areas. The Latin Americans themselves may be avoiding the themes mentioned above precisely because they are so delicate—for them as well as for ourselves. How, then, are they to be treated? That question is unavoidable if it is relevance we seek. By this time, I hope it will be clear that I do not think the instrumental devices of research collaboration or interdisciplinary approaches will in themselves provide such relevance.

Thus far I have been dialectically counterposing political commitment against professional integrity. Perhaps the search for a "useful social science" (and now let us join the terms consciously) lies in enlarging the areas of meaningful research choices by viewing political commitment and professional integrity not as opposites, but as mutually reinforcing partners. The more simple professional ends are sought, the less meaningful is the body social to the academic life, and therefore the narrower is the range of possible academic endeavor. The more simple political ends are sought, the less social science is able to provide competent analysis. Social utility and social science utility ultimately demand the same conditions: relativistic, merit-based social systems to support relativistic, merit-based rational undertakings. What is useful to the methods of the latter supports the existence of the former. A truly competent social science investigating truly significant social subjects can in the long run be useful only to rational societies. Social science is thus by this definition irrelevant in the long run to irrational social orders. I will not enter into the argument as to whether an authoritarian society can be a rational one. Empirically, Latin American authoritarianisms have been able to consume "rational" approaches (pragmatically self-testing ones) only in the short run of their first months in office. In intermediate runs they have all fallen over their internal mythmaking. It is small wonder that empirical sociology is invariably the first victim of authoritarian government in Latin America, and that the "technocratic" social "scientists" who lend their services to such regimes quickly end up in jail or consular posts in Belgium. Social science cannot be relevant to antiscientific governments of the stripe we have seen in Latin America. When we know enough of the social process so that social scientists can be relevant for the establishment of static totalitarianism and thereafter pass into oblivion, we will have arrived at the black utopias of Huxley and Orwell. That kind of relevance is suicide.

In sum, then, my doubts about the efficacy of multidisciplinary and international collaboration stem from my belief that many of the proponents of those approaches are suffering from misplaced hope. They confuse the instrument with the end. No matter the nationalities of the actors or their disciplinary identifications, in the beginning there must be competence and the understanding that professional and social integrity are goals to be simultaneously pursued, for to separate them is to kill both.

1970

Politics and Studying Societies:
The United States
and Latin America

To an Englishman, Camelot is the site of a medieval romance. To an American, the name suggests the Thousand Days of Kennedy's political dash and derring-do. To a Latin American, it means "sociological espionage." In 1964, the Special Operations Research Office of American University was granted an initial $6,000,000 for a three- to four-year period for the study of the conditions leading to internal strife in Latin America. The money was made available by the Department of the Army, then as now charged with counterinsurgency programs, and was to be spent in research that would be prescriptive as well as diagnostic—that is, research which would point out cures for, as well as causes of, civil unrest. The idea was spawned in the early Kennedy years, when "internal warfare" was a popular term because it was thought that the Cold War was likely to turn into a series of bush engagements instead of eventuating in a single nuclear spectacular. The staff of S.O.R.O., comprised in large part of scholars of liberal political persuasion, took its task as being to discover how to work fundamental social change in Latin America, and eventually elsewhere in the developing world, without courting the kind of civil violence that might tempt the protagonists in big power disputes to try to settle their differences in contained battles on other people's lands and bodies. Small wonder that, in what may now seem an age of innocently hopeful reform, they should have titled their undertaking "Project Camelot."

The evocation of the Arthurian legend is painfully fitting to the

131

case. Good knights, doing their good deeds, symbolize the best behavior of an enlightened elite. By inference, then, their presence signals the existence of depressed and dispossessed people. The dismantling of Project Camelot was the work of some of those designed to be its beneficiaries, Latin American scholars who protested that their fate should not be in the hands of benevolent Launcelots, but rather in their own. When in early 1965 the unclassified project became known to a group of Chilean social scientists, they set up a hue and cry whose echoes continue unabated. Through an intricately intertwined series of events, the project was canceled, hearings were held in both the United States Senate and the House of Representatives as well as in the Chilean Congress, many articles and eventually even books appeared on the subject,[1] and the word *Camelot* passed into standard cultured Spanish as signifying any scholarly attempt to study Latin society that might conceivably be turned to the political advantage of a foreign power.

The collapse of Project Camelot revealed deep schisms between the Department of Defense and the State Department concerning the propriety and usefulness of overseas social research, with the latter department generally reticent about the validity of such undertakings and certainly opposed to Department of Defense sponsorship. Early on, a governmental committee was established to assess the possible damage to foreign relations that might ensue from federally subsidized research; the committee still functions. In the academic community, the incident led directly to the organization of the Latin American Studies Association, and several of the disciplinary professional associations passed resolutions attempting to define the ethics of the academic-governmental relationship. A growing accent on collaborative United States–Latin research undertakings is another direct consequence of the possible loss of Latin America as a social science research site, a danger highlighted by the Camelot debacle, but actually antedating it.

The strength, durability, and extent of this crisis in academic international relations obviously far transcend the particular case in point and involve much more than the fears of Latin Americans and the guilt of North Americans. This author's murky crystal ball revealed to him in 1965, "It is very probable that, after the passage of a little time, American social scientists will once again be able to work with relative ease in Latin America."[2] The sentence could be made

[1] See the works cited in footnote 8 of the previous essay.
[2] K. H. Silvert, *The Conflict Society*, rev. ed. (New York: Harper Colophon Books, 1968), p. 159.

accurate by substituting "with care and caution and on selected subjects" for "with relative ease." The statement's tendency toward correctness stems from the undeniable cultural strength of the United States in this hemisphere, the growing rigor and innovativeness of American social science, and the continued recognition by some Latin Americans of a need for reliable social science tools in national development. The incorrect emphasis of the prediction came from a failure to recognize that Vietnam and the urban racial crisis would join to become crowning facts of American public life, involving the university as the principal site of confrontation. In such a situation, Camelot assumes the role of passing incident, with the general question of academic-governmental relations up for debate. Launcelot must now share the stage with Louis XIV, Machiavelli, Marx, Bakunin, Hitler, Coolidge, and Cohn-Bendit. Still, the saga of the good knight's passage through difficult times may serve to illuminate the problems of retaining virtue unsullied in a time of questioned standards and faltering banners.

The prime problem raised by Camelot for all parties concerned is that of the relevance of the scholar and the university to political affairs. In the United States the issue demands some definition of academic freedom for professors and students when government-sponsored research is undertaken, of academic freedom and the simple choice as well as the priority of choice of research, and of the proper relationship between a researcher and the subject of his research. In Latin America, the form of the problem is entirely political: the relationship of social science knowledge to indigenous political leaders and also to the ability of the United States to manipulate the domestic polities of those republics. In practice, in the immediate aftermath of the Camelot collapse American scholars worried about academic freedom, while Latins worried about sovereignty. We asked a question about universities; they asked a question about governments. A strange contradiction then developed: Americans became concerned about whether or how to make their social science findings available to government and still defend university autonomy and academic freedom; the Latin Americans continued to care not a whit about the propriety of academic-political relations, and merely argued that.working for the United States government was a sin. They blithely continued mingling their own academic, ideological, and governmental roles inside their own countries.

Whatever slurs may be cast on the ability of social science theory to explain, in this case standard developmental concepts permit us to mold our understanding of these differing constructions of the Camelot problem into significant generalizations. Development is universally held to involve increasing specialization and what is clumsily called institutional differentiation—that is, the carrying out of sets of behavior patterns with emphasis on the specific functions being performed, and with a minimum of cross-institutional interference from the hierarchies established to carry out other sets of behavior patterns. For example, the _developmental_ consequence of separating religious from political institutions is not only to create specialization in order to permit more efficient functioning, but also to prevent secular criteria from staining sacred ones, and vice versa. This setting off of clusters of activity is a necessary precondition for permitting merit criteria to operate effectively in the selection of leadership. The American reaction to Camelot was a sign of modernization as defined in this sense; that is, the definitions of the "proper" functions of the polity and the academy were at issue against the background of a conviction that each has a sphere legitimate to itself. The Latin reaction was a global rejection of the United States, advanced without putting into question the desirability of the discharge of multiple functions by Latin American scholars. The Latin American view realistically reflects the elitist recruitment patterns of their institutions of higher education, the scarcity of trained persons, and the consequent necessity for scholars to occupy many different posts. The part-time status of most Latin American professors is a reflection not only of low university budgets; at least as importantly, it is also a symptom of severely limited trained manpower. The long-standing struggle of Latin American universities to achieve autonomy from their governments is not balanced by a professorial respect for the difference between academic and ideological-political activity.

With the passage of time and the march of events since 1965, positions vis-à-vis foreign research and assistance have hardened into at least four clearly discernible camps in Latin America. The far leftists, whose attacks are loud and sometimes effective because they influence less radicalized nationalists, take the stand that any increase in organized social science knowledge is undesirable because Americans know better what to do with such knowledge than Latin Americans do, so that the United States' already great power over its "colonies" is heightened. A definition of "sociological espionage" from this quarter was recently given as follows:

> Sociological espionage is a vast mixed enterprise in which agencies of the American government, jointly with the international academic community, give structure to the means that assure the empire a systematic flow of reliable and detailed information on what the people of a

region think, say, feel, need, have, believe, fear, respect, love, and hope for. . . . Sociological espionage is an enterprise employing different arms from the revolver and the mask; it tries to put the most refined techniques of social science fieldwork at the service of imperialism. It may or may not be secret; in reality, only a small number of the projects of this type are surrounded by the mystery and the security measures typical of conventional espionage. . . .[3]

This analysis also argues that publication of the results of social science studies does not in itself answer to the canons of academic freedom and social responsibility: "Research whose results are accessible and understandable only to the privileged is not objective; it may be technically correct, but it is socially partial. It is not neutral; on the contrary, it is only another piece in the apparatus of exploitation." One may legitimately draw the castrating conclusion that social science research is objective and neutral only under circumstances in which all persons concerned are equally able to consume it. Still, there can be no disputing the claim that good research can increase the power of rulers. If entirely malignant motives are ascribed to the United States, then it must necessarily follow that all social scientists who publish their findings are witting or unwitting tools of imperialism and repression.

A second major source of opposition to empirical social science stems from the corporativist right, the falangist groups that are increasingly evident in some of the most important Latin American states. Their hostility has manifold roots, particularly stemming from distrust of local social scientists, who are, in the vast majority, of center to left political persuasion, and from dislike of the idea that human response can be quantified. Their notion of individualism denies that attitudes can or should be abstracted from the whole of personal experience. They react to questionnaires like the primitive who thinks that to take his picture is to steal part of his soul. The application of the antiscientism of such political groups was experienced in the first weeks of the administration of General Onganía in Argentina. One of the inaugural acts of that government was to set the police on the professors of the Faculty of Exact Sciences of the University of Buenos Aires, and soon after that to close the Institute of Sociology. Virtually all empirical social science work in Argentina now is undertaken by private entities. Similar pressures are being sternly applied in Brazil today, while in Mexico the social sciences have always lagged far behind international standards of excellence.

[3]"La polémica sobre el 'Proyecto Marginalidad,' " *Marcha* (Uruguay), February 28, 1969, p. 19.

Mexico's single-party system, with the intellectually suffocating rhetoric of its ideology, has not provided a hospitable ambience for necessarily controversial social thought.

Most social scientists in Latin America are midway between these two extremes of left and right anti-Americanism. The more humanistic and ideologically sensitive of them worry deeply about American support and the employment of modern techniques and theories, but persist in their belief that they can accept collaboration and even funds from abroad without losing their freedom of inquiry. They defend themselves against charges of guilt-by-association by pointing out that a kind of Gresham's law of contamination is presumed by their attackers to their immediate left. Staining comes only from the bad side, and never from the good. Persons holding these views feel themselves under attack from right and left in their own countries and are often indirectly protected by foreign contacts in Europe as well as the United States. Among them are the best of Latin America's social scientists, and from their ranks come the directors and staff members of the most productive social science training and research centers. Although few of them approve of United States foreign policy, they see this country as complex and to one degree or another capable of positive democratic influence as well as negative authoritarian influence. They are the persons whose integrity and beings must be most highly respected by American public and private agencies if they are to be of service to their disciplines and to the future demands of their own countries. They are to be found in such private institutions as the Vargas Foundation in Brazil, the Colegio de México, and the Di Tella Institute in Argentina. But they are also in the State University of São Paulo, the University of Chile, the National University in Bogotá, and in such religiously affiliated institutions as the Catholic University of Chile.

A final set of attitudes belongs to the *técnicos,* Latin America's crop of technocratic social scientists willing to work in any political environment. Most of them are economists. That discipline, strongly devoted to model-building, metrical techniques, and the belief that economic theory is universally applicable, is a propitious field for the apolitical. In addition, the Latin political situation in the new military dictatorships permits the institutional acceptance of economists. The reason is that economic endeavors in Brazil and Argentina, to take the two most important cases of the new military governments, are permitted to be managed by the Liberal elite—by persons espousing a classical free-enterprise approach to development. Police, education, religion, and the management of provincial governments are kept in the hands of Conservatives or neo-falangists. It is this truce among the bickering members of the upper groups that has given some stability to those two countries, permitting a measure of economic healing to take place in conjunction with a "moratorium" on democratic political activity. Needless to say, the attitude of the *técnico* is that he will take assistance from wherever it may appear, and that his worries about sovereignty will reflect the attitudes of his political supervisors.

Analogous American attitudes are easily identified. At one end are those who believe in a total separation of the American university from the present political system, as evidenced in movements to ban ROTC from the campus and to deny all federally sponsored research. At the other end are the persons who are persuaded that we are in an ultimate national crisis of survival, and that all our efforts must be bent toward unquestioning and unswerving support of the government and all its works. Neither set of views answers to the attitudes or problems of most persons engaged in Latin American studies, nor will analyzing them serve to tell us what some of the major post-Camelot currents have been.

The tribulations of Latin American studies in the United States during the past thirty years are probably as much a problem in the sociology (and stylishness) of knowledge as in the allocation of funds and ascription of importance. Long looked upon as the least prestigious of the area concerns, Latin American studies have still not advanced to the point where practitioners are generally seen as being as academically advanced as their colleagues in African, Asian, and European affairs. When Camelot broke, only one of the eleven most prestigious political science departments had a tenured professor of Latin American politics.[4] As of this writing, the number has risen to two, and in the coming academic year Columbia and Yale should join Stanford and Wisconsin in having tenured staff in this field. The picture is even spottier in sociology and economics, although much better in anthropology and history, and of course positively strong in language and literature. In only three of these prestige universities do Latin American area centers have a continuous history going back over fifteen years, and even in them advance has been erratic and in several instances the centers have fallen almost completely apart. On the other hand, Latin American area centers have a long, stable, and productive history in such universities as Texas, North Carolina, Tulane, Vanderbilt, and Florida. The

---

[4]The list includes Harvard, Yale, California (Berkeley), Chicago, Princeton, Columbia, Michigan, Wisconsin, Stanford, California (UCLA), and Cornell. Albert Somit and Joseph Tanenhaus, "Trends in American Political Science: Some Analytical Notes," *The American Political Science Review,* Volume 57, Number 4 (1963), p. 936.

implication is obvious: second-best fields can best be left for second-best universities. Foundation and government funds tended in the post–World War II era to flow to Soviet, Chinese, and Middle East studies, with only the Carnegie Corporation paying limited attention to Latin American studies between 1947 and 1955. Matters then languished until the emergence of the Castro government in Cuba, when the Ford Foundation came into the field and government assistance became intensified. It might be noted that the Latin American area was the last regional field to be supported by the Ford Foundation, which entered it in 1959.

Although sustained academic and foundation interest in Latin American affairs has been late to arrive on the scene and was indubitably spurred by the emergence of Latin America as an actor on the scene of global confrontation, that area has for long been a sphere of diplomatic and military interest on the part of the United States. The partisans of Manifest Destiny included Cuba in their plans from the early days of this republic. The "special interest" of the United States dates from the verbal expressions of the Monroe Doctrine. It continued through the Mexican War and the Maximilian episode in Mexico. The Spanish-American War was followed by the declarations of Woodrow Wilson concerning the particular duty of the United States to help maintain stability, financial probity, and, when possible, democratic governments in the Caribbean. A sturdy band of historians wrote accompaniments to these occurrences,[5] but the lack of interest on the part of other social scientists is notorious. Perhaps the prestige of such studies was low because the practitioners were poor, or perhaps the practitioners were poor because the prestige was low. Or perhaps the practitioners were poor because the state of social science theory and method was so ethnocentric that it was difficult to study a Western social case that has been extremely erratic in its peaks of development and troughs of underdevelopment. Whatever the reasons for the lag, and however one may judge the quality of the work of Latin Americanists as compared to those of other area specialists, Camelot struck when the field was beginning to move rapidly ahead toward consistent fieldwork of sophistication and theoretical imaginativeness.

This flowering on the North American side was meeting an equally flourishing situation in Latin America, where green but sturdy social science plants were growing in many important academic centers. Indeed, this very growth has further tangled the

[5]See Howard F. Cline, ed., *Latin American History: Essays on Its Study and Teaching, 1895–1965*, published for the Conference on Latin American History (Austin: University of Texas Press, 1967).

matter of United States–Latin academic relations. Some Latin American researchers have been forced to abandon or change their own work because of the reluctance of some social sectors (particularly intellectuals and upper classes) to respond to interviews. As Latin American scholars begin to suffer from some of the same debilities that confront North Americans, they also have begun to develop a trade-union mentality in protection of their guild interests. In some cases they would like to impose their own estimation of "proper" research and "proper" theory, and of course they resent being treated as second-class citizens in collaborative relations. Almost as soon as he returns home, status dissonance confronts the young scholar trained abroad. Bearing his fresh doctorate, he is a scarce and valued commodity in his own country, an apt candidate for what has felicitously been called "premature promotion." Still, on the international scene he is at an assistant-professor level, unequipped with the books, articles, and general experience that would permit him to compete on prestige terms with the more distinguished visiting scholar from abroad. These sources of insecurity are, of course, reinforced by the often confused domestic conditions in Latin America that we have already mentioned.

In the meantime, the flow of North American students and scholars and other visitors to Latin America has continued unabated, a drain on resources, patience, and time. The Latin American Studies Association has so far been unable to persuade the American scholarly community to reduce the flow and to increase the ability of North Americans to benefit from their Latin American experience while leaving something for their hosts other than a sense of annoyance. The disturbance is caused largely by coveys of students from small colleges and universities, many of them sectarian, and by graduate students sent unprepared by departments whose professors know little about the Latin American scene or who has been doing what where. While the Latin American Studies Association is attempting to put some order into the North American side of matters, the Latins have organized the Latin American Social Science Council (CLACSO), to promote intra–Latin American coordination of universities and centers and of their endeavors in applied fields (urban planning, for example) as well as the standard disciplines.

We are clearly in a difficult state of transition in hemispheric academic relations, as well as in domestic academic-political relations. The Camelot episode underscores the mutual interdependence of the two crises, for neither is susceptible to independent solution in any country of the two Americas. United States foundations, as the major external source of funds for social science research and training in Latin America, must accept a measure of responsibility for the degree of advance in Latin America that has permitted these crises of development to occur. They must exercise a restraint informed by the difficulties of the situation and the necessity to respect the autonomy and intellectual vigor and independence of the persons whom we assist. Such a policy must seek the positive support and participation of serious Latin scholars, lest the foundations find themselves playing the role of Launcelot—or of his steed.

Whatever our sensitivity, however, neither the foundations nor the American community of scholars will escape charges of being mercenaries in the employ of evil. This writer, in his role of scholar, long ago made a personal peace with the problem: this resolution is that we must maximize our opportunities to accomplish significant, relevant, and replicatable work in a world that has not trapped us in a totalitarian monolith. The fact is that social science findings may as well be used for democratic as authoritarian purposes. Maximization of the libertarian trend requires that the researcher truly be "clean" in the sense that he have no vested *scholarly* interest in the particular policies of any state, although he certainly must seek as a citizen to protect the scene that supplies him both his living and his data. In other words, as scholar he must be bound by as few policy investments as possible, and as citizen he must strive for the social climate of freedom that permits science to flourish. A careless slipping back and forth between governmental and academic roles threatens scholarly integrity; a denial of the responsibilities of citizenship endangers the mutually nourishing relationship between science and political liberty. The fitting role of the academic social scientist (as distinct from a government-employed one) with respect to the world of the state can be outlined as follows:

(a) The social scientist can generate and make available new data, useful for governments, the private sector, and anyone else concerned.

(b) He can order these data to permit informed guessing about the nature of the lacunae, a prerequisite for proper simulation techniques, as well as a source of caution in the interpretation of available data.

(c) He can indicate relevant theoretical patterns for the interpretation of the data.

(d) He can—explaining himself carefully—indicate the probabilities of effectiveness of various selected courses of action.

(e) He can indicate which choices are foreclosed by the adoption of given courses of action.

(f) He can indicate which new choices will be made available by the adoption of given courses of action.

When the writer first proposed these limits, which exclude proposing policy, he added the following explanation:

> Needless to say, very few, if any, scholarly documents submitted to any government have satisfied these difficult requirements. The temptation to take the easy path straight from description to prescription is great. But to go past these limits is to assume a vested interest in the ensuing policy itself, thereby rendering the scholar suspect in further objective analysis. Of course, I also continue to insist he is not peculiarly competent to make such value judgments. There is, however, always one overriding value decision the social scientist must make; that is, whether he will lend his talents to any government seeking them. I should suggest that if the government asking assistance is likely to use its powers to restrict that very freedom of inquiry essential to the academic task, then the social scientist is committing professional suicide, not to speak of what else he may be helping to do to existing or possible democratic institutions.[6]

Camelot tells us that long-range academic goals can be attained in common at the international level only if the scientific basis of the undertaking is also held in common. The discrimination of the academic task from the policy one, with the connections clearly delineated so as to allow each its area of legitimacy, provides the only assurance of lasting institutional health. The problem is as endemic for Latin Americans as North Americans, although the paths to resolution will necessarily differ. A measure of the professional and political competence of social scientists will be how they construct their own houses and thereafter keep them in order.

1969

---

[6]The above list and the passage quoted can be found in K. H. Silvert, *op. cit.*, p. 153.

IV. Problems

The Kitsch in Hemispheric
Realpolitik

THE WORLD did not wait while the United States disentangled itself from Vietnam, experienced Watergate, and entered into stagflation. Even the Latin American states—"static," "chronically unstable," "militaristic"—continued on their increasingly rapid evolutionary ways. Now, in the mid-1970s, American policy-makers are facing a different Latin scene from the one that they saw as a gray sameness when the "low profile" was announced in the first months of the Nixon administration in 1969. Cuba is back as an active participant in hemispheric affairs. The Mexican government has broken its diplomatic isolationism of over forty years and is seeking collaborative political relations with its sister republics. The OAS and its dependent agencies have shriveled, the Economic Commission for Latin America has lost its gloss, and the Inter-American Development Bank is pursuing "safe" financial policies, but the foreign policies of individual Latin American countries are becoming more adventurous. Perhaps most important in the international political scene is the attempt to organize for the purposes of diplomatic collective bargaining. Whether they are to be found through some formal heir of the regularized foreign ministers' meetings or another device yet to be created, the search is on for a common set of political interests that can be pursued jointly by Latin American governments themselves. Obviously, it will be difficult to stitch together such disparities as those represented by Chile and Cuba, Peru and Nicaragua, or Argentina and Brazil. But domestic political scenes—which will determine external stances as Latin governments continue to grow more national and thus more powerful—will not

145

remain unchanged. The roots of a common interest lie in desires to control the national fates: to assert sovereignty, contain multinational corporations, promote national development, confront problems associated with population, urbanization, and international market-places brokered by the powerful and bereft of the self-policing of supply and demand. The reasons for combination exist; the vessels and the ideas are as yet embryonic.

Washington will have to stir itself belatedly to recognize the latent and the actual changes in Latin America. But what the United States government can "see" in Latin America and what it can imagine doing in terms of what it thinks it sees are related to its past perceptions and policies and to its generalized view of the world and of how one practices diplomacy within it. I do not wish to enter into debate as to whether or not the United States has recently had a policy toward Latin America or whether even in recent American history we have had a single and consistent policy toward such a diverse area. The reason I evade the debate is not a matter of empirical determination; that task could be accomplished readily enough. Rather, my avoidance of the theme has to do with doubt concerning the definition of the word *policy*. If we mean that within the decade from 1965 to 1975 we have had a firm definition of our own national interest, an application of that interest to a realistic assessment of the situations of the Latin American states, a categorization of those states by type for differential policy application, and then an evolved set of mechanisms for the pursuit of our interests—then we have had no policy. But if by that word we refer to a generalized posture, an attitude, a vaguely followed set of instrumental guides, and organized interests pressing for certain goals—then, indeed, we have had a policy. The "low profile" is as appropriate a title as any for that bundle of traditions, attitudes, and practices.

The substance of the "low profile" has been a mechanistic and eclectic issue-by-issue approach to Latin America that characterizes contemporary American foreign policy in general. Our past stance toward Latin America can be taken as a possible preview of what we can expect elsewhere as the managers of the political systems of the major nations and power blocs seek "normalization." The fact that Latin America poses no threat to vital American interests means, in the minds of the crisis managers, that it is a stable area that needs little attention. In this view of the world, the decency or indecency of domestic political doings have no place in international affairs. Only if internal factors seriously threaten primary or secondary interests will actions "appropriate" to each case be taken. The discipline and predictability of overtly defined policy about anything other than national security are absent; order and sense are to be inferred from watching what the United States does, and not from what its leaders say. This style of diplomacy may be a foretaste of future international politics everywhere as America discards its role of global policeman and faces "realities."

Whatever the administration's motives, in the hemisphere an international politics of "realism" (*Realpolitik*), supported by a vague and situationally undefined willingness to employ military might (*Machtpolitik*), has led to a crass and ineffective foreign policy (*Kitschpolitik*). The proponents of "realist" politics invariably content themselves with the "concrete" and "positive" facts of social life. Natural resources, population size, urbanization, military preparedness, and industrial development are for them "hard" facts, the "real" ones. Ideologies, norms, values, personal crotchets, and ethics are "soft," the claptrap in utopian minds. It follows that an efficacious politics flows from accepting the physical bounds of situations and seeing those bounds as inelastic parameters, or fixed limits, constants for the purpose of working out given policy problems. Values are to be shunned, and an effective politics must be "pragmatic." This construction turns night into day: it is hardly pragmatic in the philosophical sense of that term, and it is fiercely—if pessimistically—ideological. This idea, like many others in our contemporary political armory, will have to be taken off its head and put back on its feet before we can go on to make sense out of our situation.

Cleaning up ideas about international politics is of particular urgency at this time, for the domestic tensions of all industrial and industrializing societies are increasingly flowing over onto the international scene. It used to be held that the United States should break out of isolationalism because all nations are interdependent, a postulate based primarily on benefits expected from trade and economic specialization and secondarily on the cultural fruits of international ties. A contemporary version of the same view emphasizes ecology, "Spaceship Earth," scarce resources, swelling populations, earththreatening weaponry, and other goads to reason and global planning. Not so often mentioned, but certainly more perturbing to national politics and thus more threatening, are the direct effects of the international order on the tug-of-war between privilege and equality that is the stock-in-trade of all domestic politics. In developing countries the craglike class structures stand opposed to the creation of national community, to the continued incorporation of populations into equalitarian participation in the full institutional panoply. The class-nation disharmony of Latin America is most nearly replicated in the United States by its race-nation split. For many years, however, United States foreign policy was intellectually divorced from domestic politics precisely on the grounds that the former involved a *status* (security) on which all could agree and the latter involved a *process* (the distribution of values, ostensibly toward an expanding equality of opportunity) concerning which legitimately expressed disagreement was the motor force of politics. Therefore, foreign policy was justifiably bipartisan, domestic politics necessarily partisan.

The distinction will no longer serve. As the wars of nation-states have long since involved total populations, with growing costs and increasingly intimate effects on the creation, use, and distribution of domestic material and attitudinal values, the international economy is also increasingly able to affect power distributions within developed as well as developing states. The most notorious instruments of these changes are the multinational corporations, one of whose principal immediate effects is to threaten the position of organized labor in the older industrial societies. Politically organized international economic structures, such as common markets, also contribute to a cross-national rationalization that tends to both stabilize and destabilize internal systems of power allocation, the effects depending on the natures and types of political-economic systems of the nations concerned. Even though the major difference between intra- and international politics remains the absence of social and political community in the latter, both arenas now are scenes for playing out the same problem—the grounds on which individual and group differences are maintained or eroded.

Bipartisan foreign policymaking is anachronistic because international affairs now involve as many ethical, ideological, and moral determinations affecting personal and national interest as does domestic politics. Latin American developmentalists have long recognized this commonality and have created theories to explain it. North Americans have been laggard in this respect, however, preferring to keep international affairs separate from domestic politics and to think of relations among nations as involving only formal structures and manifest "leaders," not the people who follow leaders and give them power. This antiseptic and asocial approach has contributed importantly to the creation of empty ideas and linguistic distortions—euphemisms that cover the carnal facts of death, corruption, sacrifice, and heroism. As we now attempt to clear away some verbal problems in understanding international affairs, we will also be dealing with domestic happenings both in Latin and North America. We should not want it otherwise if we have any pretenses toward respect for all persons or toward the application of reason to the solution of problems that are increasingly worldwide and, thus, the problems of everyman as well as of every state.

Let us look at some aspects of hemispheric politics in which domestic and international affairs have become twisted, and illogically related.

Isolationism and Internationalism, Unilateralism and Multilateralism. The United States has been dealing with Latin America on a country-by-country and case-by-case basis. A small genuflection has been made in the direction of Brazilian hegemony, indicating the "realistic" acceptance of that country's potential power and hinting that it may become the surrogate for the United States in policing South America. But Brazil has a limited capacity for such a role, and other Latin American republics are organizing themselves to inhibit the possibility. In the meantime, the United States government is encouragingly reactive to Mexico, broadly hostile and punitive to Cuba, puzzled about and increasingly ineffective in influencing internal Argentine events, defensively protective of the Chilean junta, quietly worried about Venezuela but content with its two major parties, eclectic about the Caribbean islands and too abstracted to pressure them severely, and so on. While the multilateral agencies are withering, we go on thinking by ourselves about Latin America, we alone deciding with whom we shall tango, with whom we shall rumba, and whom we shall snub.

The forgers of this approach call themselves internationalists, and accuse those who disagree with them of being neo-isolationists. But unilateral moves into unbalanced bilateral relations plus a shunning of multilateralism add up to nothing more than isolationism practiced overseas. The functional distinction that should interest us is not between the misleading words "isolationism" and "internationalism" but between acting alone and acting in concert with others. Acting alone involves working abroad with no entangling alliances— with no acceptance of the mutuality of obligation, no felt need to compromise, and no desire to establish a community of interests involving the happiness of living and sharing together. Conversely, acting multilaterally implies attempting to *create* interests the sharing of which can generate a complex and broad basis for international comity, in much the same way as one seeks to create national community within one's own borders.

These behavior patterns are not, of course, specific only to hemispheric relations. Solitary internationalism has characterized the way in which the present American government has treated

Chinese and South and Southeast Asian politics, to the dismay of Japan and most other nations friendly to the United States. The monetary crises of recent years provide an even starker example of our style of international sociability.

The Ideology of Value-Free "Pragmatism." Among the unhappier legacies of the complacent fifties is the idea that industrial, democratic societies had solved their basic problems and needed only to continue to administer into being the better world past whose threshold we had already stepped. No overarching questions about the total system remained to be asked. Only subversives, malcontents, and the emotionally disturbed still insisted on the need for explicitly held ideologies. The proponents of this argument acted in unwitting ideological good faith as utopian democrats. But they did not know and did not foresee, and very few have subsequently admitted that their views have served to usher in not an age of expanded participatory democracy, but an ideology and a practice of technocratic management that profoundly threatens free institutions.

Even though events of the past decade have clearly demonstrated that in the formal institution of the American state as well as in the informal workings of the polity, there are underlying structural problems that tap the ethical and moral roots of beliefs and thus are *necessarily* ideological in implication, the notion that techniques alone can solve our problems remains with us in both international and domestic affairs. The pretense is made that politics can be understood and administered in an essentially value-free way, as a play of effective desires among participants in the "game." In this construction, balance-of-power politics abroad are the same as interest-group politics at home. One must simply accept the rules of play, and let power plus perceived interest work themselves out—all the while making certain that one's own power and explicit recognition of interest are maintained at as high a pitch as possible. If the system and its rule remain unchallenged, then it is indeed possible to act without questioning basic premises, thus pretending to amorality and ethical neutrality, to being "practical" and "pragmatic" without asking what we are being "practical" and "pragmatic" about. Certainly it is sometimes useful to assume an anethical position within a value-freighted system, as in the doing of science. But that contained neutrality is not possible when systems themselves are in contention. Fundamental choice is unavoidable, and thus amorality is impossible, when the survival of societies and their systems of behavior and beliefs are at stake. Under such conditions neutrality slides either into morality or immorality, depending on one's values. There are no *technical* solutions to basic *policy* problems, only political ones. And *all* political solutions are seated in ideologies—systems of belief that interpret the past, justify present behavior, and seek to control the future in desired ways.

The more advanced Latin American countries have the historical opportunity to attempt many alternative ways of organizing their societies. No longer held in the firm grip of Iberian tradition, freed from slavish dependence on foreign models whose attractiveness diminishes every day, and with goodly numbers of urban, literate, and reasonably well-educated persons who can be recruited to active civic life, perhaps a dozen countries have the opportunity to move effectively and firmly toward structuring new ways of social life. At issue are patterns of participation, the nature of political-economic relations, the kinds of national consciousness that will be forged, the nature of and restraints on state power, the building of appropriate legal and educational institutions, and the many other fascinating problems that must be solved in order to build the structures and articulations of complex social life. There are also stern limitations on the freedom of choice of these countries. Needed are intelligence, capable administrators, support rather than hindrance from overseas, a willingness to be playful and experimental, increased economic productivity and equity in distribution, stable international markets, and ideologies supportive of both rationalism (a way of thinking) and rationalization (a way of organizing). All these elements are in short and irregular supply. Particularly lacking are models, physical and ideological. Arid technocracy and mechanistic balancing are no substitute for the satisfying excitement of systems of thought that directly address themselves to how people do and should go through their lives. If those idea systems deal with participation, belonging, and dignity within a frame of secular rationalism, they can establish an ordered relation among goals, expectations, and means in creating the power that comes from public agreement with political policies. This consensus helps to provide the political wherewithal to assure sufficient success in ordering social events to warrant continued public enthusiasm as the difficult processes of development proceed. The decay of democratic idealism is not merely the loss of an old and sentimentally cherished ideology, or of the power of moral leadership; it is also the loss of a moral reason for working development with efficiency and dignity.

Because systems themselves are at issue in Latin America, a truly realistic hemispheric policy will need to make its moral basis clear. To continue a pretense of "pragmatic" amorality is only to invite self-delusion, unreason, and, hence, failure. Bertrand Russell put it more elegantly:

> ... the power conferred by technique is social, not individual.... Scientific technique requires the co-operation of a large number of individuals organized under a single direction. Its tendency, therefore, is against anarchism and even individualism, since it demands a well-knit social structure. Unlike religion, it is ethically neutral; it assures men that they can perform wonders, but does not tell them what wonders to perform. In this way, it is incomplete.... The men at the head of the vast organizations which it necessitates can, within reason, turn it this way or that as they please. The power impulse thus has a scope which it never had before. The philosophies that have been inspired by scientific *technique* are power philosophies, and tend to regard everything non-human as mere raw material. Ends are no longer considered; only the skilfullness of a process is valued. This ... is a form of madness. It is, in our day, the most dangerous form. ...[1]

Nationalistic Antinationalism.   The United States, from the heights of its development and its history of democratic sophistication, is beset by the same fundamental political problem that the more advanced Latin American states have as they push to choose the corner of the modern estate in which they will live. The primary public question of countries like Argentina, Chile, and the United States has to do with the form and content of national community— with the nation and with nationalism. In contention are two opposing views of proper and feasible national organization:

- A national society organized to provide equality for all before its diverse institutions. A society whose power is molded from the positive consent of the governed. A relativistic, secular, and rational society, in which a contained and accountable government is accepted, for the immediate purposes of conflict resolution, as being the ultimate mundane arbiter of secular dispute. A society that attempts to mitigate the effects of social class through merit selection and equality before the laws and to guarantee a minimum decent level of existence for all its citizens.

- A national society organized to maintain hierarchy and existing privilege. A society that exhorts its people to support the state for reasons of grandeur, mystical or otherwise, while at the same time it assumes the necessity and righteousness of the uses of overt coercive power, sometimes in massive doses. An absolutist

[1]*A History of Western Philosophy* (New York: Simon and Schuster, 1945), p. 494.

state that demands that it be taken on faith as the legitimate ultimate arbiter of secular dispute. A society that justifies the effects of social class, equates achievement with moral worth, and applies moral, ideological, class, personality, and ethical criteria in its selection procedures. A society that at best defines social decency in only material terms and prefers the argument that God helps him who helps himself.

An anomaly describes the relationship between belief in the value of an open national community and most consciously held ideologies of nationalism: throughout the Americas, the two attitudes are usually considered opposites. North American liberals and Latin American center-leftists who espouse the value of an egalitarian national community have ceded nationalist appeals to the jingoists who praise the value of hierarchically stable, class-bound authoritarian organization. In other words, the self-professing nationalists in both culture areas of the hemisphere oppose the extension of the national community on conditions of equality to all citizens, while the ashamed nationalists want a complete social nation but blush to exhort the loyalty that supports legitimacy.

The contradiction between belief in the value of building a national community and the current ideologies of nationalism has served to weaken national communities and therefore to make the democratic solution of problems difficult, and sometimes impossible. Antinational nationalist governors demand loyalty from everybody, but in turn extend their own loyalty only to citizens of proper "standing" and beliefs. The more nationalistic in ideology the political leaders are, the more prone they are to disown some of their own citizens as heretic and to make common cause with their ideological brethren across national boundaries. (International military and police activities in the Western Hemisphere are clear day-to-day proof of the primacy these ideologists give to their political values over their loyalties to fellow nationals.) The results are as clear in Argentina, Uruguay, and Brazil as they are threatening to become in the United States: nationalistic governors erode the power of the social nations they lead, weakening states in their international relations both politically and militarily, and crippling the ability in domestic affairs to identify and deal flexibly and equitably with problems surging up from rapidly changing economic, technical, and demographic factors.

A Committed International, Nationalist Policy. This essay is, among other things, an attempt to revive the forgotten half of a famous pair of articles that appeared in *Foreign Affairs* over twenty years ago, signed by one Mr. X. There the argument was advanced that containment of Soviet expansionism might well be necessary as a temporary expedient, but that the long-run *justification* for the immediate behavior of this country must rely on the quality of its national life, on its worth as a decent society *per se*. Because Latin America does not threaten North American security in any military sense, containment or its analogues are not at issue; the justification for behavior certainly is.

In a time of increasing entanglement of domestic with international affairs, we have no sound choice but to want for others what we want for ourselves. What we should expect is not any instant equalization of physical conditions; such a desire is impossible of fulfillment and in any event flies in the face of cultural, ideological, and historical differences. Therefore, what we can rationally desire in common has to do with a process—the procedures by which societies can satisfy material wants for their populations and find ways to organize themselves so they can constantly expand their ability to reduce alienation and free creative abilities of all kinds. If that commitment is rejected, another must be taken—its opposite, perhaps. Such a policy might seek to institute those procedures that assume that socially created hierarchy is an eternal necessity, given innate human corruption, and that the good society will be attained when classes are stabilized, everyone knows his place and is made content with it, and status can be transmitted through the generations. Yet a third alternative is to seek order and efficiency within existing frames through the establishment of a merit-based technocracy. Political leaders and managers would no longer be selected by election, nepotism, or buddyism, but by objective tests of capacity, and they would run the present structures, although somewhat more efficaciously than they are now run. Regardless of the option selected—whether participatory democracy, corporatism, or technocracy—certain trends will have to be faced by everyone. Among others, they are:

- The increasing unity of national and international politics, already stated.

- The increasing unity of political and economic power. Unhappily, the time of a clean differentiation between the economy and the polity is over in erstwhile liberal, Western, capitalistic societies. In most other countries, the idea never gained ideological or structural hold. How to maintain economic incentives in a time of general collectivization is a critical issue for us all. How to maintain democratic mechanisms in a time of economic gigantism is an even more important issue.

- The increasing intimacy of global communications. The promise held out by a world television network involves potential access to cultural richness and variety. The threat is the opposite: the swamping of cultural uniqueness, with a concomitant loss in the ability to judge among workable alternatives and a consequent impoverishment of values.

- The increasing power of governmental authorities to control individuals. The days are numbered of the traditional authoritarianism, in which the dissident can withdraw from politics and remain safe, hidden inaccessibly in institutional nooks and crannies. Now, even in tiny Central American republics, the total control of governors over preliterate populations can be extended to individuals by modern techniques, bypassing institutional protections. Totalitarianism is no longer a threat only to developed countries.

- The increasing independence of industrial development from education. Capital-intensive industries using imported technicians no longer need draw on skilled and semiskilled populations for their work forces. The productive side of industrial society needs many fewer educated persons than it did even thirty years ago. Education will increasingly have to do with consumption, a fact that deeply affects the distribution of power as well as goods and that permits us to raise questions about the intrinsic functions of an educational system and its role in the development of individuals for their own sakes instead of for a series of economic roles.

This list could be much longer, of course. The point, however, should be clear: there are constraints stemming from important problem areas that everyone will have to consider. But each ideological group will define its own problems into existence—for, after all, a problem is brought to life only by our heads and our passions.

Problems in the Definition of a Hemispheric Policy. The contradictions described in this article impregnate the recent history of United States–Latin relations. We have a static policy for a rapidly changing hemisphere, a policy offhandedly seen as a part of our general defense of raw national security, against which no important threats come from the lands to our south. Otherwise, we have no statement of our interests. There is a vague feeling that American private investments should be defended, and that somehow Venezuela is more "important"—or more easily influenced—than is, say, Argentina. Even our ideas about what we do *not* wish to see in the hemisphere have become muddy. This policy of misplaced concreteness cannot last much longer. Because it is unrealistic, passively reactive, and out of intellectual control, it can satisfy no group—whether business, governmental, or academic—nor the country as a whole.

If we are to act on the assumption that many Latin American nations are soon going to take their places in the world as powers of the second and third rank, then the United States must prepare itself to compete in the hemisphere as it does in Europe. The ends for which this country competes, the means it will permit itself to use, and the ways in which it attempts to give structure to the conditions of the competition depend primarily not on inputs from the hemisphere, but rather on domestic political dynamics. In short, some of the contradictions on the home front need resolution before policy, deeds, and words can be brought together on foreign fronts.

If the line of argument so far has any validity, and if we search for an effective policy, then the basis for recreating a Latin American foreign policy should first be to strengthen the national community of the United States. This task should be guided by an ideology that insists that rationalism be applied to measure the proper balance between means and defined ends. This writer, then, has made some value commitments: he believes rationalism is possible in human affairs, that it is preferable to irrationalism, that the play of rationalism requires self-correcting, relativistic, and free social institutions; and that from this combination flows the power to pursue rational purposes, including increased power through time to pursue such objectives. The internal conditions for the creation of such a foreign policy involve, consistent with the analyses above:

- A reinforcement of America's social nation: that is, the incorporation into participant, ordered, and creative social life of as many persons in this society as possible. No social task is more important than this one. No social sacred cow is worth preserving if it inhibits the growth of nationalism of this kind.

- The recognition that acting as an isolate abroad is as inefficient and eventually self-defeating as it would be in national social life. A concomitant is the realization that internationalism depends on social nations, and the two can be mutually reinforcing. They are opposites only when made so, an act to the detriment of both. Even etymologically, it is impossible to imagine fruitful relations among "nations," if there are only states, but no nations. In other words, the fecund participation of individuals and groups at international levels depends upon a prior assembly of individuals into groups within their cultures. This statement has been true of cosmopolitan elites for centuries. Let it also become true for the humblest among us.

• The conscious creation of systems of understanding and explanation, backed by adequate information subject to test in a competitive market of ideas—what the Latin Americans call *concientización,* an arousal of consciousness. If these ideas are to be supportive of secular national community and interacting participation, they must also be pragmatic in the true sense of the word. Secrecy must be abandoned, information made freely available, the grounds for governmental decisions made public, and ends and means conceptually laced together.

And what should be our hopes for Latin Americans as a result of our interaction with them? Why, that Latin Americans should develop the same general values, of course, and find their own ways to work toward them within their particular cultural contexts. And if some Latin American governments do not pursue such ends, what should we do? Do not support those trends, as we do now, but also do nothing that would damage the integrity of our national interest by doing to others what a decent person would not do to his fellow citizens. And if some Latin American governments do pursue such positive ends? Help them in any reasonable way, avoiding paternalism or any other attitude or action that may impede the development of autonomous, interactive, cooperative, self-sustaining national-international life.

1975

Acknowledgment: This essay is a slightly revised version of the one by the same title that appeared in *Latin America: The Search for a New International Role,* Ronald G. Hellman and H. Jon Rosenbaum, editors, pp. 27–38. © 1975; appears by permission of the publisher, Sage Publications, Inc.

The Relevance of
Latin American Domestic Politics
to North American Foreign Policy

FOR YEARS it has been customary to say that one cannot speak of a "Latin America"—and then to proceed to do so anyway. The reason, perhaps, is that for some purposes "Latin America" does indeed exist, but building categories in which to place Latin American events and situations is difficult and controversial. Categories are statements of theory. The taxonomer justifies the limits he establishes by saying that they will group factors, situations, relations, dynamics, or what have you because of a commonality—*one that he imputes to them*. Further, he argues that his system of boxes is useful for understanding, description, prediction, diagnosis, or whatever else may be his goal. Accordingly, categorical systems should not be lightly accepted; they set the agenda, suggest what is significant and what can be neglected, and tag what is variable and what is constant.

Latin American politics cannot be discussed with refinement without passing through such a self-conscious construction of categories. Perhaps we can speak with sense about Latin America's generic characteristics: language, ethos, religion, world position, or historical experience. But any similarly generalizing political statements are absurdities. They are of the order of Latin America's "chronic political instability," the "hot blood of the l atin temperament," or the "need for personalistic, charismatic figures in a population that admires the 'macho' spirit." Those stereotypes could as easily be given an opposite twist. For example, political turmoil reveals Latin America's unquenchable thirst for better and more

159

open governance. Or, Latin Americans are willing to risk their lives in the pursuit of the ideal of improved governance. Personalism and charisma are elitist excuses for governments of force, evidence of the unwillingness of ruling groups to accede to the never-ending popular quest for a meaningful and effective voice in affairs of state. Even though we know that every stereotype contains some truth, let us not fall into using such statements, for the obvious reason that we have no way of knowing how much falsity is mixed with how much truth.

Left with the categorical task as an imperative, I find that an ethical question arises. This is not the place for me to indicate fully the theory lying behind my selection of categories or to expound the tastes and passions lying behind the theory. Consequently, I will hew as closely as possible to conventional wisdom, in the expectation that such an approach will be less coercive of the views of my readers than would the presentation of a more idiosyncratic set of conclusions from a hidden array of normative and hypothetical premises. In addition, I will cast this essay in the form of a line of argument in order to highlight the links in the reasoning.

I assume that one of the basic elements in politics, whether domestic or international, is power taken pure. Power can be viewed as the ability to force others to do what you wish them to, despite their opposition. It can also be taken to mean, even in the absence of an antagonist, the simple ability to take effective action. For instance, power can be seen as placing fluoride in water systems despite opposing pressure groups, or as having the knowledge of what fluoride can do, or even as having water systems amenable to fluoridation. I will take power in all of these senses in this analysis.

I also assume that power—as coercive ability, knowledge, and control over available instrumentalities—is always in its applications mingled with preferences. "Pure" power and "pure" ideologies, preferences, and tastes come together to give us effective desires, the political analogue of what economists call "effective demand." But the subject is infinitely more complex for political than for economic thinking. There is rarely a clean test of the quantities of power "actors" bring to political drama, or melodrama. Political victory is only sometimes unequivocal for individuals, and almost never so for states. And, more important, the origins of power have to do with social organization, classes and "races," idea systems, and profound cultural values as all of them filter through consensus, legitimacy, institutions, and policy.

Uncomfortably difficult as these themes may be, they are the subject matter of international as well as national politics. I will understand the term "international politics" as follows throughout this essay: it is the power-infused relations among formal states in pursuit of varied conceptions of the national interest and concerning all subjects that become consciously attended, from war to cultural exchange. This definition does not cover all relations among nations, of course—only those that fall into the overtly political sphere. It is for this reason that I have chosen to use the term "international politics" and not the more inclusive "international relations." Now, what should we want to know about the way in which domestic factors fit into these statements?

- We should want to know something about the *kinds* of power that can be brought to bear at any given moment by governments.

- We should want to know something about the kinds of power that can be brought to bear *for certain purposes* by governments.

- We should want to know the range of alternatives that can be seen by governments, interest groups, intellectuals, parties, and other interested and organized groups in a society.

- We should want to know something about tendencies in the above three respects.

The first categories in which we should be interested, then, concern the patterns through which societies create and order public power. In Latin America, generally speaking, they are:

1. *Patrimonial states.* In a patrimonial state, a small ruling group uses a large group of non-nationally organized persons for economic purposes of a low order of complexity. Only very small numbers of people can be recruited for tasks at the national level, for there is hardly a "nation" in other than formalistic senses. If the upper groups are cohesive, such governments can make firm pronouncements for their own limited purposes. These political structures are fragile and weak in the face of external threat, but they can be persistent if internal division is avoided and social change at lower levels is not promoted. Haiti, Nicaragua, and Honduras are classic examples of this kind of governance.

2. *Partially "organic," corporate states.* The purpose of corporatism at grand social levels is to permit the growth of institutional differentiation and specialization in the accomplishment of tasks, but without scrambling the class order. Hierarchy is stably incorporated within this kind of state. The corporate pillars, classically, are the clergy, the landowners, the industrialists, the military, the bureaucracy, the merchants, and the trade unionists. The concept of citi-

zenship exists in such situations, but it is strained. The notion of
citoyen coming to us from the French Revolution is that all persons
are equal before the state; corporatism provides a minimal equality
within an occupationally derived, structured system of inequality.
Although no Latin American country is an example of full organic
corporatism, some show more than a few signs of such organization.
Mexico's political party structure is corporate in form; the thinking
of Chile's incumbent government is overtly corporatist, and it is
pursuing policies to bring such a state into existence; Peronism and
the present Brazilian military government have both shown strong
traces of this persuasion.

3. _Liberal partial nation-states._ The nation-state seeks to integrate the universal _citoyen,_ who can overcome the class-based accidents of birth and assume equality of condition before the state. No
nation-state anywhere has achieved the goal of complete equality of
condition in political matters. But some have come closer than
others. Clearly, the political goal of Allende's administration in Chile
was to mitigate, if not erase, class-rooted impediments to complete
citizenship. Substantive equality before the laws and structures of the
state was much more present than absent for most members of the
Argentine and Uruguayan upper and middle groups throughout all
of this century, until very recent years. It was the loss of this class-
related quasi-equality that caused great distress in Brazil after the
coming to power of the military in 1964. The attempt to build the
social nation characterizes the present Venezuelan polity. The class-
inhibited partial nation-state is the political form that has been most
characteristic of Latin American ideals (not practice) during the past
fifty years. Attacks upon it, made in the attempt to substitute corporatism, provide the fundamental pattern of domestic political strife
in the more complex societies.

The emergence of the nation-state as ideal form has given rise
to two fundamental areas of political clash in Latin America, as well
as in the Western world generally: the clash between nation and class
at the level of total social organization and that between sacred and
secular legitimation within the formal state itself.

The original idea of the secular nation-state was that it would
provide arenas, or "marketplaces," in which equality of condition
could play itself out in a rationalistic interchange which, it used to be
supposed, would allow ever-growing efficiency within a self-correcting
and thus self-sustaining mechanism. Further, a secularized natural
law provided freedom to choose one's formal religion without effect
on one's other social roles. To be within a pertinent jurisdiction was

the requirement for triggering equality before the laws. Citizenship also carried with it equality before the ballot box, the ultimate definer of policy legitimacy. The use of capital, reason, or skill to gain advantage in the economic marketplace was not to be reinforced by monopoly, nepotism, political influence, or any other extraeconomic factor. Finally, public education was to assure an equalization of skills, despite the facts of class origin. These were more or less the ideals, and however imperfectly they were realized, in many nations they promoted mass mobilization of populations for new economic tasks and the emergence of popular (and populist) nation-states that could count on the willingness of masses of citizenry to die in defense of the polity. They contributed as well to strengthening middle classes and to changing the nature of upper classes. However, nowhere has the construction of national communities of universal membership come to completion. In every case, including that of the United States, national movements have created vast new social and political powers, and they have also created a class order that can effectively resist the incorporation of all persons within the community on conditions of essential structural equality. This is what I mean by the clash between nation and class.

The second clash—that between secular and sacred legitimation of the state—has to do with whether the form of the state should be suitable for the pursuit of national ends or for the attempt to restrict the further expansion of national community. Although written in a somewhat different context, the following paragraphs from a recent book review illustrate the point most adequately:

> Popular sovereignty is an awesome idea precisely because it means nothing less than the existential freedom of a people to be responsible for its own fate, without recourse to any "father." The regicides created this terrible and magnificent freedom, the only one commensurate with the fullness of human potential. With the execution of Louis, they could solemnly declare to the nation: "From this moment, one will no longer write the history of France, but rather the history of the French."
>
> Yet the rule of one man with his entourage can reemerge whenever a people, for whatever reasons, renounces the practice of its sovereign judgment, abandoning itself to that slow erosion of responsibility which turns citizens into subjects. Similarly, the "abiding pretensions of monarchy" are also the ones of all those who assert the power to rule alone . . . .[1]

[1] Review by Richard Mowery Andrews of Michael Walzer, ed., *Regicide and Revolution: Speeches at the Trial of Louis XVI* (New York: Cambridge University Press, 1974), in *The New York Times Book Review*, June 9, 1974, p. 3.

This concern is not appropriate to those relatively few Latin American countries that have hardly begun to grapple with the question of national community: Haiti, Nicaragua, Honduras, and, to a limited extent, El Salvador and Ecuador. But the problem shapes national politics in all the other Latin American countries, and it affects elites everywhere. In all countries, of course, there are major segments of the population totally outside the "national question": the Indians of Mexico, Guatemala, Peru, and Bolivia, seminomadic populations in Brazil and Paraguay, and persons living on society's margins in both rural and urban areas.

As I see it, then, the three grand families of Latin American politics are those of patrimonialism, of antinational sacralism, and of pronational secularism. Note that so far we have been speaking only by implication of authoritarianisms, totalitarianisms, and democracies. The reason is clear: national community is a precondition for both the secular republicanism of democracy and the sacred paternalism of totalitarianism. Political situations in nonnational societies are in a class by themselves, producing authoritarian regimes with characteristics far different from either the voluntarism of the perfectly integrated society of autonomous persons or the coercive control of totalitarianism. Our first set of categories had to do with social organization as inferential of power creation. The second set, that of the two fundamental clashes, had to do with the quintessential problem of all national states. And the third, the usual display of kinds of political systems, dealt with the formal structures evolved for the day-to-day governance of administration, and for the definition and solution of problems. It is clear, however, that some rough relationship must exist between the degree and nature of national social organization and the kinds of political systems they permit. Thus, with a rough set of guesses concerning degrees of national integration, cohesion, and citizenship (all of which we have derived from economic statistics, patterns of urbanization, literacy, and mobility, knowledge of cultural and racial homogeneity, extent and complexity and completeness of social services, and our hunches concerning citizen loyalty and anticipatory obedience to law), let us range the Latin countries on an approximate scale of national community.

The most complete *social* (not *political*) nations are:

> Cuba
> Chile
> Uruguay
> Argentina

Countries with harsh class divisions, but with strengthening traditions of participation and social access to national institutions, are:

Costa Rica
Venezuela

Countries with harsh class and regional divisions and with racially reinforced stratification, but with growing access to national institutions (except, generally, for effective and continuous political participation), are:

Mexico
Brazil
Peru
Colombia
Panama
El Salvador

Countries with harsh class divisions, very sharp urban-rural differences, some racially reinforced stratification, and little growth in access to national institutions, including the political, are:

Guatemala
Paraguay
Ecuador
Dominican Republic
Bolivia
Nicaragua
Honduras
Haiti

(I have omitted formerly British Caribbean republics from this list, for by tradition and circumstance they comprise a special problem.)

It should now be obvious, given the bases of this argument, that the countries which can effectively choose quasidemocratic or quasi-totalitarian forms of governance must come from the top half of the total list. This exercise is not an idle one. If it had been gone through at the time of the Bay of Pigs invasion, the planners of that operation might have been less ready to apply a technique learned from Guatemala, one of the most fragmented of Latin American countries, to Cuba, a country socially ready for nationhood. Similarly, it was nonsense for an Assistant Secretary of Inter-American Affairs to warn a conference several years ago that the United States "is on a collision course with Haiti," implying that if we did not treat "Papa Doc" well, he would opt for a *fidelista* course. But it was *not* nonsense to have viewed the urban guerrillism of the early 1960s in

Venezuela as bearing a functional relationship to the choices that
had recently been made in Cuba. The two countries share many
characteristics, and until the past decade their potentialities were not
radically different. In short, this array of cases suggests to us the
limits of choices open to the societies concerned. It also suggests that
as one goes down the list, leadership can express widely varying
opinions—being unconstrained by the complexities of autonomous
followership—but that the ability of leaders to act on attempts at
far-reaching and profound change is limited. Thus, the governments of Arévalo and Arbenz in Guatemala (1946–1954) could call
for revolutionary change, but they could not manage to bring it
about with a population more than half of which was Indian, more
than three quarters of which was illiterate, and about 90 percent of
which was rural.

This categorization helps us in prediction and also assists us to
understand some of the reasons for the present array of types of
governmental situations. Let us go down the list again, applying easy
(and necessarily somewhat slovenly) labels to the types of governments involved.

In full crisis of nation vs. class	*Cuba:* a socialist authoritarianism, totalitarian in national political affairs, participant and democratic in many local affairs
	Chile: a totalitarian military corporate state in the making at both national and local levels. Not yet fully settled down
	Uruguay: a totalitarian semicorporate state under military tutelage
	Argentina: a quasidemocratic state, unstable, undergoing an attempt to establish a traditional liberal democracy with a populist cast, but liable to fall into a militaristic totalitarianism
Building the nation, not yet at nation-class confrontation	*Costa Rica:* a traditional liberal partial democracy
	Venezuela: the same
Totally mixed situations, politically and structurally	*Mexico:* a mixed situation, with some elements of corporatism, some of liberal partial democracy, and remaining strong vestiges of patrimonialism, especially in rural and Indian areas

Brazil: a mixed situation under military control, with some elements of corporatism (strong), some of liberal partial democracy (weak), and remaining strong vestiges of patrimonialism in lower groups in both city and country

Nationalizing elites, lagging populations

Peru: a developmental military rule attempting to move from patrimonialism to some of the choices open in the Mexican and Brazilian scenes

Colombia: a civilian regime, using the forms of partial liberal democracy within the social structure and social habits of patrimonialism

Panama: an essentially patrimonial and clientelistic state with some of the trimmings and promise of traditional liberal democracy and some of the drives of the Peruvian leadership

El Salvador: the same as Panama

Prenational

Guatemala: classbound military patrimonial rule, traditional in a slowly modernizing social setting

Paraguay: the same

Ecuador: the same

Dominican Republic: the same, but with civilian oligarchical government

Patrimonial

Bolivia: the same politically, with little social modernization

Nicaragua: the same

Haiti: the same

Honduras: the same, with some autonomous movement in rural areas

I find this ordering useful. It permits me to "hear" better when someone says that "Latin America is beginning to come on the world scene in an autonomous way, and we should start thinking of the region as we do of Europe"; I immediately screen out all but the five or six first countries on the list. Or, when others tell me that Latin

America will be comprised of client-states for many generations to come, I nod, thinking about the bottom half of the list. Also, it should be noted that all five of the lowest-ranking countries, as well as some others, have in the past been the objects of direct military intervention by the United States. Nonnational states geographically close to a major power are always inviting targets for the impatience of military intervention: they are pushovers. At the other end of the list, covert activities have an inviting chance of succeeding when countries find themselves in the ultimate crises of national being and therefore are beset by empowered groups of citizens willing to seek assistance from abroad to confront their profound crises at home. It is this kind of opportunity that the United States has taken in Brazil, Chile, and other such countries.

At this point, we begin overtly to enter into the discussion of intervention and, more broadly, of North American stimuli to and reactions toward Latin American situations. Let us turn to the narrower matter of interventionism first. Obviously, the United States "intervenes" by existing: our cultural and ideological impacts on Latin America have been strong and continuous for a century and a half. Also, the nature of our economic system and our variegated monopolistic-monopsonistic presence in some countries at given times constitute a critical element in influence, a fact that has been taken as the basis of *dependencia* thinking in Latin America. Approaching the subject with such breadth, however, precludes concrete discussion. I prefer, therefore, to limit my discussion to political affairs, handling economic and cultural dimensions as they become the subject matter of political intercourse and somewhat controllable through political mechanisms. Some of the patterns of what may vulgarly be called "interventionist" international politics are as follows:

1. *Coercive intervention.*   The direct use of armed forces, almost always in smaller, weaker, and neighboring republics, has been becoming passé as the Cold War recedes and security is redefined.

2. *Indirect and implied coercive intervention.*   The indirect use of coercion is carried on through covert operations, such as operational activities undertaken by intelligence agencies, that are violent by implication or actuality. A major case is the training of Latin American armed forces in techniques of civic action and internal policing. These programs were related to doctrines of internal warfare common in the early 1960s, but of course they have been employed by some Latin American armed forces in the creation of political devices and forms unforeseen and unintended by at least some United States advisers.

3. *Ideological interventions.*   There are many examples: to wit, the Alliance for Progress, the *abrazo* for the democratic friend and the handshake for the authoritarian enemy, the Hickenlooper Amendment, the individual actions of some United States ambassadors.

4. *Economic interventions.*   These especially include protection of individual United States enterprises and the establishment of policy in the Inter-American Development Bank, the World Bank, and similar agencies. The Eximbank has an interesting history in this respect. (Such interventions are also heavily freighted with ideological considerations, of course. The blockade of Cuba, the policy of economic denial applied to Chile under Allende, and certain reticences in Peru since the mid-1960s are examples.)

5. *Cultural interventions.*   Examples of these are the USIA, bilingual schools, traveling exhibitions, scholarships, and the academic developmental activities of USAID.

We shall not avoid interventions, and, therefore, we should not seek to avoid intervention*ism*, conscious control over how and why and for what ends we intervene. At this point, however, there is no choice but to express some values. Given the differing Latin American situations, no single set of interventionist techniques—for good or ill—can very well be employed. Therefore, I should like to suggest an overarching criterion: to the extent to which we may pursue policies to influence Latin American countries to change in any direction, we should always seek to increase the ability of Latin American polities effectively to make ever-broadening sets of choices. The implications of the statement are:

1. National communities—"terminal communities," as Rupert Emerson called them—permit the creation of the greatest amounts of social power. Therefore, all other things being equal, we should support nation-building endeavors; they provide the "effectiveness" in the choice-making.

2. Democratic organization permits self-correction and the mechanisms that provide widening sets of meaningful choices reinforced by public acceptability. For that reason we should support, when we can, partial democracies wherever we find them and recognize the costs of their absence.

3. Academic freedom and university autonomy, civil liberties in their full range, and the existence of strong artistic and intellectual communities are critical components in injecting relativism and sense into choice-making. Traditional patrimonial authoritarianisms permit limited freedoms of that sort much more than do dictatorships that are totalitarian or becoming totalitarian. We have many governmental devices to encourage the creation of autonomous

practices. These devices should be employed, and we should not hesitate to be a haven for persons who are threatened because they have exercised such freedoms.

Taking two limiting cases may help to spell out the meaning of the posture in foreign policy decision-making to which I have been referring. They concern such atrocious political behavior as torture and mass murder, on the one hand, and the issue of socialism, on the other. Let us start with atrocious practices. Even superficial thought reveals how widespread is such behavior; after all, the United States is widely accused of atrocities at home as well as in Vietnam. It may be that as many as 300,000 persons died, some the victims of quite spectacular techniques of murder, in Colombia's *violencia* between 1948 and 1960. A dwarf in the Dominican Republic was alleged to have specialized in biting off testicles in the Trujillo period; it is said that an iron maiden was in use in Venezuela during the Pérez Jiménez era; impalement is not an unknown police practice in Guatemala; torture, sometimes to the point of death, has been taking place regularly in Brazil for most of the past decade. In short, the film *State of Siege* dramatically understates the actual situation in many countries. If we declare beyond the pale every government, Latin American or otherwise, that engages in atrocities against at least some types of persons or population segments, then we should end up talking only to ourselves—and that in growls, I suppose. Our first task must then be to decide which type of horror may legitimately be an issue of intergovernmental concern. As an individual citizen, I reserve the right to oppose as best I can any and all atrocities. But in an epoch of moral cicatrization and the rapid evolution of an American policy of quietude on this score, I also want to build a reasonable case for governmental action in opposing such activities.

Briefly, I should want my government to seek to remind signatory states to the Universal Declaration of Human Rights of their obligations under that statement. And, more activistically, I should like my government to apply moral suasion against and, if necessary, to adopt a policy of cool and sharply limited diplomatic interchange with all states that commit atrocities *as an intrinsic and institutionalized part of the governmental process.* I think a legitimate case can be made that both Brazil and Chile have employed torture and political killing as consciously adopted policy. Brazil has done so in order to still opposition from the Liberal elite, from potential trade union leaders, and from intellectuals. The economic development policy of Brazil demanded making the country attractive to capital flows from abroad by restraining unionization (not a difficult job), by ousting or

weakening certain national industrialists, and by silencing the voices
of left nationalism. Relatively little killing was necessary; torture and
attendant fright not only broke the nascent urban guerrilla movement but also stifled most public protest and muted demands for
internal equity in income distribution. Brazil's governors think the
price low for a high rate of industrialization, on which basis they
promise to permit the better society to be built. Others disagree. As
for the Chilean incumbents, they have destroyed the country's political party system, its national trade unions, and its interest group
structure. In the absence of legitimating institutions which permit
the agglutination and expression of opinion and consensus, they are
left with the practical necessity of substituting the coercive effects of
fright for routine acceptance of law. They argue that they were
forced to such extreme measures in order to forestall civil war.
Others disagree. In any event, in both cases the practices continue
long after the end of the heat of revolution and the taking of
revenge; in both cases the practices are part of day-to-day governance. But there the resemblance ends, for Chile is on its way to
totalitarianism, and Brazil's polity is still far from being able or
willing to range the power of the state against individuals standing
alone and naked without the protections of station, class, sex, age, or
institutional buffering. To put it another way, in Brazil there are still
places to hide, to express dissidence, to wait for a better day, to be
silent. In Chile such havens are hard to find. The difference is akin
to that which distinguished Nazi Germany from Franco Spain. That
distinction is not an innocuous one; for many millions of persons it
has been the difference between life and death.

The suggestions flowing from this analysis should now be quite
obvious. They are:

- Except for routine diplomatic relations, the United States government should in no way assist by word, economic aid, or any other
action any Latin American government that is totalitarian. All such
governments *must* rule through inducing fright; all such governments sooner or later fall into lunacies, for by definition they exclude the practices of self-correction. No Latin American government is as yet in this happily exclusive club, but Chile is on its way.

- The United States government should publicly state its displea-
sure to any government using terror as an instrument of governance and should channel any activities beyond entirely diplomatic ones in such a way as not to reinforce the specific governmental agencies employing terroristic devices or to reward the
use of atrocities.

The finding of fact in these cases will not be easy. But it can be done. I am well aware of the arguments of the day that "nobody appointed the United States to be the world's policeman." Even though those who make such declarations have long actively advocated and pursued the attempt to turn us into the Global Cop they now reject, I agree with the statement.[2] My purpose in making these recommendations has to do not with Latin societies, but rather with our own. Total abandonment of judging others and attempting to make them abide by international law is only the antechamber to our continued abandonment of respect for our own international commitments and our own democratic history. Moreover, judgment is like interventionism: neither is avoidable, for to eschew judgment is of course to make a judgment. If, however, pleas for human decency and freedom come from governments that do not themselves respect such values, they can have little effect.

A second limiting case concerns socialist regimes. The only recommendation I can logically fit with my prior statements is that if the socialist state is truly a total dictatorship, then we should extend no friendliness. But we now know that socialism is not automatically totalitarian. It is also no assurance of democracy or even of its own major promise, egalitarianism. (Neither, of course, does capitalism assure democracy.) Economic systems and types of governance are not in a one-to-one relationship, as anyone who is not a crude economic determinist knew long ago.

I hope it will be recognized that in actual practice our government has treated attempted socialisms in Latin America, no matter what their political color, as I have suggested we treat totalitarianisms, and it has treated harsh authoritarianisms and nascent totalitarianisms with the love and affection I should like to see lavished on more relativistic, pragmatic, and open societies. I do not view this selective diplomacy with equanimity. It reveals in our own governors a hidden basic preference that frightens me.

I do not at all wish to imply that we should view with equanimity the stripping from American citizens and companies of their assets by a nationalizing or socializing foreign country. But we should banish religious fervor from our reaction; after all, every major

---

[2]I do not agree, however, that Americans do not have a sense of mission. Most of us are infused with the democratic ethos, and we would like to see other countries pursue the promotion of personal and group freedoms. Some say we have neither the knowledge nor the power to pursue such goals; others say—with Kennan—that our own international situation should serve as moral example; still others, especially liberal Democrats, are more activist. The real issue is what modalities and techniques we can and should employ in helping to build a decent world.

economy in this world, and most minor ones, are either completely or heavily collectivized—not subject to the accountability of a free market, and monopolized, planned, relatively noncompetitive. The real issues have to do with private *versus* public collectivization, with which segments of the economy have been removed from the market, with the nature of planning and the degree to which given national economies contain government or are contained by government. We will have to live through great tensions in the continuing adjustments of economies and polities into a new accommodation that will, I hope, permit economic activity and democratic life to be mutually reinforcing once more. We must expect more socialization and nationalization in Latin America, unless all those countries turn into corporatisms for the protection not of private enterprise, but merely of private ownership.

Up to this point the discussion has centered on macropolitics. Before concluding, I wish to mention some common difficulties as examples of ways of testing less dramatic but perhaps no less important levels of policy. These themes are obvious, and they affect all nations of the world in varying degrees: ecological matters, population dynamics, urban-rural relations, education and citizenship, education and employment, patterns of industrialization, and communications, as well as many other themes. If the stakes are global, they are also particular to each nation and to every person. Thus, these themes are obviously testing grounds for styles and types of international relations and organization. We can mingle multilateralism with bilateralism in reconciling the universal with the particular aspects of these matters. Indeed, one of the better ways to test the utility of my earlier typologies is to learn to what extent a nation either recognizes or has any interest in any of these subjects. For example, countries at the top and bottom of the array of states tend to have little problem with excessive population expansion. The least well developed "benefit" from high death rates, as in Haiti; the most well developed have self-governing populations, as in Argentina. The in-betweens have rapidly expanding populations, as in Brazil, Mexico, and Costa Rica. The least well developed, such as Honduras, have few ecological problems. The most well developed, such as Argentina, have populations that worry about the environment. Again, the intermediates, such as Mexico, Peru, and Brazil, emphasize the quantitative over the qualitative.

But matters affecting the nature of populations, especially noticeable in education and communications, are of a different order. They are unavoidably ideological in nature. In the last century education was seen as preparing universal persons of culture who would then build their economies, polities, and societies. In this century education serves to supply manpower; labor is seen as a commodity, becoming but another factor of production. Communications, to take another example, can be taken as instrumental for sales or for "preparing" persons for occupational roles. Or, education and communications can be promoted as a good *per se,* as an enrichment of human experience and understanding that is valuable in itself. The transfer of international experience and knowledge in these fields is a first-order task with profound long-term political implications.

I shall enter into no further detail because the task of policy prescription should not be confused with the equally difficult job of operationalizing policy, of adjusting preestablished structures of thought to the facts of given cases. Policy is not a simplistic statement of preferences, nor is it a set of *ad hoc* adjustments to exigencies. Rather, it is an explicit preference system that includes guides for application and a statement of appropriate styles and instruments of application. In this view, policy is akin to the common law, and opposed to civil-law pretensions to the anticipation of all possible human behavior.

It is precisely because policy contains statements of goals that I began this essay with an apology for my inability to reveal all the premises lying behind my statements. In closing this argument, however, I should admit and clarify at least one assumption. I have deduced the arguments in this essay from Latin American cases, but I have also suggested prescriptions that may well have much wider application. Do I see those prescriptions, nevertheless, as being in any way intimately and particularly linked to the countries of the Americas? The answer is that I do indeed see such a connection, that I presume the existence of a "special relationship." Thus, I see these policy suggestions as having possibly more pointed and meaningful application to United States–Latin American relations than, say, to United States–Central African relations, or to United States–South Asian affairs. I cannot "prove" my point with "hard" data, or make more than a reasonable case for it. But I do not rest it merely on old-fashioned Monroeism, pan-Americanism, or similar romanticisms. Instead, I see the particularity in Western hemisphere affairs as having something to do with the following elements:

- Republicanism is a long-standing common ideal of governmental structure in the Americas.

- The ideal of egalitarian democracy has, except in some countries in very recent years, comprised a key element in the ideological constructions of all reigning groups.

- Capitalism, as a market economy of private participants, has also until recent years been a dominant ideological commitment, if decreasingly an actual practice.

- Until very recently, all states as they have grown competent have moved toward an extension of educational systems and other aspects of public welfare.

- The existence of class and racial barriers has been generally seen as undesirable, even while the privileges they confer have been enjoyed and defended.

- The crises of republicanism and of class and nation have become the common property of all the more developed societies, including the United States.

One could extend this list, concomitantly introducing elements that more clearly distinguish American from Western European experience. But I wish only to suggest that it is reasonable to assume that indeed there has been a "Western Hemisphere Idea." Even if structures and practices have partially belied the idea, the common historical commitment is a subtle and profound potential instrument for collaborative and controlled change.

1975

Turning Ideals into Reality:
Democracy in Latin America

A MOVE from paternalism to fraternalism in hemispheric relations was the essential recommendation of the report of the Commission on United States–Latin American Relations, commonly called the Linowitz report, published in 1975.[1] Since making its pronouncement, the commission has been criticized by conservatives for proposing a giveaway—giving Cuba back to the Cubans, the Panama Canal back to the Panamanians, and other such unthinkable propositions. And the left has criticized the commission for failing to recognize that the solution to Latin and North American troubles lies in the establishment of socialism. The report has been very favorably received by many center and center-left Latin American newspapers, as well as by many persons in the liberal wings of both major United States parties. An unexpected dissent, however, has come from the adherents of a pro–Alliance for Progress view. Their ideas were publicly aired in *The New Republic*, by Arthur Schlesinger, Jr., on January 4 and 11, 1975, with the satirical subtitle, "A Light Skiff on a Deep Ocean."

It is to these last antagonists that I address this essay. I do so not because they are the commission's most acerbic critics, but because the questions they raise far transcend the document at issue. Vulgarly put, what is in contention is how American liberals should think about the Cold War, the relationship between democracy at home and democracy abroad, the proper uses of American power

[1]Professor Silvert was a member of the Commission on United States–Latin American Relations, and the previous essay in this volume represents his contribution to the commission's report. —*The Publisher*.

overseas. In pondering all of these points, Mr. Schlesinger and I share a commitment to democratic values. But we differ in how we try to make those values live, in how we seek to avoid having democracy's defense mechanisms destroy the host body.

Schlesinger accurately points out that the report barely mentions the word *democracy,* that the commission would have the United States diplomatically recognize all Latin countries regardless of their political bent, and that there are no prescriptions for dealing differently with totalitarianism *a la chilena* and fledgling democracies *a la venezolana.* The report's strong statements against violations of human rights, he legitimately argues, are not a substitute for policy discriminations based on other measures of the politically decent. And again he is entirely correct. But he is wrong, I think, in assuming that the commission cared not a fig for the growth of democracy in Latin America, or that in its recommendations it intended to surrender a concern for the growth of democratic *substance* (not necessarily *forms*) in the Latin nations.

My understanding is that the commission rejected the alliance's "embrace for our friends, and a handshake for our enemies" for several reasons. Even during the incumbency of President Kennedy, the cool hand was mailed for the Bay of Pigs, gloved for clandestine operations in Ecuador, and beringed for diddling with electoral politics in Peru. For its part, the *abrazo* (embrace) pushed many Latin governments into national planning they could not intellectually control, promised poor people that they could be economically better off even without increased political power, and promoted trade unions on the basis of how their leaders felt about Slavic affairs. Second, the feeling was that fine-tuning other people's polities is as much beyond our capabilities as fine-tuning our own economy. Third, governmental ideological pretensions are mistrusted in this age of the grand lie. But that last reason is put negatively and does not do justice either to my own thinking or to that of a majority of my colleagues on the commission. We thought much more positively, and thus consciously tried to erect a policy that would oppose meddlesomeness, let alone interventionism, and that would yet be consistent with democratic aspirations in Latin America and at home. Schlesinger totally missed this point.

He writes that the report's recommendations are "random," that there is no line, but only a statement of scattered and trite observations. Here we enter into implementation, into how our own and other people's social good is to be promoted through foreign policy, and here I disagree entirely with his judgment. The essential line of the report is as follows:

• In recent years many Latin countries have markedly increased their political, economic and social capacities; further, they have moved toward genuine autonomy in their international relations.

• The United States has lost some of its power to influence the politics of other nations, although we remain far from powerless.

• Ideas about how to achieve social change and the good society are in disarray almost everywhere.

• Raw physical security and the Cold War have ceased to be keystones of North American foreign policy debates; at the same time we are less certain of the stability and purposes of our major national institutions.

• Whatever the panoply of international agencies and transnational "actors" (mostly corporations), the nation-state is still the "social community of last resort," the only scene within which equality before the law and other elements of political freedom can be effectively sought. That statement does not belie the fact that torture and atrocities take place within nation-states. The issue is not *whether* to engage in "nation-building," but what *kind* of nation is desirable.

The commission thought it beyond the capacity or will of the United States to dictate what kinds of nations the Latins should build for themselves. We thought it enough to state that it was time to stop trying to hinder the building of national communities—in other words, to get out of Latin America's way, letting those countries find their own path to wherever they may be going. Each country will have to make its own revolution, just as we made ours. If we can provide expert help, some money, and meaningful goodwill, then fine. But in no case should we employ covert or overt force of a military or economic nature to enter directly into the internal play of Latin American politics. We thought this prescription good for both the United States and Latin America, and that therefore it could be the basis for a foreign policy of mutual self-interest. The relevant portion of the commission report reads:

> Of late, the United States has faced a variety of challenges: unemployment, racial conflict, the long war in Vietnam, and a major crisis of governmental leadership—all of which have seriously tested the coherence of the United States as a nation. This testing is likely to continue amidst the developing energy crisis, commodity shortages, and inflation now facing the world. All of this is bound to affect U.S. ways of thinking about the international community. What is most needed at this point is an international policy that will not further strain the

nation, but rather contribute to solving some of these problems. Significantly, the process of nation-building in the Latin American countries also depends on the same sort of international policy. Thus, a commonality of interest exists between the United States and Latin America at this juncture. The shared experience of working to solve problems which the United States and Latin America face can only serve to strengthen ties between the peoples of North and South America.

My view is that the United States is out of control because our systems of economic and social accountability are breaking down. We combine depression with inflation because market mechanisms can no longer control the gross outlines of economic behavior. We get Watergates because we have been losing the meaning of citizenship, because the parties and the formal institutions of the several governments under which we live have become clogged, bureaucratically self-serving, and sensitive to only a limited array of organized pressures. Certainly the way out cannot lie in a vapid internationalism or an equally vapid appeal to the good natures of our governors and the technocratic managers of our economic machinery. A democratic solution must lie in boldly rebuilding the national community; it must have to do with making citizenship once again meaningful, with welcoming all of our fellows into the social nation in an equality of condition (not of hollow "opportunity" alone), with deciding that economics will become the slave of our policy and not the other way around. I do not believe that the solution to the problems of democracy lies in international rationalizations worked by transnational managers, latter-day Realpoliticians, or military-political missionaries. When democracy gets into trouble, the solution lies in more democracy—and not in the nostrums of snake-oil salesmen on white horses.

The commission report says that in basic policy what is good for us is also good for Latin Americans. The first step is to give them room by removing the threat of the varied forms of interventionism as a continuing part of their domestic political constraints. The second is to begin to treat them as fully functioning members of the international community, like other self-respecting states. Thus, we should help them to deepen their autonomy through everything from making technological information available to encouraging their participation in intraregional and global relations. We should attempt to even out the terms of trade and to help Latin American countries to understand and bargain with governmental and private economic agencies. In short, all the specific recommendations are pointed toward reinforcing trends within each Latin American country toward strong nationhood. The objective is to promote collective bargaining in international affairs, leaving behind the American indignity and the Latin irresponsibility involved in paternalism. I think none of the commission members expects such an outcome to lead automatically to democracy. But certainly, whatever the causes may be, past relationships have not promoted such democracy either—even with the Alliance for Progress. So, we were content with attempting to further the essential precondition for democracy, which is the formation of responsible national community.

My own greatest area of dissatisfaction with the commission report concerns the failure to discriminate between strictly defined totalitarianisms, on the one hand, and quasidemocracies and varied kinds of authoritarianisms (but not full-blown totalitarianisms), on the other. The other commission members refused to accept my suggestion that we propose that the United States treat a country like Pinochet's Chile as it treated Allende's, or as it is treating Cuba. I can understand and respect their desire, however, to prevent diplomatic recognition, economic embargoes, military intervention, and "destabilization" from becoming "variables," real options in the hands of our policy-makers. Their view is certainly eaiser to implement than my own and more consistent with the primary line of the commission report. The commission's general sensitivity to the issue, however, is revealed not only in the strong human rights statement, but also in the appeal to make our country a haven for political refugees of any hue and an active participant in attempts to ameliorate the effects of official terror.

Schlesinger also faults the report for not having gone more deeply into problems caused by United States private investments, "the question that probably poisons United States relations more than any other." He applauded what was said, but failed to recognize what was implicit—that we in the United States will have to develop the clout to control our own economy, as each Latin American country will have to control its own. Where, in the absence of a global government, is that international political power that will permit the control of global corporations? The control can come from nowhere but national states and the international organizations of those states, such as the Andean Group in Latin America. As of this writing, some Latin American countries are organizing themselves for a forthcoming meeting in Buenos Aires to apply a legally binding code of conduct on transnational corporations. The United States, in company with Brazil, is hindering the full spelling out of those controls. The sense of the commission report opposes such a blunting of an attempt by Latin American countries to control their national destinies. Thus the report implies that the American government should not attempt to regulate the operation of American companies, say, in Mexico. That job is for the Mexicans, and we should officially owe no more to companies working there than we owe to any American citizen.

Schlesinger concludes by calling the report "shallow," a wasted "opportunity to educate a future administration," and "a sorry retrogression from an earlier ideal of a hemisphere united by devotion to democratic institutions." In this case shallowness may be in the eye of the beholder. Turning democratic ideals into reality must also involve hewing close to the truth, eschewing self-delusion. Mr. Schlesinger should not have misquoted the report; accuracy would have strengthened his case. He writes that "one would not recognize the Alliance for Progress from the description given in the report—as a Cold War instrumentality dominated by the 'overriding goal' of 'military security.' " Here is what the report says:

> Over the past 25 years, U.S. primacy in Western affairs has been achieved at high cost—contributing to inflation, a war orientation in industrial development, political discord, and extensive secrecy in government. It is no small wonder, then, given an atmosphere of primary concern for national security, that relations with the less powerful nations, and Latin America particularly, were shaped largely by that concern. The Alliance for Progress was in some measure an attempt to accommodate security considerations with concern for the domestic welfare of Latin American nations. The Alliance was a reflection of generous intentions and Cold War considerations.

The commission decided to enter this decade and acknowledge the end of the Cold War in its classical form. The political "reality" that we recognized is that working toward a hemispheric policy based on freely established interests demands that we promote the power and authority of the Latin countries themselves, for without strength there can be no real freedom of choice. The *realidad* we took into account is the still uneven but vastly changed potential of most Latin American countries. And that's good, for only the grown-up can be ethical. Children can be but naughty or sweet, but adults can choose either the sinfulness of dictatorship or the morality of democracy. It's time for the United States to chuck the notion that it must guide its Latin children, if only because a lot of them are already taking off. Latin America is having its bar mitzvah, and the least we can do is go to the party, pen and pencil in hand.

1975

Frames for the
Caribbean Experience

IF IT IS TRUE that only inane generalizations hold equally for all of the political units in the Caribbean, it is also true that seeing each one as unique is intellectual laziness that must impede understanding and policy decision. The first task of this essay will be to lay out the broad similarities and differences among the multitude of Caribbean polities.

Let us first list some of the generalizations that apply rather more than less to the entire area, and later turn to criteria for dividing the islands into discrete families. A very persuasive case is made by Professor Gordon Lewis in *The United States and the Caribbean* (edited by Tad Szulc) for weighing the islands' histories in terms of three grand periods: the slave-holding colonial epoch, the post-Emancipation or Independence period, running from the beginning of the last century to the end of World War II, and the contemporary era of growing domestic autonomy, even within a structure of relationship to a metropolitan power. This commonness of background promotes similar social explanations, despite striking cultural differences. At least as important, however, is a second overarching likeness: the intertwining of color and class differences that defines the social structure of each of the islands. The felicitous word *pigmentocracy* applies to some degree everywhere, from mulatto-black Haiti to Latin Dominican Republic.

Another constant is the small size, in both area and population, of all the islands. We are accustomed to recognizing the self-reinforcing effects of race and class when they are mixed together, but we have little to go on in discussions of the effect of size of human unit on the quality of human interaction. Small-group specialists in the social sciences sometimes attempt to generalize their findings to nations. Though few scholars accept that procedure without grave reservations, it is still somewhat difficult to disentangle the idea of city-state from that of nation-state. In the Caribbean we are invited to speak of small states and mini-states; perhaps the better designations would be town-states, city-states, and small nation-states as descriptive of unit size, but not necessarily of unit quality. In any event, the matter of size invariably introduces a fourth common element, worry concerning the viability of these insular establishments. How small states are to survive in a big-power world is a question not only of international politics but of access to markets, of fitting institutional arrangements in which "small" does not necessarily spell "weak," of the proper use of complex modern technology, and of the many other problems that flow from political economies of small scale.

Whatever the problems, however, the Caribbean is not to be classed with the world's *Lumpenproletariat* of underdevelopment. In *per capita* income terms, most of the islands are on the high side of the intermediately developed, with Puerto Rico falling into the statistical bag of the developed. This common income fact is clustered with other shared economic phenomena: weak economies dependent upon a few exports, spotty concentrations of natural resources, high rates of under- and unemployment, elevated dependence on external sources of capital and technology, and too great market dependence on too few consumers. The demographic facts of Caribbean life reveal generally high population densities, whether in Hispanic-, French-, British-, or Dutch-influenced areas; literacy rates that range from reasonably acceptable to high, coupled with low attainments at advanced educational levels; strong migration tides in response to low economic opportunity at home; and those other manifestations of populations mobilized for participant national life but not blessed with the institutional orders that will permit their full integration into their societies.

Although the list of commonalities is not exhausted, only one more significant constant will be mentioned here: the pervasive and continuing influence of Western culture, no matter what the particularities of historical growth, metropolitan power, economic situation, or even class order and nature of institutional structure. A stubborn attachment to the language of democracy, even in contemporary Cuban ideology, is a recurrently mentioned symptom of this Westernization. Language, ideal patterns to be emulated, school curricula, ideology, and many other aspects of life-style testify to what is not an ornament but a primary mover of Caribbean events.

MODERNITY AND DIVERSITY

The recitation of these common characteristics and their synthesis into an overall picture serve at least the negative purpose of telling us what the Caribbean is not. Great droves of peasants living at subsistence are not the fate of the Caribbean; nor are the countries like some of Africa's new states, damned by tribalism and uncertainly held together by thin veneers of foreign-educated elites. Conflict between church and state is in the past, and battles against colonial overlords do not loom in the future. The meaning of these and other indications of complexity is that the Caribbean's problems are not solvable through simple quantitative changes: more food, fewer people, increased housing, more or less of what is. Rather, the problems are qualitative as well as quantitative: the ways in which communities are to be organized, the nature of national identities that are to be forged, the substantive meanings of varied styles of integrating individuals and groups into national and local and supranational communities, the mix of ideologies that can explain and rationalize and stabilize the processes of change. In sum, most of the Caribbean islands have developed enough internal strength through institutional complexity and specialization to begin to determine the shapes of their own social fates. This is the positive meaning of their common heritage and their common being today. Within their likenesses, however, they are sufficiently different so that they can neither coexist under universal sociopolitical umbrellas nor carelessly transfer experience from one to another.

One way of classifying the Caribbean societies would be in terms of general social effectiveness—a typology that would combine criteria of economic viability, political organization, race and class, cultural cohesion, historical relationship to European and American powers, and contemporary international relations. To employ such a classification, we must begin by defining what it is that we mean by effectiveness, or viability, not of any kind of society, but of one that pretends to fit and enjoy the modern estate. We need not stretch for esoteric criteria. The following list is suggested, in no particular order of significance:

(a) A viable modern society possesses mechanisms for the orderly transfer of political power through time.

(b) A viable modern society possesses an urban life-style. Such societies do not necessarily include large cities, but an urbane and worldly quality characterizes social relations. Another way to put it is that the secular city increases freedom of choice in personal relations and consumer habits. "City air makes man free" is a medieval legal dictum still meaningful today and not belied by the fact that some urban situations imprison man. That is, it is possible to live in cities and not be urbane, and possible to be urbane and live in the country. It is the quality of urbanity that is important, not ecological fact.

(c) A viable modern society possesses an industrial life-style. I refer not to labor within industrial complexes, but to the consumption of industrial products and to work relationships determined by merit through impersonal market mechanisms. It is not necessary that a particular country have either large cities or a massive industrial complex in order to enjoy a ramified communications system and an open class structure that permits individuals to find their places according to their talents and desires. If this looseness of association between physical plant and human orders did not exist, it would be impossible to explain the relative degree of advance of Costa Rica within Caribbean basin countries, or that of Denmark within Europe.

(d) A viable modern society organizes itself in a community pattern whose largest unit is the nation-state. The earmarks of national community are that all men are equal before the laws and the community's institutions, no matter what the accidents of their birth or their systems of beliefs are. What is required in return of the citizen is his recognition of that community as deserving of his ultimate loyalty in the event of international conflict or of such other conflicts as those arising from religious, economic, or ideological beliefs and interests. The national community is the organizing unit for the legitimacy that produces the consent that in turn makes possible governmental effectiveness and the settlement of dispute in such a way as to avoid ultimate showdowns and promote the acceptance of interim working solutions.

(e) A viable modern society possesses an educational institution that is open to all and that empowers individuals, without regard to class or color, to participate in the national community and share in the industrial and urban cultures of the modern situation.

(f) A viable modern society possesses a system of explanation of its existence—or an ideology, or an appropriate set of ideologies—that reinforces fitting human relations, rationalizes "national identity," and stabilizes the intricate social relations that build flexibility into modern secular societies.

Various authors have spoken of the difficult search for national identity and national organization in the Caribbean. I have suggested the above criteria to define the elements of the modern national society and to give a basis for judging the ways in which given Caribbean societies are near to or distant from national status. The question is being begged as to *why* such desires for national organization are almost universal in the developing world. Perhaps the developing states want to emulate the experience of the developed world; perhaps something in the nature of man channels his gregariousness into the largest vessels he can find. Whatever is the case, we surely are dealing with a combination of factors. In any event, we cannot address ourselves to a general discussion of the Caribbean societies without somehow dealing with a political desire that is also a program for overriding social organization.

We have neither the data nor the space rigorously to characterize the Caribbean societies by these criteria. Nevertheless, even a summary exercise in organizing our materials along these lines should reveal developmental gaps and policy problems among our cases. To begin with the thorniest case, Cuba, we find that the Castro government has been strongly pursuing the creation of many aspects of national community but has made little progress in institutionalizing its political process. Even confirmed *antifidelistas* are usually willing to give Castro's government high marks in such endeavors as education, race relations, medical attention, and the mobilization and integration of lower-class elements into national life. Even Castro himself gives his efforts low marks in lessening personalism, ordering administrative procedures, organizing the mechanics of national economic life, and inculcating a full range of attitudes toward work and social life that will lessen the need for coercion and exhortation. Within the Hispanic portion of Latin America, Cuba has become one of the most secularized and national of all states, able to survive an amazing array of adversity stemming from internal disarray as well as external opposition. The explanation does not lie merely in the relatively high degree of advance to be seen in pre-Castro Cuba; the failures and successes of the present Cuban government could not have occurred without that regime's inheritance from the past, but they also could not have happened without the personal, ideological, and international power configurations created by the principal actors in Cuba's post-revolutionary drama.

The Dominican Republic, to remain within the Hispanic orbit, does not by any means exhibit Cuba's degree of national organization. Ranking low on almost every indicator suggested, it reflects clearly in its politics a population left grossly unprepared to comprise a national citizenry. Generations of authoritarian rule have deprived government of legitimacy and thus of continuity, have contributed to a class structure that impedes social mobility, have supported an economic structure antagonistic to the development of urbane people and industrial organization, and have prevented the growth of indigenous systems of explanation that can provide the dignity of social self-awareness. The potential developmental advantages of an ethnically homogeneous population and of an agriculturally rich island have thus been washed away in a tide of greedy authoritarianism swelled by international fear and shortsightedness. The Cuban and Dominican cases are very well worth this contraposition, for their divergent histories, even within similar geographical and cultural settings, underscore the autonomy of human action and power.

If Cuba is to be counted among the most national of Caribbean states, although in twisted form, and if the Dominican Republic is one of the less national, Haiti can be counted as the least national of all. Often called the Mississippi of the Americas, because its vital statistics always put it in last place among those countries belonging to the Organization of American States, Haiti lacks a social recruitment base for a politics of national development. Its leaders may have the education and the will to mold world ideologies to their perceptions of Haitian needs, and even to create original systems of thought, but the ready creation of an articulated and self-aware popular following is probably not possible under present social conditions. Cuba's leaders profited from the ease of their campaign of national mobilization; recent experience in the Dominican Republic reveals that a reasonably large percentage of its population, too, is organizable for nation-building ends. By this critically important measure of readiness for modernizing change, Haiti probably falls entirely short: any nationalistic government it may have in the future is condemned to mobilize its population through the dangerous exercise of charismatic appeal and force.

Jamaica and Trinidad, the two largest British-influenced independent states, show strikingly differing configurations from Cuba and the Dominican Republic, let alone Haiti. Traditionally economically monocultural like their Hispanic neighbors, tied to specific international markets for both purchases and sales, lagging in higher educational facilities, and weighed down by even more rigid class systems, Jamaica and Trinidad are similarly in crises of national identification within their particular institutional structures. These countries are still able to operate within neoparliamentary governmental forms; party politics and economic power and color and class have become entangled in a form of pluralism that has thus far permitted constitutional process to overcome political disturbance and has bought some time for the working out of the processes of egalitarianism that are important to nation-building because they mitigate divisiveness. But high unemployment rates in these contexts are not only economic facts; they are also descriptive of alienation from the other institutional mainstreams of national life. The ethnic mosaic of Trinidad, the Guyana-like ethnic confrontation opportunistically fomented in Trinidad's recent party and ideological history, and the remaining color resentments of Jamaica provide fertile soil for future conflict, especially if such differences continue to be reinforced by class divisions. Great social distances between strata of these countries' populations prevent the emergence of the urban and industrial life-styles within which other diversities can be maintained, and both the quality and quantity of their educational systems are insufficient for the state of readiness of their populations. Still, neither of these countries is paralyzed by castelike exclusions, although desperate class antagonisms are entirely possible. Their relatively high degrees of attachment to institutionalized political process and to the rule of law are assets that should not be squandered in a narrow drive for economic growth, one of whose ends must be precisely the enrichment of the political structures that already exist.

Frank McDonald, in his article in the collection mentioned earlier, *The United States and the Caribbean,* makes all of these points about the British-influenced states. He emphasizes, moreover, that all the Commonwealth states, not just the larger ones, suffer from a lack of economic autonomy, reflected in the maintenance of systems of social exclusion that prevent national consciousness from becoming effective. Black Power movements in these islands have become anti–foreign white and economically collectivist; this is the means toward social cohesion within the islands and perhaps among them. Yet color consciousness is still reinforced by class lines, which in turn are an immediate reflection of raw economic circumstances. As McDonald demonstrates, drives to dismantle this linkage of color, class, and economics are common to all the formerly British islands, whether they are large or small, whether they are politically independent or have the status of associated states.

At this point in our discussion it should be apparent that the conditions of effective nationhood are holistic: all of them are needed, in one or another effective combination. We can draw a further important conclusion: nationhood, in the sense in which we are using the term, does not depend on formal political sovereignty but on the appropriate organization of community. A third conclusion is that population and territorial size influence the paths along which nation-building proceeds but are not determinants of nation-hood. When it comes to nationalism, Anguillans share the restless-ness of their maritime neighbors in the largest Caribbean states, such as Cuba and Jamaica.

Now we can situate Puerto Rico, the Virgin Islands, and the Dutch and French islands in their fitting places in this discussion of diversity within sameness. Puerto Rico is an integral part of the complex mainland economic structure, no longer condemned to producing dessert crops for export and to importing luxury goods for its resident elite. Its educational system is complex, and it has a large floating population able to move back and forth between the island and the major cities of the mainland. The weak fabric in the web of Puerto Rican social development is political in the grand sense: a confusion of cultural identities, a lack of ideological convic-tion, discomfort with the juridical structure of the state in its rela-tions with the United States, a suspicion that the Puerto Rican experience is not transferable to neighboring islands because of the special relation with the mainland, and a lack of definition of how much responsibility to accept as a part of the United States and how much as Puerto Rican. Surely problems of class, color, employment, economic development, educational growth, and the role of religion in cultural life remain important. The point being made here, how-ever, is that economic change and closely allied occupational mobility have tended to lead the parade of Puerto Rican developmental elements; the lagging aspects are primarily political in nature. Con-versely, in the Commonwealth Caribbean formal solutions to politi-cal problems have preceded economic elaboration and some mea-sure of self-determination. In both places, the strands of national integration are strained by this uneven development.

Even a hasty reduction to speculative generalizations, which is what we have been about so far, leaves us with an appreciation of variety and of potential. Only the mean-spirited will see the Carib-bean's mixed development in a pessimistic light, for they are the ones who equate complexity with trouble and go searching always in vain for the one magic button that will bring social contentment into being. But we should learn from worldwide experience that there is no single secret to be found. As the Caribbean islands have been assuming their own political and social identities, breaking away from the culture-bound nostrums of their respective colonial offices, they have also begun to be the site of the arguments and strategies for development under test elsewhere in Latin America, Asia, and Africa. It is to the Caribbean variants of these recipes for change that we now turn.

IDEOLOGIES OF DEVELOPMENT

For the purposes of discussing strategies for change, the Caribbean should be thought of within the more general Latin American environment. Not only are Cuba, the Dominican Republic, Haiti, and sometimes Puerto Rico normally classified as being within Latin America, but also the loosening or breaking of colonial ties throughout the area points up analogous situations that make some Latin American experiences increasingly applicable in the Caribbean basin. Like the islands, Latin America is an intermediately developed outpost of Western culture. Also as in the islands, political autonomy is threatened by economic fragility and dependence. Employment problems, desires for industrialization, class and race complexities, the "special relationship" with the United States, internecine quarrels, and many other problems are endemic to Latin America, as they are to the Caribbean. Ideological disputation concerning the most viable as well as the most desirable paths to development is now virtually the same throughout the Caribbean as it is and has been in Latin America for the entire post–World War II period.

There are three major linear approaches to development, discussed in the following sections:

The Economic Approach. The classical developmental strategy, consciously attempted in Latin America since the mid-1930s, argues that industrialization is the road to emancipation from one-crop, exploitative relations with the developed world. Industry was to bring in its train educated people, opportunity as well as desire for advancement, the creation of middle-class interests, and political pluralism and democratic process. Instead, some of Latin America's economically most highly developed countries have found very different ways of life. Argentina has been in political disarray for forty years, Mexico has become a single-party authoritarianism, Brazil is in the grip of the military, and Uruguay is in an unhappy torpor. Not even economic emancipation has flowed from industrialization, for the new factories have increased the need for foreign exchange to supply constituent parts and to satisfy increased effective demand. Inflation and industrialization, increased inequality of income distribution and industrialization, and political instability and industrialization have been the correlates—and not the automatic path to social decency that was initially projected. The reasons for these occurrences have been debated endlessly, of course. Some twelve years ago, it began to be fashionable to declare that the quality of population must make a difference, and the era of social development opened.

The Social Approach.   The social development argument is that economic advance is a necessary but insufficient condition for development; individuals must also escape from their class positions and make themselves more productive and more rational consumers. The favored method is education, of course. But social development programs, supported after the establishment of the Inter-American Development Bank by "soft" loans administered through the Social Development Trust Fund, also included assistance for housing, the establishment of cooperatives, and many other devices to close the gap especially separating lower- from middle-class groups. The Alliance for Progress was designed to combine economic and social developmental approaches, permitting Latin and North Americans to work together in a complex mix of private and public funding, with expenditure patterns sufficiently flexible to fit each country. It would be unjust to label this attempt a failure, for it did not have the time, the funds, the ideological decisiveness, or the sure knowledge to work through to completion. If self-sustaining and free societies were to be the fruit of these programs, however, it is obvious that Latin America did not respond; there are more overt governments of force in Latin America now than before the Alliance was launched, a statement that should not be seen as describing cause-and-effect.

The Panacea of Political Union.   Not since the nineteenth century have political men placed much faith in constitutions and political forms as means of assuring the good public life. This shying away from the political dimension of development has been reinforced by the entrance of international organizations and banking agencies into development assistance; the overt exacting of political conditions for aid smacks of interventionism, an increasingly unpopular concept in international affairs despite the frequency of its real occurrence. Instead, faith in form has been transferred to pressures for regional organization. The dream is old in Latin America, dating from Independence and the Bolivarian ideal of Gran Colombia. Earlier in this century, Peru's Aprista party pushed for a gigantic Indo-American structure to balance the Latin against the Anglo-Saxon in this hemisphere. Within recent years we have seen the collapse of the Caribbean Federation and the hesitant gropings of such emulations of European experience as the Latin American Free Trade Association, the Central American Customs Union, and, most recently, the Andean Group. Latin Americans have entered into these economic arrangements with scarcely hidden hopes of eventually being able to arrive at an overarching political union. Unhappily, only modest (though important) economic gains have been their lot, and in no case have planned goals for organizational growth been met. The economic sense of these arrangements is clear: they are designed to create larger markets for Latin America's industrial plant, to rationalize production and achieve economies of scale, and to permit a relatively free international flow of investment capital among Latin American countries. There is a scarcely hidden debility, however: the horizontal expansion of markets across international borders may well have the effect of inhibiting the vertical growth of markets within countries that would permit greater equity of income distribution. In any event, the success of none of these agencies has as yet been sufficiently sustained to permit rigorous judgment of their areas of efficacy.

The three approaches we have discussed can all be labeled reformist. There are also revolutionary approaches to development, coming from both right and left; their common element is that they assume that iron control of the state is the independent variable from which will flow other aspects of development. That is, they do not assume that formalistic political arrangements, economic change, or social preparation will lead to desired political change; their view is that the political organization must first be seized and then employed as the instrumentality for socioeconomic development, which in turn can assist in political evolution. Many variants of these views are under experimentation in Latin America. A few are summarized as follows:

Tutelary Military Governments. The present governments of Brazil and Peru are both cases in point, despite the fact that the former is frankly rightist in color, the latter inclined toward a quasipopulist nationalism. They are revolutionary not merely in the sense that they supplant constitutional civil government and (in the case of the Brazilians), employ novel forms of political torture and repression, but that they also change the power distribution system. The Brazilian government has supplanted the traditional Liberal element in that country's upper class and has stripped the intelligentsia of its power; the Peruvian administration has broken the power of the landed aristocracy and is beginning to change the life-chances of rural and urban lower-class persons.

The two governments vary widely in their approach to economic development. The Brazilian government employs the power of the state to constrain wages, suppress effective trade union organization, and inhibit economic nationalism, thus promoting foreign investment and encouraging local entrepreneurs by guaranteeing high profit margins. The Peruvians are moving toward a state capitalism as rapidly as their techniques and understanding of the politics of the situation permit them to do so. It is this difference in attitude that in turn probably makes the major difference in the amount of repression exercised; indeed, the Peruvians have engaged in only the most minimal exercise of police control of the opposition.

The Trujillo administration in the Dominican Republic and the first Batista administration in Cuba were early forms of tutelary military government. A contemporary case is that of Nicaragua.

Falangist and Other Populist Movements of the Right. No mature fascism has ever managed to take office in a Latin American country, but nationalist, corporativist parties have existed since the 1930s, and they have been revived in modern form in Argentina and to some extent in Brazil. Radical Peronism, as it has developed in the past decade, is moving into an alliance with certain groups of Argentina's left. More than a simple alliance of convenience among groups sharing respect for the same violent means, a National Marxism is developing that has already gained significance in Argentina's internal politics, and has some chance of spreading in a Hispanic world accustomed to thinking of institutional organization in corporate terms. The formal organization of the Mexican polity is already quasicorporate; although that country has its peculiar mix of authoritarianism and democracy, it is not a fascism in any classical sense of that word. The Caribbean has been little influenced by these currents that are perennial in other Latin American countries, and there is little reason to think that the former British, Dutch, and French areas are susceptible to this kind of ideology.

Nationalist Socialism. To a social scientist or anyone interested in the sociology of knowledge, Cuba is one of the most fascinating cases of guided social change to be found anywhere in the world. For the moment, leave aside the grisly facts of Cold War, the inflamed rhetoric on all sides, and the dryness of statistical numbers games. Castro and his associates are attempting to create an absolutely egalitarian, national community based on a theory of value that has nothing to do with economic criteria, and everything to do directly with the affective meaning of man's activities in his community. Only Maoist China approaches the degree of radical innovation being pursued by Cuba's leadership, who unabashedly speak of the creation of a new man—new in his sense of good and bad, in his world view, in his approach to work and labor, and in his identification with community. Obviously, we cannot know whether Utopia will become Havana. But the very radicalness of the present Cuban vision has served to limit its attractiveness to mass groups in other countries: the price in cultural change seems impossibly high, the concatenation of leadership elements and followership dedication and North American *laissez-passer* too accidental to permit easy replication. Thus it is entirely understandable that the Cuban case has been self-isolating in the Caribbean.

Our earlier attempts at typology-building may demonstrate their usefulness again at this point. Haiti, the Dominican Republic, and such states as Jamaica and Trinidad do not at this time have the available masses to make possible a repetition of the internal dynamics of the Cuban Revolution. If elites in alliance with limited numbers of others can make an armed revolt, they would not find it as easy as in Cuba to integrate great groups of lower-class and lower-middle-class persons into national institutional structures. Still, all such matters are relative, and long-term predictions in such a matter are feckless. Whatever the future may hold for the Caribbean as a whole, whatever the real degree to which the Cubans approach their ideal state, that country is now unequivocally the most secular and socially national state in the Ibero-American world. Whether it will become even more isolated from its geographical and cultural neighbors or more meaningful as an example depends rather less on Cuba than on conditions in the surrounding area.

The search for national viability and adequate ideologies is just beginning in most of the Caribbean. The role of the industrial states, and especially of the United States, will continue to be critical in this unfolding odyssey.

INTER-AMERICAN RELATIONS

The concern of the United States for the Caribbean and its long-standing readiness to act unilaterally in its perceived interests are well documented. From the earliest days of the republic, some political men have seen Mexico, Central America, and the Caribbean as crucial to United States national development; later, some definers of Manifest Destiny included much Caribbean real estate in what was to be the Greater America. It was only much later, however, near the turn of this century, that physical force accompanied political and economic interest into the region. Since that time, to some degree all Caribbean governments have had to mix into their political analyses the facts of United States cultural, economic, political, and military behavior.

American intentions are, however, not easy to guess. Often North American attention is directed elsewhere, and Caribbean policy has been conducted by military and diplomatic persons accountable only routinely for their actions, isolated from high policy levels in the absence of crisis situations. In addition, before World War II American activities in the Caribbean were carried out in a simplistic conviction of what was right and good, unencumbered by the ideological and scientific doubts that have crept into foreign political and economic relations in the past thirty years. Most important, however, is that American policy has been and is ambivalent in motivation. For example, President Nixon was quoted in the *New York Times* on October 1, 1970, as telling Yugoslavia's President Tito that "all nations should respect 'the rights of others to choose their own paths' "; he "applauded Marshal Tito for giving heart—by his independence from Moscow—to those who chart their own political course." If that statement were taken literally, then one could confidently have stated that all North American armed and covert intervention in the political affairs of Caribbean states would be eschewed during President Nixon's tenure. And, indeed, there is a long-standing American tradition favoring self-determination. Still, one can always argue, as Dean Rusk essentially did during the Dominican crisis of 1964, that any leftist revolution favors Communists, that Communists are part of an international network, and therefore that American intervention to counter leftist revolution is necessary in order to preserve self-determination. The fact of the matter seems to be that the United States has acted overtly in countering recent leftist moves in at least three Caribbean states, but has been able or willing only to harass the most important case, Cuba. Even if American policy has a clearly discernible bias, it lacks explicitness, evenness of application, and consistency either of criteria or of interpretation of adduced fact. The reasons for this confusion are many.

First, as is notorious, there is a genuine and profound confusion among Americans concerning the proper role of this country in the world. This primary puzzlement is certified by uncertainties concerning the effectiveness of American developmental programs overseas and by more than a little suspicion that aid is often counterproductive, always interventionist, sometimes arrogant, always the product of guesswork, and all too often a preliminary of military commitments to protect what have become vested interests.

Second, the American public has been slow to understand the relationship between conventional weapons and the marriage of missiles to thermonuclear explosives; policymakers, too, are con-

fused about the optimal mix of military men and equipment necessary in present world conditions. This uncertainty is compounded in
an area close to the United States, one that traditionally has been
designated as obviously vital to national security, as our "backyard,"
as the ultimate test of our determination to protect ourselves, and so
forth. In the past, when distance was a critical military matter and
the United States was comfortable behind its ocean bastions, no
American government could, with domestic impunity, look lightly
upon a military threat implanted in the Caribbean. It is not that
today's situation is entirely different but that it is sufficiently
changed to demand more subtle judgments than in the past. For
example, when President Kennedy took to television to warn the
Soviet Union to withdraw its missiles from Cuba, he made a point of
saying that we would remain within the bull's-eye of Russian IBM's
whether the missiles were in Cuba or elsewhere. He was trying to
introduce psychological software into what is too often treated as
only a question of hardware.

Third is the very complex set of United States attitudes toward
Latin America and the Caribbean. There can be no certainty in
describing these attitudes, of course, and even less sureness in ascrib-
ing them to significant sectors of the American population. For
example, Midwesterners know little of the black population of the
West Indies, but observers of the racial scene in the East, as well as
in such Canadian cities as Toronto, know of the leadership role
carried out by Caribbean migrants and recognize a cultural difference between American and Caribbean black populations. Where
Spanish-speaking populations mix, for example, it is well known that
Cubans are much more prepared to assume middle-class roles in
American society than are Puerto Ricans or Dominicans. Indeed, the
motion picture *Popi* was built around the theme of the favored
reception given to Cubans in New York, and the discrimination
practiced against Puerto Ricans.

The cloudy and unevenly distributed perceptions of Caribbeans
are hardly cleared up when matters of ideology and national security
enter. From the beginning, the Cuban Revolution has provoked very
sharp reactions in the United States; they do not need repetition
here, except for the comment that Cuban events have so deeply
affected North American attitudes as to give tone to American
politics. Few ordinary Americans react profoundly when economic
interests are threatened in the Caribbean, but certainly their feelings
are sharpened when Russian nuclear submarine bases are reported
abuilding in Cuba, when they are warned of threats to the Panama
Canal from Communists in Guatemala, or when they are told that

Guyana is becoming a Communist outpost on the South American continent. Military actions in the Caribbean, then, cannot solely be responses to real military activities by others; they must also be military aspects of political pressures and appreciations inside the United States. It is in this way that the Cold War must intimately affect United States–Caribbean relations so long as United States–Soviet relations rely so heavily on psychological elements in order to avoid nuclear ones.

Another complex psychological strain is set up by the tension between domestic and international needs in the American polity. If the United States wants to abandon the role of world policeman, does it also want to lay down its variant of the White Man's Burden? Does it wish a "special relationship" with Latin America, and a particularly special one with the Caribbean because of geographical proximity? Confusion is amplified by the relationship of Britain, France, and the Netherlands to the Caribbeans, with many Americans not knowing which islands are independent and which in juridical relationship to a European power. Thus, concern with other than Haiti, Puerto Rico, the Virgin Islands, Cuba, and the Dominican Republic is often seen as merely juggling the hot chestnuts of others.

This kaleidoscopic set of public attitudes gives government and pressure groups broad freedom of action in all matters except those concerning Cuba. Even the latest Dominican invasion, although it occasioned a wide wave of antiadministration rhetoric and caused the first open break between Senator Fulbright and President Johnson, was generally viewed as a spark off the Cold War–Vietnam–Middle East bonfire. Soon that incident passed into mythology as a great administration victory, and little mention of it is now made outside circles of specialists. In the absence of conviction and the presence of confusion, the definition of issues remains securely in the hands of government officials and groups with special interests in the Caribbean—a leeway not at all conducive to policy continuity, for it promotes reactions on the basis of personalities and transitory perceptions and explanations, instead of actions bounded by established understandings and limits.

These relative uncertainties concerning United States intentions and behavior in the Caribbean are little cushioned by the international political position of the independent states of the area. Unable to form their own federation, uncertain about the costs and advantages of membership in the Organization of American States, and developing independent foreign policies, they are in no position to engage either in collective bargaining or in hard horsetrading on their own. Three recent conferences sponsored by the University of the West Indies on political and developmental problems of the area document the difficulty of these island republics in finding a comfortable niche for themselves, whether with surrounding Latin American nations, the United States and Canada, or their former European colonizers.

For their part, the Latin American nations, when they bother to consider the non-Latin Caribbean, are as ambivalent as the United States in their attitudes. Long accustomed to thinking of the Organization of American States as Latin America *cum* Anglo-Saxon North America, they are not entirely enthusiastic about an influx of new English-speaking small states. In addition, to the shame of many of them, they are not overjoyed at the prospect of commingling with "black" states—even though they are very quiet on this point, of course. More basic to their doubts, however, is their essential disdain for the OAS as an effective international mechanism. They are more comfortable with their United Nations Economic Commission for Latin America, and with the Inter-American Development Bank, than with an OAS they have for so long seen as merely an arm of United States foreign policy.

Certainly for the near future, then, the United States will remain the single most important international influence on the Caribbean, with effects varying with the degree of internal cohesion of each government, the country's relationship to Europe, and the nature of political events inside the country and in the United States. Such influence is obviously dangerous not only to the Caribbean but to an overextended and uncertain United States. In recognition of the unforeseen effects that always flow from overt intervention, the Kennedy administration added after the Bay of Pigs what was in effect a nonintervention political corollary to its Alliance for Progress, then in full process of formation. The policy, expressed almost explicitly, was that the United States would not intervene in the internal affairs of any Latin American government unless there was an obvious, overt *Cold War* threat to American national security: that is, unless the link between a Latin American state and the Soviet Union was express and military in direct implication. Otherwise, the worst that a Latin American state could risk was the economic, political, and social disfavor of the United States—a cold handshake instead of a warm *abrazo*. Coupled with avowed friendship for constitutionally chosen civilian governments, the policy bade fair to reduce military adventurism in Latin America and to remove American policymakers from necessarily tricky and projective decision-making.

Unfortunately, the Kennedy policy of restraint and attack (the latter element clearly evidenced during the Missile Crisis) was short-lived, coming to a resounding end with the Dominican intervention. Its revival would be a stabilizing force in the hemisphere and would give room to the Caribbean states for that internal experimentation through which they will have to pass to attain the internal strength that is their only long-term guarantee of integrity and security, as it is that of the United States.

CONCLUSIONS

The Caribbean states cannot give themselves the luxury of fooling themselves with the mythology of the large states. Such countries as the United States and Russia can delude themselves into thinking that their space and resources somehow give them a telluric kick, that coal and iron and frontiers make the man. The Caribbean islands would do better to make the simpler and more accurate presumption that in social matters there is only one natural resource: human beings themselves. Athens and Florence are more appropriate models for Tobago and Antigua than are Germany and Sweden; Israel and Denmark are more fitting prototypes for imitation by the Dominican Republic and Jamaica than are France and Canada. The lesson that emerges from barren Athens and desert Israel is that the quality of the population is the ultimate determinant of development. The Argentines, comfortable in their spacious and rich homeland, can allow their lush farmlands and fat cattle to make up for the deficiencies of their political organization. The Caribbean peoples, crowded onto their beautiful islands, do not have such margin for error.

The reformist finds it difficult to work directly on the quality of individuals and the nature of social organization: those problems are at the heart of grand politics, and the reformer seeks other ways to affect such matters. A major unanswered question both of development theory and international development policy is how to manage such basic change without courting highly risky and often counter-productive turmoil. Whatever the specific paths that may be chosen and the ideologies fashioned to justify and guide further change, the process will be eased and rationalized by a clear understanding that the Caribbean needs simultaneous centralization and decentralization. That is, the rationalization of relations among the islands needs to take place together with the deepening of community identification within each state. Viewed in this light, federations of any sort, or arrangements like CARIFTA, are no substitute for the erosion of class and color lines within each island, the development of over-arching national institutions and the guarantee that all persons will have access to those institutions, and the creation of the other hall-marks of the modern estate. Conversely, insular political cohesion is not a substitute for a rationalization of international economic relations, common diplomatic fronts, the creation of a viable set of international political relations, and those other devices, practices, and habits of mind that contribute to effectiveness at home and abroad.

Steps toward the creation of national and international power in the Caribbean can be eased by the understanding and sophisticated assistance of the great powers, near and far. Whether they have the generosity, the will, and the skill to do so is a moot question.

1970

V. Projections

Latin America in the World
in the Year 2000

THE WEAKNESS of history is that it has no future. And the trouble with the future is that we do not know what its history will have been. Sending the mind into the future is consequently a chancy business, but it is the only way of getting there short of clairvoyance or patient survival.

Rational projections into the future should not be leaps to a single predictive point but attempts to paint various historical situations within which ranges of social happenings can occur. Even with this limitation, simulations must be created within systems of constraints; the soothsayer must decide what spread of change he is willing to allow for. For example, there are those scientists who argue that the history of the future may well be lived and created by humanoids of biologically different construction from our own. They mean not merely the biological "manufacture" of supermen, but the use of genetic control to change the very mechanics of our physiological construction. If future men have eyes permitting them to see about them in a 360° arc, one may expect intellectual reflections of such perceptual difference. Other scholars maintain that as we learn more of "biological imperatives" such as "territoriality," we can decide to what extent the nobility of the savage can be promoted, to what extent a search for social peace may be hopeless, and perhaps even how to engineer "instinct" out of our systems if we deem it ethically desirable to do so.

I intend to avoid arcane discussions of this nature. Instead, I shall hold invariate man's physiological and instinctual apparatus, assuming that no scientific control over them will have significant social effect before the end of this century. Much more important to this essay, I shall presume that the available choices of the forms and justifications of human organization will not be increased. That is, no totally new kinds of societies will emerge, and no completely new ideologies will be generated. I do not mean that ideas and procedures and systems will not change, but rather that those changes will be variations on existing themes. Socialism, capitalism, communitarianism, and such other code-named mixed economic systems will still be with us. Democracy, communism, falangism, fascism, and *caudillismo* will remain possible political forms. Social class will not go away. Special interests will continue to press their cases. Ethnic diversity and class distinctions will continue to perturb the integration of national communities. And national communities will continue to find difficulty in reconciling internal with international interest. The newness and freshness of coming situations will arise from the interactions of these elements, not from new ones. The implications of this construction, then, are that this essay must examine possible new syntheses, without presuming great change in the very building blocks of political thought and action.

The most easily measurable changes in society are likely to come in the related areas of technological innovation brought to bear on economics and communications. Automation and the automatic factory are certain to continue their advances. The variety, speed, and social penetration of communications systems will continue to increase, but the content of communications and their significance in social organization and idea systems are variables that do not follow directly from the mere fact of the existence of the systems. Recognizing economics and communications as two areas of almost certain great physical change does not imply that we must necessarily accept a set of ineluctable qualitative consequences as flowing from those material changes.

The introduction to this essay would remain incomplete without a statement of my approach to the study of societies. The preceding emphasis on the necessity of synthesis as well as analysis and the suggestion that material change varies somewhat independently of qualitative consequences imply a multivariate approach: a denial of linear and deterministic theories. I presume that the explanation of social change can be covered reasonably well by indicating the conditions necessary for any given occurrence and adding the sufficiency through examining their interrelations. In macrosocial analysis, for example, one should know the power of the actors in any given circumstance, their normative systems, their relationship to the institutional structures of society, and the idiosyncratic factors of personality. Proper analysis is not attained by holding three of these elements stable and varying one. Rather, it is their simultaneous variance, measured by the differing patterns into which historically they do fall and potentially can fall, that permits the perception of the necessary as well as sufficient conditions leading to social happenings.

Although those four elements are not the only ones, and they could be expressed in much greater detail, I am suggesting that as one cannot think of data without theory, one also should not think of analysis without synthesis, of necessity without sufficiency. A statement about causation involves the probabilities of the play of elements *within* complex independent and dependent variables, as well as probabilities of interaction *between* independent and dependent variables.

Another element in my personal view is that I see politics as the study of the distribution and uses of public power. Naturally, the creation of power is related to social class, the uses of it to normative systems, and the channels of its application to institutional orders—all affected by the personal idiosyncrasies of the actors involved in their differing positions. The particular study of international relations may at first appear simpler than intrasystem studies, for international affairs *par excellence* reflect the facts of power relatively unsullied by other considerations. But scholars in the field have long sought to relate internal to external matters, giving rise to such well-known schools of thought as geopolitics, present attempts to see the world as the scene of international class conflict, and such racist arguments as those of Gobineau or the exponents of a softer "White Man's Burden" argument. I shall attempt to relate the expression of power internationally to the patterns of generation and maintenance of internal power through an analysis of the prime variables I have already mentioned.

It has often been said that in predicting what groups or individuals will do in the future, the most relevant data are what they have done in the past. The control one must put on such a construction is to remember that there is no logical necessity that what has happened before must happen again. The fact that the sun rose yesterday is not proof in itself that it will rise tomorrow. The point of looking at the past for clues is not to predict a recurrence of events, but rather to discern their patterning, to discover how they have taken place as a clue to the ways in which future probabilities will unfurl themselves. We will not attempt to predict the sun's rising in itself, but rather the array of circumstances that (all other things being equal) will bring with it yet another dawn.

I shall now turn to an analysis of United States–Latin relations in the past, as a test of the analytical model I shall later attempt to employ in discussing the array of future possibilities. This procedure will make explicit my presumptions, and permit the reader more ably to defend himself against the projective portion of this paper.

HEMISPHERIC INTERNATIONAL RELATIONS:
A HISTORICAL ANALYSIS

Let us consider first the power the United States has exercised on Latin America, and then the Latin American side of the influence balance. North American power is not a constant; it has varied by time and by place, and the places have varied through time. Let us not tarry for any description of the emergence of the United States from its colonial period through the critical period of the Civil War to its present position as a dominant world power. We all know that this growth has been quite consistent, particularly so since the onset of the Second Industrial Revolution after the Civil War. We also are all aware of the shifting world power patterns that have affected the relative standing of the United States in the global scene. Two axioms of American power in the hemisphere are obvious: United States influence has grown consistently heavier through time, and the influence has spread farther and farther down the South American continent through time. Less obvious is the probability that the nature of the influence has changed. During the early era of Latin American independence, United States power was felt largely in ideology and law. Many early Latin American constitutions were modeled on the American document; even in statutory law, such as Guatemala's Livingston Code, such appropriate models as the Louisiana Civil Code were adapted to the needs of the new Latin nations. Ideologies of libertarianism, republicanism, and nationhood drew on French and American precepts, which in their turn relied heavily upon English doctrine. But American political and economic penetration was relatively light and was concerned principally with such neighboring states as Mexico and Cuba, from the earliest days the object of attraction to North American expansionists with their notions of Manifest Destiny. Within half a century of the establishment of the United States, Mexico felt the use of overt power. But as late as World War II, the United States still drew its defense perimeter only through the bulge of Brazil.

Through time, both the pace and the extent of United States involvement in Latin America have increased. For example, before

World War II Great Britain, Germany, and Japan outstripped the United States as Latin trading partners. For a generation after the war, however, the United States held an almost monopolistic position in Latin American trade. Now, even though the classical partners have reappeared, the United States still holds hemispheric preeminence.

These trade patterns have always been unequally distributed. For long, the major American investments were in Cuba and Venezuela; the latter country still holds the major single cluster of American economic investment. From the Latin American point of view, of course, even small foreign investments in such countries as the Central American republics may have contributed importantly to political events in those countries. From the North American point of view, however, the unevenness of investment has not been directly reflected in politics. The evidence appears to be that the political interest has washed slowly and more or less evenly down through the Caribbean to the northern tier states of South America, and that it now embraces the entire hemisphere.

To these variables of time, place, and economic and political influences, let us add two integrating concepts: types of United States influence and the groups within the Latin American countries reacting to those influences. First, the types:

1. The most obvious and public influence is direct intervention, military or paramilitary. The cases are many: Haiti, Nicaragua, Panama, Honduras, Mexico, the Dominican Republic, Guatemala, Cuba, and certainly many others, known, suspected, or unknown. Overt military occupations have more often than not ended in the implantation of a "safe" dictator with some military or police training (Trujillo, Somoza, etc.) and eventual withdrawal of the overt investment. Then long periods of despotic rule of a traditional type have usually followed. It is impossible to know whether the development of such countries as Honduras, the Dominican Republic, and Nicaragua would have been substantially different without this kind of intervention. But Panama and Guatemala certainly have been fundamentally affected, the former in its very existence, and the latter in its present decay into years of violence directly related to American assistance in the overthrow of the Arbenz regime in 1954. It should be added, however, that this kind of action is sporadic and even to a certain extent casual. The 1965 intervention in the Dominican Republic, for example, was "accidental" in the sense that the combination of United States leaders involved took an action "inevitable" for them, but probably remote for other leaders. Thus, direct intervention is the influence most susceptible to variability.

2. The second level of effect may be said to be the reflection of the long-term national interests of the United States as defined through explicit or implicit policy statements. These statements tend to build whatever stability there is into the hemispheric policy of the United States. The best-known example is the Monroe Doctrine. Although its meaning and effectiveness have changed through time, the Doctrine's basic sense is that the United States has a special interest in and responsibility for Latin America. This particularity of concern does not necessarily exclude that of other states, but it is considered to override other nations' interests in times of stress. Another example, of implicit policy this time, stems from North American beliefs in a modified capitalistic market system. When translated into the private ownership (but not capitalistic market system) of most of Latin America, American private enterprise tends to Social Darwinism. Business that operates in an ambience lacking effective political and social constraint and that is equipped with a high capacity to compete can degenerate into rapacity. The common result is that American business is looked upon with high suspicion by many Latin Americans simply because of its power relative to that of local institutions and groups. (This suspicion differs with the type of enterprise; there is an important difference between reactions to public monopoly and extractive industries, on the one hand, and to light industrial and commercial activities, on the other.) The American commitment to a particular type of economic organization defined as "correct" also exemplifies a kind of moralism in our international stance that may be highly offensive to other nations, whether they are led by conservatives or liberals. Thus, when the United States cuts off foreign aid to Argentina and Peru because those governments threaten to cancel oil contracts or to engage in other disapproved economic activity, a strong conflict of values is involved. The actions of the United States stem from conviction about the correctness of given economic beliefs and the sanctity of contract and private property, as well as from conviction about the virtuous use of power. Many Latin Americans see such action as a violation of their sovereignty in its most profound sense—that is, as sovereignty somehow reflects the state of being and becoming of a people.

National interest thus should not be seen as a mere military or defensive question. It also involves a desire to see others live in accord with whatever world view one's own people may have—by one's own values, with one's own institutional referents, and following one's own ways of conducting affairs. Clearly this latter view has been denied by some United States leaders; but it has also been expressed in deed as well as word. It is the rare culture that can prevent itself from seeing others in its own image. Given the facts of international power, few nations have not attempted to impose certain elements of their own image on others when able to do so. And yet American public demonstrations against the Philippine campaign of T. Roosevelt, the nonintervention policies of F. D. Roosevelt, and the succeeding years of Good Neighborism and the Alliance for Progress have all reflected a counterdesire, the containment of this aspect of American power. This dialectic reflects domestically what have in truth been major differences in the United States approach to Latin America.

3. The third level of influence is the most pervasive, and the least susceptible to control by anyone. It is the cultural influence of a nation that is powerful intellectually and technologically as well as militarily and economically. The most common examples of this weighty influence are linguistic: the "new" Spanish of *parquear, troque, breque, estok, estándard,* and so on—meaning "to park," "truck," "brake," "stock," and "standard" (as in "standard of living"). Much is also made of the movies and TV as contributors to the "revolution of rising expectations," or what may better be called "the bedazzlement effect," leading to social paralysis at least as often as to action. In any event, the influence is much broader than even these examples might indicate. Faulkner and Hemingway and others have contributed much to a generation of Latin American novelists. The social science explosion of Latin America is the result of a direct exportation of American theories, models, and techniques. And with them goes much ideology. The training in the United States of Latin American military officers, for example, is specifically designed to impregnate them with North American ideas of proper civil-military relations.

It is in this area of happenings that one must search for some explanation of the widespread grief felt in Latin America on the deaths of Presidents Roosevelt and Kennedy. The joke references may be illuminating. There is the hackneyed one, that when the United States catches cold Latin America contracts pneumonia. Or, Latin Americans are vitally interested in the present American campaign because they want to know who their next president will be. What I think is being expressed is that the very posture, the "psychic" stance, of the United States has an immediate effect on the choices made in many Latin American polities. For example, the Dominican intervention, when linked to Vietnam and certain military policies undertaken in Latin America, as well as the general tone of the Johnson administration, persuaded many Latin Ameri-

cans that the United States welcomed right-wing military movements. President Onganía of Argentina was reportedly bitterly dis-
appointed that the United States did not welcome him as warmly as
it did his Brazilian prototypes. Earlier, they had overthrown President Goulart to the apparent satisfaction of the United States. The
result of this projection was that the Argentine and Brazilian armies
mobilized during the Dominican crisis to intervene in Uruguay and
Bolivia in the event that the governments of those countries threatened to go leftist. Not all Latin countries react with this sensitivity,
however. In general, it may be said that those in which the internal
political forces are delicately balanced try to read into American
policy the factor that will send the balance in one direction or
another. This kind of anticipation is of long standing in Latin America, stemming from the last century, and will be discussed more fully
below.

Some other recent examples of attempts to anticipate American favor may help to explain this point. In late 1947, in anticipation of United States approval and assistance, President González
Videla of Chile broke the Popular Front that had governed the
country since 1938. (The approval, but not much assistance, was
forthcoming.) It is possible that the Castelo Branco revolt in Brazil
would not have occurred when it did had not President Kennedy
been assassinated, an act leading in the first week of Mr. Johnson's
presidency to the firing of Teodoro Moscoso and thus an indicated
change in United States governmental attitudes toward revolts in
Latin America. Center and center-left presidents (such as Leoni of
Venezuela and Frei of Chile) have complained that they knew that
the United States supported them but that if they were overthrown
by a military coup the United States would also support the new
military rulers. Their complaint was that adventurist military men
were as certain as they of this American stance, and therefore emboldened in their ambitions.

These attitudes of Latin Americans are based on guesses. Sometimes they reflect real American policy decisions that must be put in
the first of the three categories in this list. But as often as not, the
hunches are derived from feelings about whether the United States
is in a period of liberalism and international confidence or in one of
international insecurity that suggests the wisdom of "safe" governments of force in Latin America.

When cultural style and political choice thus interact, conscious
choice becomes difficult. Some of the less recognized but still important defeats for American policy in Latin America come from a
disjunction between verbal expressions of desire and Latin Ameri-

can perceptions of basic United States posture. Thus, American diplomatic pressure against recent military coups in Argentina and Peru, among other countries, was unavailing. The coups came, and indeed the combination of security considerations and the attitudes of American policy-makers supported the presumptions of the Latin Americans: their coups were recognized and normal relations quickly established. Opposite events have also occurred. The Good Neighbor policy and the Kennedy period of the Alliance for Progress strengthened social democratic and Christian Democratic elements in Latin American politics. These shifts in American political posture, contained as they are within the standard spread of our own political occurrences, thus provoke wide swings in Latin American government and help to institutionalize political instability there.

LATIN AMERICAN INTERNAL POLITICS AND LATIN FOREIGN RELATIONS

A standard sociological way of stratifying Latin American populations is as follows: (1) the Indian populations, outside the stream of national politics entirely; (2) *mestizo* rural villagers, on the fringes of national consciousness and culture; (3) recent lower-class migrants to the cities; (4) urban industrial lower classes; (5) middle-class groups; and (6) upper-class groups. A social psychological dimension is then normally added to these caste-class differentiations. The rural villagers and recent migrants are usually classified as "mobilized" but "unintegrated," meaning that they have lost their "folk" culture, but have not as yet taken on the routinized behavior patterns and identifications of a citizen integrated into the national society. The artisan and unionized lowers, the middles, and the uppers are then normally divided into "traditionals" and "moderns." The definitions vary, but these are the ones I employ:

- A *traditional* person is a ritualist in his reasons for behavior; he views his behavior as universal in effect, or "organic," as having an effect on all else and as being imbued with moral significance; he is resistant to change, for the existing order has moral sanction by definition.

- A *modern* person is rationalistic in his reasons for deciding on action; he is relativistic in that he assumes his behavior has limited influence, in recognition of institutional and role differentiation; he is anticipatorily self-adjusting to change.

To the class and value breakdowns above may be added groupings of Latin Americans by institutional affiliations relevant to international politics: that is, parties, pressure groups, interest associations, and so on. Now, if we add these three elements together, we
can say something about the effectiveness (the power or class factor),
the uses of that power (the value factor), and the customary behavior
and institutions adding the style component to public behavior as
well as providing the organized means for its expression. Figure 1
helps to simplify what would otherwise be a long and arduous
typology by presenting a composite of political party arrays.

The leadership of all these parties is upper-middle-class and
upper-class in status, although the social origins of the leaders
often reveal a high order of upward mobility. The leftist groups
are strongly influenced by leaders of urban origins; on the right
the Liberals are also urban. Conservatives, Radicals, and Christian
Democrats count important contingents of rural influentials among
their leaders. The followers scatter widely: Conservatives rally some
rural labor to their banner; Liberals attract lower-middle-class entrepreneurs and some artisans in search of "stable and honest government"; the Radicals, Socialists, and Christian Democrats appeal
strongly to middle-class groups; the Communists, *fidelistas,* and
Trotskyites are basically middle-class parties with some trade union
support; the leftist corporativist parties are the most populist of all
the parties, appealing to limited middle sectors and to broad sectors
of the recent migrants to the cities, and semi- and unskilled labor.
(*Peronismo* is an example. For more on this subject, see Gino Ger-
mani's works on the "popular masses" in Latin America.)

The ideological attitudes of these groups toward the United
States are as follows:

All groups on the traditional scale culturally reject the United
States, but support anti-Communism and the Cold War. Thus, a
minister of corporate leanings could say, "We reject that Liberal
capitalism that leads to atheistic communism." The point is, of
course, that to the eye of a Counter-Reformation man, the Soviet
Union and the United States must look more alike than different.
Thus, we find rejections of capitalism, Protestantism, and Communism in the same breath. Nevertheless, such groups generally support American foreign policy as they define it, and seek alliance with
counterpart groups within the United States.

The Christian Democrats share many of the corporativist views
of the Conservatives (from whose midst they historically sprang), but
reject present United States foreign policy, support a progressive
Alliance for Progress view, and in their turn also seek to make

FIGURE 1

A General Typology of Political Groups in Latin America

Fascists	Falangists	Corporativists				Conservatives

TRADITIONAL SCALE

Left   *Right*

Fidelistas	Trotskyites	Communists	Socialists	Christian Democrats	Radicals	Liberals

MODERN SCALE

common cause with such elements as Kennedy Democrats, for whom they feel a special affinity.

The Liberals—much like Taft Republicans—support American foreign policy as evidenced in its Cold War stance, applaud American industrial culture, and resist competitive American industry and business. These groups, usually strongest among industrialists, often oppose such specific American policies as inflation control, for they see high but not runaway rates of inflation as permitting hidden profit-taking, and thus as conducive to development. Liberals share many points of view with Radicals of the right, and in general the Radical parties even of the left (not shown in the figure) spread between the pro–United States views of the Liberals and those of the Christian Democrats.

The democratic Socialists are profound admirers of American culture and resist the specifics of United States foreign policy. The Marxist left sees the United States as inevitably imperialist and thus as an ineluctable political enemy. But the Marxists, too, may sometimes admire what they see as the cultural and technological victories of American capitalism and therefore seek a partial emulation. The greatest single difference between Christian Democrats, social democrats in general, and democratic Socialists on the one hand, and the Marxist left on the other, is the way they view the susceptibility of the United States to pressure and change. They all see the United States as imperialistic. But the democrats think imperialism is a policy and not a necessity, and the Marxists think it culturally determined and unsusceptible to change without social revolution in the United States. In practical terms, then, the former seek alliance with the United States as government, and with sympathetic pressure groups inside the country, while the latter espouse nationalistic revolution in their own countries as their only genuine defense.

Nationalism is then linked to attitudes toward the United States in ways much more subtle than the workings of simple xenophobia. The Conservatives are antinational, in the sense that they reject the supremacy of a secular nation-state. This view is shared by the left traditionals, but the Conservatives substitute a nationalism of the right, a clericalist and xenophobic attempt to return to an idealized medieval state. The modern groups all accept the idea of the secular supremacy of a nation-state, reject right-wing nationalism, and then divide on the imperialism question, as I have indicated.

These attitudes, when run against power as class expression and power as institutionally specific, comprise the minimum paradigm necessary to understand the internal roots of Latin American foreign policy. There is no space to spell out the full range of relations here, but the description of a few polar cases may help suggest the limits. In terms of class power, we have at one end a country like Guatemala, of whose 4,000,000 population perhaps 350,000 form the entire core of what can be called national, participant citizenry: the civil service, the army, the professionals, the white-collar employees, and so forth. The remainder of the population is Indian, illiterate, rural, below fourteen years of age, and so on. At the other end, we have Argentina, where perhaps 45 percent of the population is in middle income and occupation groups, two thirds are urbanized, 90 percent are literate, and so forth. Over half the total population votes in national elections. Naturally, Guatemalan leaders can have few followers, but Argentine leaders have large committed or "available" masses (to use Raymond Aron's expression) as followers. In a real sense, then, Guatemalan leaders have license to choose widely among ideologies, but little power to recruit mass defenders. The opposite would seem to be empirically true of the Argentines in situations short of total crisis, when populations may be forced back to their basic social premises.

When the groups we have described are related to value systems, it becomes apparent that the patterns of conflict run not only *across* class lines but, probably more important, *within* them. That is, intraclass conflict, as engendered by differing perceptions and thus differing definitions of group interest, describes the major lines of political division. Upper-class groups fight upper-class groups as well as other interest levels. In order to explain this phenomenon one is forced to discuss class and values simultaneously. And then, of course, there should be added the experience of organization, the technology of politics. This ingredient is the institutional dimension of which we have been speaking. Again, space precludes detail, but in general the Radical parties and the Marxist left are the most professionally organized and impersonal groups. The traditional left corporativists tend to be conspiratorial and badly organized, while the Liberals and Conservatives have small organized pressure groups but generally scorn stable and extended party organization.

What this complex picture implies for inter-American policy is that no country of Latin America has sufficient intra- and interclass cohesion to have the politics of a true nation-state. Nor does any one have a strong institutional structure that can plaster over class and value conflict. (The only possible exception to these two generalizations is Cuba, which for good or ill may be Latin America's first nation-state in the social sense of that term.) Thus, opposition to the United States remains largely at the verbal level, and the temptation to employ the United States as a force in internal political decision looms large in all countries. To be entirely explicit, Latin America's weak governments, reflecting internal schism, make it possible for political groups to impute desires and attitudes to the United States that can be used to tip the balance of internal politics one or another way. It is through this mechanism that the cultural stance of the United States, mentioned above as the most basic influence on Latin America, is linked to their internal power constellations. This articulation of United States and Latin relations is what makes the post of American ambassador such a critical, delicate, and difficult one in many Latin American countries.

The stigmata of schismatic politics are not spread equally among the Latin American republics, of course. Ideological identifications do tend to bleed across frontiers, but in ways that tend merely to reinforce the general "feeling tone" of the continent as it is related to more general inter-American pressures. For example, at this moment [1968] the major Latin American countries are being ruled by relatively softly authoritarian governments: the military, quasi-falangist regimes of Argentina and Brazil, and the single-party system of Mexico. There are small islands of Christian and social democracy (Chile, Venezuela, Costa Rica, and so on), and the remainder are rather traditional Latin American authoritarianisms of combined civil-military stripe. The democratic regimes worry that they will be infiltrated by the authoritarian ones, and the latter worry that the former are islands of Communist penetration. But little occurs other than verbal hostility, an occasional attempt to propagandize. There are only a few cases of overt action: the attempt of Trujillo to assassinate Betancourt, the successful assassination of Trujillo, with its international overtones, tension between the late President Somoza of Nicaragua and President Figueres of Costa Rica, the rumors of mobilization of the Argentine army on the Chilean frontier on the occasion of the last polarized presidential election in Chile, and so on. These incidents are relatively rare, and are not often taken into routine consideration in Latin American policy-making.

The verbal interplay of Latin American international politics naturally reflects the class facts of leadership and ideological commitments. Formal and informal organization both are functions of these factors. For example, the Economic Commission for Latin America (ECLA) reflects a reformist, industrially oriented, Keynesian approach to economic development. It has been a major factor in promoting the Inter-American Development Bank (of similar ideological persuasion) and the Latin American integration movement. The latter, with headquarters in Buenos Aires, is consciously attempting to link Liberal industrialists, Radical politicians, and co-operative trade union leaders, among others, toward the end of building a Latin American common market that can also eventually become a political union. The ultimate aim is to generate sufficient power so that Latin America can confront the United States not in enmity, but as equal partner, *à la* Western European powers. The Organization of American States, on the contrary, has been seen widely as reflecting Latin American surrender to United States suzerainty in the hemisphere. Whether the OAS is entering on a new period of growth remains to be seen.

The Central American customs union and the Latin American Free Trade Association (LAFTA) are still entirely economic entities. In my opinion there is little chance for either to proceed in the near future to full common-market status, let alone to any semblance of political union. It is not merely that vested economic interest in Latin America's growing industrial sectors is already far enough advanced to make economic collaboration difficult, but also that there is little experience in intra-Latin diplomatic collaboration except for the most formal variety in the United Nations, ECLA, and the OAS. The critical task facing Latin America, however, is extension of markets, not laterally by international expansion, but vertically by intra-national social growth. The integration of Latin America is no substitute for the internal integration of the Latin American republics.

PROBABILITIES

In beginning the projective part of this essay, it will be useful to set the limits of probabilities by examining the indisputably marginal cases—those that define absolute limits. Each of these polar cases in truth voids the possibility of effective international action. They are:

(a) *Armageddon, the Wagnerian solution.* Nuclear warfare that destroys civilization would render the year 2000 moot.

(b) *Frozen balance-of-power, the Orwellian solution.* The famous projection, *1984*, posited the division of the world into three great power blocs, each under the leadership of a central power: the United States, Soviet Russia, and China. All other states were satellite dependencies of one of the three, with internal politics rigidly hierarchized and controlled, warfare ritualized and perhaps even the figment of manufactured news, and "international" relations reduced to playing out the formal rules of a charade.

In this strange world of ours, we should be wary of lightly

labeling any alternative as impossible. But certainly these two pure situations are unlikely. The first presumes a suicidal lunacy on the part of the leaders of the nuclear powers. The second assumes the utter powerlessness of Western Europe, the impotence of the Third World, and a failure of such internal dynamics as can be seen everywhere, and which are especially evident in the internal turmoil of the Eastern bloc. The Orwellian view also implies a desolate view of "human nature," denying the meaning of a possible very long-range trend toward greater human rationality and social decency.

The more likely social solutions are in the realm of mixed situations in which "greater" and "lesser" are more appropriate adjectives than "hellish" or "heavenly." Nevertheless, some social conditions that may be acceptable or even positively rewarding for some can be devastating for others. Even in Nazi Germany, as close to hell as we have recently come, millions of good burghers pursued their ways in relative placidity, and the sounds of genocide did not stop citizens of Warsaw from parading in their Sunday finery on their way to worship. It is erroneous to examine mixed situations by thinking in terms of averages, and thus washing out the absolute misery they may cause in given social groups. The reader should keep in mind differences in human benefit and deprivation inherent in the facts of stratification by race and class.

The dimensions of change that, as a minimum simplification, need to be taken into account in describing the limits of mixed situations are as follows:

(a) Changes in the relations of the great and the secondary powers.
(b) Changes within the great and secondary powers.
(c) Changes of international relations among the Latin American countries.
(d) Changes within each Latin American country.

These elements are a crystallization and a justification of the previous sample discussion on the history of inter-American relations. That section of this essay attempted to suggest the possible interacting effects on hemispheric relations of changes within the United States and within the several Latin American societies and the manner in which international influence reflects momentary, long-range, and cultural factors. I presume a continuance of internal change within definable limits, a continuation of the three levels of international interaction, and continuing pressure toward changing power balances by shifting alliance and integration patterns. Remaining for explicit discussion are the sets of economic and demographic changes in Latin American societies that I presume to be likely, and the ethical judgment of alternative possible directions of change.

In economic and demographic terms, I assume the following to be likely trends in Latin America:

(a) The rate of population increase will continue to be high for most of the remainder of this century, but will taper off in the more developed urban areas, as is already evident in Buenos Aires, Montevideo, and elsewhere. I do not assume that population pressure will become so acute as to be a cause for political action in itself.

(b) Urban clusters will increase in size and in numbers, and percentages of population living on the farms will decrease. But absolute numbers will go up both on the farm and in the cities.

(c) Sophisticated technology will increasingly be imported into Latin America, and industrial and service economic sectors will continue to grow absolutely and to absorb increasing percentages of the employed population.

(d) Rates of literacy will climb, especially in the newly industrializing countries such as Venezuela. In addition, access to higher education will grow even more than it has in the past five years, with a particular increase in secondary school attendance.

A sharp implication of these points is that we should turn our attention to absolute numbers, instead of being mesmerized by percentages that blur objective achievements by *per capita* rates. The striking physical changes of the past forty years in Latin America are likely to continue. So is the increase in the absolute numbers of educated and reasonably well-to-do urban persons. These absolute changes will work relative changes in the realm of political organization, making possible alternatives only weakly felt at this moment.

These demographic and economic changes, however, do not bring in their wake any single necessary kind of political change. Industrial urbanization and a literate population are as compatible, in the relatively short run between now and the year 2000, with totalitarian as with libertarian public systems. The same theoretical independence of socioeconomic from political factors must pertain for the world powers also. We may expect the following in the United States, Western Europe and its cultural counterparts (Canada, Australia, New Zealand, and so on), and, to a more limited extent, in Soviet Russia:

(a) In these countries, the ecological facts of urbanization will be qualitatively modified by technological advance in industry, agriculture, and communications. The countries will be able to become nation-city-states. That is, national and urban life-styles will permeate all regions of the countries, and make it possible to follow a modern way of life inside or outside cities as physical entities. No groups, either ethnically or socially defined, will remain outside the polities: pariah groups and "underclasses" will not exist as such, although certain self-selected marginal groups and individuals may be ostracized for reasons of social style. The truly national society will exist in which all groups have some access to or some role to play in all institutions.

(b) Economic factors will be increasingly seen as secondary to social and political decision-making. The harder facts of ideology, culture, taste, and style will become increasingly important in determining the course of national political affairs. I do not mean that class structures will not exist, or that more privileged groups will not coexist with less privileged ones; I am saying only that economic factors will come to be seen as merely instrumental to other considerations concerning the value and purpose of life.

Japan will probably follow the same paths as the European countries. China and India will have continued their economic development, although the former will probably be more successful than the latter in achieving high rates of economic growth, still assuming no intervening major armed conflicts. Because these countries come late to industrialization, but also because both have for long had major urban concentrations, one should expect that their economic progress will take advantage of their late appearance by the employment of highly advanced production techniques and the organizational tools of modern team science. China will certainly continue to employ labor-intensive devices for quite some time, but such a procedure for the generation and employment of capital is not incompatible with a selection of other appropriate and highly advanced techniques of production.

Whatever the tone of the political orders that accompany these probable socioeconomic changes, the almost certain consequence is that the primary and secondary powers will be stronger than ever, not only in terms of arms, but also with respect to their ability to mobilize major masses of citizenry and to count on their loyalty through periods of armed international crisis. Whether this power is based on freely extended legitimacy, or on coercion made exquisite through the employment of sophisticated control devices, effective "massification" of society will permit high levels of social mobilization.

Another consequence of technological sophistication and mass mobilization is that the administrative comity of centralization and decentralization will become apparent. That is, old arguments as to the desirability of centrally governed as opposed to locally based administrations will be as passé as the arguments as to whether city or country life is more desirable. In synthesis, then, we may expect more powerful political units buttressed by complexly interwoven local and national administrations, the conversion of economics into an institution clearly dependent on choices made on political and social bases, and the consequent emergence of an array of ideological and socially stylistic choices that can be more firmly defined for more persons throughout society than ever before.

On the international scene, one may expect reflections of the greater specialization and social synthesis that will be apparent at the domestic level. Two essential directions are possible:

(a) The international community may be an interacting group of highly autonomous national units, their viability made ever more apparent by the self-sufficiency stemming from their strengthened national cohesion and the conquest of some of the problems of economic scarcity. Nations may choose to sacrifice the cultural and economic gains possible through rational international arrangements in order to gain security through autarky and isolation, formalized by international agreement. This alternative is not impossible, especially if the proliferation of ultimate weaponry provides every major nation with the weapons of absolute offense. In a way, the Cold War was prevented from erupting by this kind of self-imposed isolation, in which the two major antagonists tacitly agreed to respect a geographical division of the world, to limit the spread of their atomic arsenal, to talk before shooting, and to avoid the physical confrontation of their armed forces everywhere except in Berlin.

(b) The international community may be the scene of higher syntheses of loyalty, beyond the nation-state. As local and national interests are now becoming compatible, national and international interests may also be put in a mutually reinforcing order. The specialized agencies of the United Nations and the drives for regional integration are all contemporary evidences of attempts to rationalize certain international functional relations. No law of social community necessarily impedes the simultaneous development of intercultural as well as intracultural and local loyalties in interacting patterns.

Let me once more state that even these administrative arrangements can proceed within both politically restrictive and politically libertarian environments. But the choice of each alternative brings important consequences for the ways in which societies will proceed through periods of crisis and change. Thus, aside from ethical judgments of political orders, there is a hard empirical difference between political processes in a relativistic and rationalist humanistic style and those in a dogmatic, ritualistic, and absolutist style. The former permit self-correcting mechanisms restricting the effects of mistaken or imperfectly informed choice, while the latter lead to rigidities and attempts to prevent change. In providing a summation of the spread of possible mixed situations in hemispheric international affairs, I shall employ the labels "best possible" and "worst possible." The valuational adjectives should not be understood as implying an unreasoning choice of one kind of political situation over another. In this choice, as in all other public ones, empirical results flow from normative evaluation.

The Best Reasonably Possible Mixed Situation

1. Most Latin American countries will achieve true nation-state status; that is, all persons will be within the national institutional structure.

2. National institutions will be sufficiently differentiated as to permit individuals to attain differing status levels within different institutions; that is, there will be a merit system of selection in educational, economic, political, and religious institutions, according to which all individuals have equal opportunities.

3. The facts of social class will be contained not only by the equality before the institutions mentioned above, but specifically in the political sphere by genuine equality before the law and the periodic ability of citizens to make effective and rational choices concerning the direction of national political life at all levels—international and local as well as national.

4. The strength generated by participant politics will be reinforced by regional Latin American organizations, permitting the area to make its voice felt as a block when necessary in international affairs.

5. Direct foreign intervention will be a thing of the past, not merely because the major powers eschew such behavior, but also because the strength of Latin American public opposition can be translated into effective armed opposition if necessary, thus raising the price of such intervention to unacceptable levels.

6. The long-term policies of the foreign powers will come into confluence with consciously derived long-term Latin American policies in order to provide a ground for equality of international collective bargaining.

7. The literacy levels of Latin American societies will be so high, and the advanced education so sophisticated, as to make it possible consciously to pick and choose among the international cultural stimuli bombarding the area—for the sake of deepening national

culture by an adequate response to international currents, instead of diluting national culture by intellectual mimesis.

8. The great powers will achieve levels of libertarian politics that they recognize as valid for others as well as themselves, thus eliminating the double standards now currently employed in distinguishing permissible domestic from permissible international action. Such a situation can occur only when the developing countries move into the category of national societies.

9. The great powers will turn away from bloc and naked power politics to a politics of diplomacy based on a rejection of the use of force and violence in international affairs, except in the case of clear and present danger to the international comity.

10. All countries will recognize that expansionist totalitarianism threatens all the previous arrangements, and thus should be contained by any measures appropriate to the immediacy of the threat and consistent with the maintenance of domestically free societies.

The Worst Reasonably Possible Mixed Situation

1. The Latin American republics will become rigidly stratified societies of privilege and deprivation; that is, only selected groups will enjoy the full fruits of national life.

2. Institutional differentiation will be denied in the name of the organic unity of society; that is, position will be the result of ascription, the accidents of birth that confer class position throughout life and determine the advantages or disadvantages to be attached to individuals and families.

3. The facts of social class will be reinforced by the above devices in order to create a self-perpetuating governing class for the long-term maintenance of authoritarian control, increasingly using the techniques of modern repression.

4. The strength of the governing elites in each country will be reinforced by international collaboration among them for the destruction of any possible opposition from within or among the Latin American republics.

5. Direct foreign intervention will be requested from sympathetic foreign governments whenever the repressive systems are threatened from within or without.

6. The authoritarian Latin American republics will believe that internationally, as domestically, the rich must get get richer faster than the poor, that the powerful must become more powerful faster than the weak, and thus that the proper international position of the Latin American states must be as client systems of the great powers.

7. The Latin American elites will recognize that their systems can be maintained on a small base of educated technocrats, and that cultural and scientific stimuli can be invited from the outside in order to avoid the creation of a self-stimulating intellectual community on the inside.

8. The great powers will recognize a continuing double standard in international affairs, treating the developing nations as they would irresponsible children: that is, applying the same standards internationally that the governing elites do domestically within each Latin country.

9. The great powers will admire the uses of force and proceed to military investment in order to nip potential disorder at the roots.

10. All countries will decide that democratic libertarianism conduces to disorder and threats to morality and the sensibilities of decent people, and thus should be contained by immediate strict control.

I trust the reader will recognize the relevance of these points to much current ideological disputation as well as to actual practice. It is depressing as well as heartening that evidence of the possibilities of both dimensions of the future can be found in the present. The lists are not intended to exhaust characteristics or possibilities, of course. Nor are they designed to intimate that all of Latin America will become one sameness, whether in the libertarian or the authoritarian direction. I leave it to the reader to use these and other elements as a kind of a do-it-himself kit for the construction of many possible combinations.

Whatever the world of 2000, from the vantage point of 1968 I am certain that it can be said that man today is more the master of his destinies than he has ever been before, or than he is usually willing to admit to himself. What we will be in 2000 is to a great extent what we will have made of ourselves—whether that be automata or free men.

1968

Index

Academic community
assistance to oppressed people,
57–58
government sponsorship of, 124
and international relations, 132–
141
tenure in, 35, 125–126
Academic freedom, need for, 66
Accountability, of institutions, 12, 91
Adams, Richard, 64
Adorno, Theodore W., 112
Agency for International Devel-
opment, 85
Agricultural Development Council,
85
Agriculture
in Cuba, 84–85
developmental work in, 48
Alienation, Marxist view of, 60–61
Allende, Salvador, 10
Alliance for Progress, 68, 177, 181,
182, 191, 199, 211, 213
Almond, Gabriel, 109–110
American University, and Camelot
Project, 131
Andean Group, 181, 192
Anthropologists, concern with
ethical issues, 64
Aramburu, Pedro, 26
Arbenz, Jacobo, 68, 209
Area studies, and social science, 10,
102

Argentina
developmental classification of, 19
education in, 18–19
extreme right nationalists in, 28
inefficacious government in, 13
integration of middle elements in,
27
Marxism in, 194
middle and upper classes in, 20
middle-class professionals in, 26
military leaders in, 26
oligarchy in, 26
per capita income in, 18
as political community, 13–14
populist movement in, 27
power base in, 217
relations with Chile, 218
relations with Cuba, 95
relations with U.S., 149
in scale of national community,
164
social joy in, 8
social science in, 121, 135
type of government in, 166
universities in, 34
urban population in, 20
Army Department, in U.S., 124, 131
Asia, Latin American interests in, 120
Atrocities. See Torture
Authoritarianism
in Argentina, 13

227